KODIAK ALASKA DEER

Stories, Sterility and Stewardship
... or lack thereof

JAKE JACOBSON
Alaska's Favorite Real Life Wilderness Storyteller

PUBLICATION CONSULTANTS
We Believe In The Power Of Authors

PO Box 221974 Anchorage, Alaska 99522-1974
books@publicationconsultants.com — www.publicationconsultants.com

ISBN 978-1-59433-796-3

eBook ISBN Number: 978-1-59433-797-0

Copyright 2018 Jake Jacobson

—First Edition—

All rights reserved, including the right of reproduction in any form, or by any mechanical or electronic means including photocopying or recording, or by any information storage or retrieval system, in whole or in part in any form, and in any case not without the written permission of the author.

J.P. "Jake" Jacobson
Alaska Master Guide #54
PO Box 1313
Kodiak, Alaska 99615
website: www.huntfish.us/
email: huntfish@ak.net

Editing by Martha Stewart.

Manufactured in the United States of America.

KODIAK ALASKA DEER: *Stories, Sterility and Stewardship* is the fifth book by Jake Jacobson on Alaskan topics.

His other books are:

ALASKA HUNTING: Earthworms to Elephants

ALASKA TALES: Laughs and Surprises

ALASKA FLYING: Surviving Incidents and Accidents

ALASKA BEARS: Stirred and Shaken

Reviews from Previous Books

ALASKA HUNTING: Earthworms to Elephants

Not just about hunting 5.0 out of 5 stars
By Roninco, October 2, 2013
This book is not just about hunting. A great glimpse into life in remote Alaska over the past five decades. Adventures from the arctic to archipelago describe personal animal and human interactions. This book is a very fun read in just a few hours.

Great read & educational, 5.0 out of 5 stars
By David A Johnson, October 20, 2013
Jake provides 46 years of natural history observations and perspectives on arctic and interior Alaska, Kodiak Island, marine habitats, plus fun perspectives on hunting, Alaskan characters and the Eskimo culture. Jake demonstrates a consistent ability to critically asses or analyze wildlife and fish populations over time and the environmental effects weighing upon these wildlife populations, from Kodiak Island to the most northerly portion of the USA, Barrow, AK.

Jake's book was entertaining while providing an educational activity, whether the reader, be the general public, naturalists, sporting folks, professional biologist, anthropologist or geologist.

Jake actively maintained a journal, recording past and present activities, recording his interesting life with its predicaments, in daily jot downs, now luckily, these interesting life glimpses are available to us regular folks, in book form. This daily journal activity, by itself, is a lesson for all aspiring writers, to instill, as a habit, into their daily activities.

Review by an Australian reader 5.0 out of 5 stars
By Robert J. Penfold, November 29, 2013
Having hunted and fished over much of Alaska over the past 35 years I have learned to love the place. Jake's book is inspiring as it describes the real Alaska, the rural lifestyle, the real people and the visitors who come to experience this great land and its significant challenges. Jakes impeccable records of instances provide great insight into the real world of the professional big game hunting guide life. His attention to detail and his affinity with nature old and new, with his collecting artifacts and jade and collecting a wide range of friends along the way add to his 40 odd years of experiencing what Alaska has to offer. As a professional hunter, his approach to good game management and good conservation and high ethics are a standout in this book. It is a great read that I could not put down once I began turning the pages. Congratulations on producing a great book, the first of many I hope. Bob Penfold Australia

A rare gem about life and hunting in Alaska,
5.0 out of 5 stars
By Utah State Aggie "Utah State Aggie"
(Salem, OR USA), December 1, 2013

Henry David Thoreau wrote, "most men lead lives of quiet desperation, and go to the grave with the song still in them." Sometimes, a man leads an interesting life. Infrequently, one leads a consequential life. Rarely the two come together. If the rest of us are very lucky, that man is also a gifted natural storyteller. Over the course of a lifetime, Jake Jacobson, dentist, outfitter and guide, entrepreneur and family man, has polished his stories like the jade and petrified mammouth ivory he has lifted from the Alaskan outback. He has entertained generations of hunting clients in the cluttered comfort of his arctic lodge. Now, those stories can reach a wider audience in this volume. All that is missing is the smell of caribou stew and trail creek berry bread wafting in from the kitchen.

Jake Jacobson has produced a beautiful little gem of a book. It is a collection of vignettes that are alternatingly moving, perplexing, heartwarming, and hysterical. A grandson experiences the magic of a first hunting trip. A famous hunting author is the butt of an elaborate practical joke. A former senator is chased from camp at rifle point. The writing style is conversational and engaging. A wealth of black and white photographs illustrate the stories.

I'm tempted to compare Jake to Peter Capstick Hathaway, Robert Ruark, or Patrick F. McManus, but that would be unfair. He's James P. "Jake" Jacobson, DMD, Alaska Master Guide #54. He is one of a kind, and this book guarantees that he will not go to the grave with the song still in him!

ALASKA TALES: Laughs and Surprises

By Ronico, November 23, 2014

A thoroughly enjoyable read! What a refreshing departure from the ho-hum of so much written material! This collection of short stories related to Alaska hunting details various aspects of modern Professional Hunting in our northernmost state. It focuses on dealing with the occasional absurdity of human nature, the vagaries and idiosyncrasies of people, including guests, guides and peripheral personnel. Jake dissects events, locating the humorous aspects of what might otherwise be completely negative scenarios. He sees the humor, sometimes adding to it, and makes the best of situations, however bizarre they might be. Legends and superstitions are explored and in some cases, exploited. If the reader is looking for relief from everyday "Great White Hunter" stories—give this publication a read. It will lighten your load and give you relief from the doldrums of average, everyday existence. This is the author's second publication ... and I hope he writes more. My ribs hurt from laughing

Don't Miss Jake Jacobson's Alaska Tales!
By Craig Boddington, December 29, 2014

I have been fortunate to spend time in the Alaskan wilderness with Jake Jacobson…aside from being a very genuine Alaskan legend—not just as an outdoorsman, but one of the early "flying dentists" serving Arctic communities—he's a real character and truly a funny guy. Read the "laughs and surprises" of his Alaska Tales, and you'll feel like you're seeing his wild Alaska…and laughing along with him.

like God, country, 5.0 out of 5 stars
By Utah State Aggie, January 15, 2015

I believe in full disclosure. I wrote one of the forwards for this book. I also believe in standing up and being counted for something you believe, like God, country, family, honor, and hard work. I wrote that forward, and I am writing this review, because I believe that Jake has produced another wonderful little book that is worth every penny of your hard earned $19.03 (with Amazon Prime!). And in case you're wondering, no, I have no financial interest in Jake's literary efforts.

Jake's first book, *ALASKA HUNTING: Earthworms to Elephants* ($17.06 with Amazon Prime. Don't be a cheapskate, buy them both!) is mostly about hunting. This book is mostly about people. Alexander Pope said, "The proper study of mankind is man". Too many of us shuffle through a grey world, staring with tunnel vision at our own feet. Jake has spent his wonderful, bohemian life training his clear hunting guide's eye not just at caribou and Dall sheep, but at all of us. He captures people in all our infuriating glory, and with all our contradictions, nobility and fallen nature. It doesn't take many of these stories to realize that Jake loves people. No one sees, and writes with this kind of detail without loving the subject. And yet he takes us on our own terms, painting a sympathetic portrait of each quirky character, hero and coward, saint and sinner. Because in the end, it is hard to tell which is which.

This book is definitely worth the money (did I mention, only $19.03 with Amazon Prime?), it is worth the time to read it. Actually, it is worth the time to read it 5 or 10 times, or maybe more. Because, trust me, you won't just read it once.

You should buy this book
By Ed Pentis, November 12, 2016

Looking at the back of the book, it said "You should buy this book. It will make you laugh." That's what I call simple and direct. And true. First I buzzed through what I thought would be the most interesting stories. That was 7/8ths of the book. Then I devoured the rest, too. Now I'm going cover to cover, and finding all these great little nuggets of info that I missed the first time…like how the long distance phone lines were in the '70s. Funny stuff, all right, and it happened to Jake…or, he made it happen to somebody else. Jake didn't spend some piddling one year in Alaska. He has spent most of his life there, so far. I wonder what'll be next.

ALASKA FLYING: Surviving Incidents and Accidents

Jake's best effort yet (and that's saying a lot!), 5.0 out of 5 stars
By Utah State Aggie, May 1, 2016

God has a special purpose for Jake Jacobson. There is no other explanation for his being here to grace us with *ALASKA FLYING: Surviving Incidents and Accidents*, the latest installment of Jake's Alaska series.

Jake is a terrific storyteller. If you have read his other books, *ALASKA HUNTING: Earthworms to Elephants*, and *ALASKA TALES: Laughs and Surprises*, you already know that. He benefits from priceless material. Jake's life, by chance and choice, is a cornucopia of the absurd, comical, heartwarming, and bizarre. He has a natural storyteller's gift. Do a little experiment; close your eyes and let your favorite hunting companion read you one of Jake's stories. You'll feel the warmth of the campfire on your hands, the arctic breeze in your hair, and hear the gentle burbling of Trail Creek in the background. Jake brings every vignette to life.

As good as Jake's previous efforts have been, this book may be his best effort yet. The other two books are character studies, filled with the quirky denizens of the last frontier. This book has a much narrower cast, essentially Jake and his planes. Jake has an almost intimate relationship with his planes. He writes about his favorite, "21 Pappa", as "feel[ing] like an extension of my own body…. That Cub, to me, is a bit like one's first kiss – memorable, unique, and never to be repeated." This is certainly Jake's most personally revealing book. In writing about those planes, and the moments they have liberated him, sustained him, and brought him close to death, Jake shows more of his own character than he has in his previous works.

As I said, I truly believe that God has a special purpose for Jake. Jake is a superb pilot, as I know from personal experience. The interior of Alaska is littered with the bones of superb pilots. Many of the stories in this book are brushes with death and disaster. No one could do what Jake has done for 45 years without being held, as he puts it, "in the palm of God's hand". Do yourself a favor. Read the book and see if I'm not right.

ALL of Jake's books are definitely "worth the read"!!
5.0 out of 5 stars
By Dr. Rick Kaufman, January 3, 2018

Jake and I went to dental school in Portland, Oregon, together…starting in '62. A "loose cannon" does not describe him very well…as he was/is always very focused…but never an "average Joe"…and always very high energy…indeed, there are additional stories that could be told about him… that are NOT in his books…which have enough real life adventure to keep the reader entranced even BEYOND the last page[s] of his books…no matter which one[s] are read…waiting with great anticipation for his next literary accomplishment! I am privileged to call him a good friend…and daily e-mails exchanged…except when he is "in the field"…or on some sort of wild assignment…just hone that even more. Dr. Rick Kaufman, Forest Grove, Oregon.

ALASKA BEARS: *Stirred and Shaken*

James Oliver Curwood would be jealous of this book!
5.0 out of 5 stars
By Utah State Aggie, August 8, 2017

I sincerely regret my reviews of Jake's previous books.

Don't get me wrong. They are terrific books, packed with intrinsically interesting material told in an engaging and highly readable style. If you haven't read *ALASKA HUNTING: Earthworms to Elephants, Alaska Tales: Laughs and Surprises,* or *ALASKA FLYING: Surviving Incidents & Accidents,* you've missed out on some great leisure reading. No, Jake's previous books deserved every syllable of praise that I lavished on them. Nor do I regret my reviews, per se. I am not a writer, at least not a writer of books. In all modesty, however, I think I am a pretty good reviewer of books. I read, carefully and thoughtfully, every word of Jake's previous volumes. I put a great deal of thought into them. I think I was sympathetic, but fair. Even though I don't have the sustained focus to write a book, for five pages or less, I can conjure up some pretty snappy prose. I'm actually quite proud of the writing in those previous reviews. But I still regret them.

They didn't leave me much room to be more effusive in my praise. This book, *ALASKA BEARS: Stirred and Shaken*, is clearly Jake's best effort yet. It is the natural order of things that the more we work on a skill, the better we get. Jake's writing is getting better with each successive book. Stylistically, the prose is crisper, and the structure of the stories is more disciplined. Jake has always been a terrific natural storyteller, but he is unquestionably getting better as a writer.

And the stories! Holy Mother of Pearl! Great bears are not just top predators, they are THE top predators. They are enormously powerful, cunning, fearless, relentless killing machines. And Jake has been their nemesis. For cunning and lethality, he has been not just their peer, but their superior for fifty years. Because of that relationship, and the respect that Jake has for these other great hunters, the book has the feel of an elegy, a song of respect and admiration. The stories, even poorly told, would be absolutely gripping just because of the nature of the encounters. Jake's writing brings each encounter to adrenaline fueled, sweaty palmed life. Previously, I couldn't imagine dropping a charging six hundred pound grizzly with a last, desperate shot at less than ten yards. Thanks to Jake, now I can. And I may never sleep well again because of it.

Look, have I ever steered you wrong? Trust me. Buy this book.

Great storyteller, 5.0 out of 5 stars
By Arthur L. Bradshaw Jr., November 8, 2017

If you love real hunting tales or some of the unusual things different people do while hunting, you'll thoroughly enjoy Jake's latest. Like his earlier books, he tells a great stories and has you both laughing and shaking your head at the people he has hosted in far northern Alaska. I tend to read a lot of hunting books and articles, about all types of hunting all over the world. "Alaska Bears" is one of the most enjoyable and readable ones I've run across in recent years.

Jake draws the reader into his campsite antics or stalking a dangerous American Grizzly Bear, 5.0 out of 5 stars
By David A Johnson, January 20, 2018

Jake, the wilderness and big game guide, dentist, licensed aircraft and boat pilot, wilderness carpenter, old friend, trick player, teller of wild tales, composer of scientific papers on both dentistry and wildlife, but mostly, a good fellow to accompany any "chew-the-fat" wilderness campfire or sitting around the finest table at a Trump Hotel. The book *ALASKA BEARS: Stirred and Shaken* is the best yet of his series of 4 books about hunting and other wildlife encounters in Alaska. There are few historical or current books that can be found that encompasses so many entertaining, interesting and learning experiences as you will find in *ALASKA BEARS: Stirred and Shaken.*

I believe that a very interesting big screen movie or TV special could be made using Jake's 4 books if correctly strung-together. This one book, *ALASKA BEARS: Stirred and Shaken* should be the main plot.

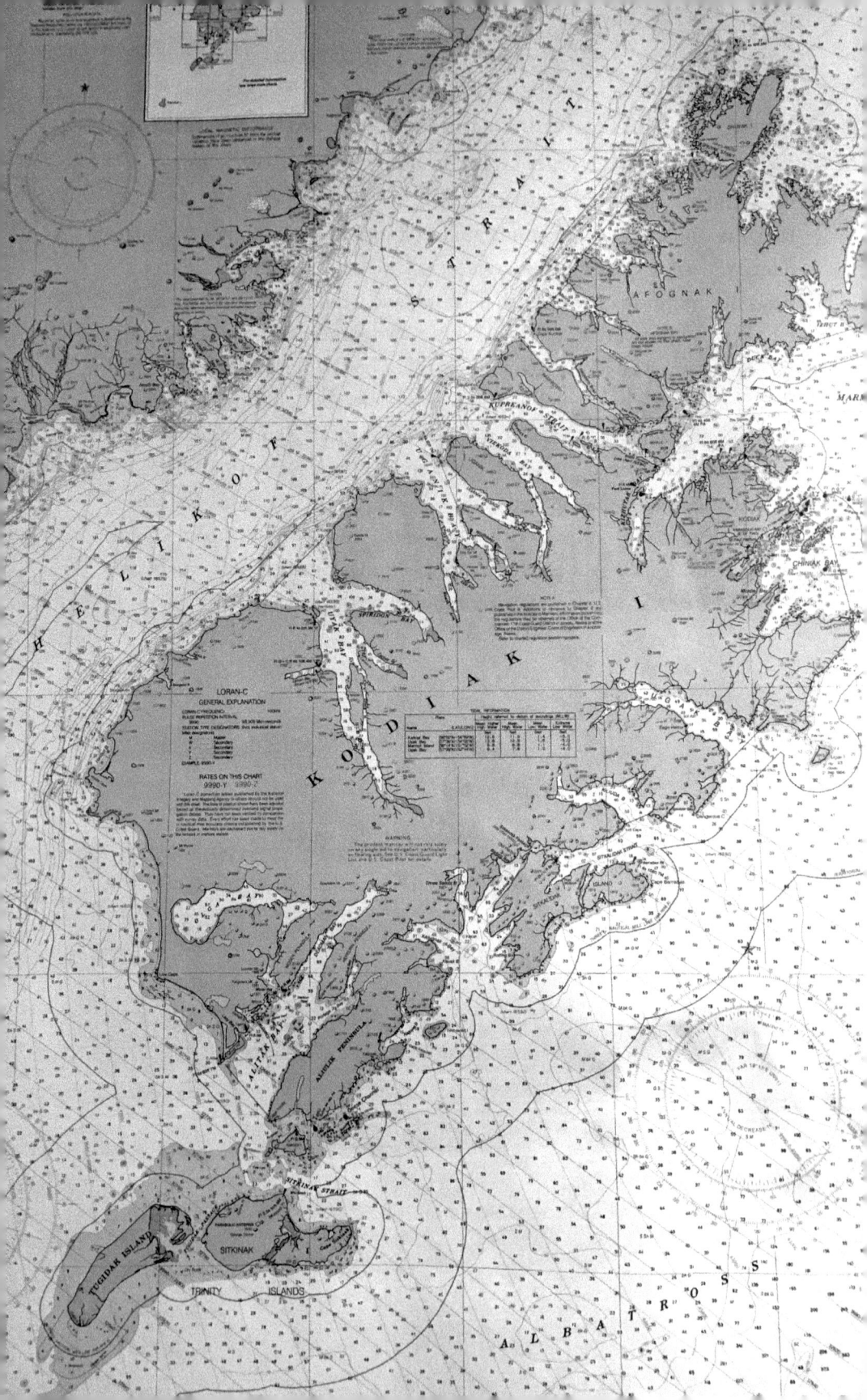

Contents

Admission to Heaven 15

I Wish I Had Taken More Photographs 17

The First Deer 23

Prehistoric Giant Deer 27

Characteristics and Origins of Deer 33

My First Sitka Blacktail Hunt, December, 1967 45

Return to Kodiak for a Sitka Buck 53

A Kodiak Skiff Hunt 59

Windage and My Longest Shot 69

An Unusually Wide Rack 73

King Crab Fishing and Deer Hunting 81

The Daughters' Deer 87

A Grandson's Visit to Kodiak 89

Walking Out 93

Hunting Solo—Not Always the Best Idea 99

The Big One Got Away 105

Dandy Buck, Bad Company on Kodiak Island 117

Care of the Meat 131

Heavy Buck Near the Beach 135

The Massive Pestrikoff Buck 145

Skip Woodward's Surprise	147
Stuck on the Beach	151
The Peruke	155
Hunter's First Buck	159
Luke Anderson's New Number One	163
An Outstanding Sitka Blacktail "cactus" Buck	165
Another Outstanding Non-typical Sitka Blacktail Buck	171
Joey's Buck	177
Norm Sutliff's Buck	181
Gary Cobban's Number One Sitka Blacktail Buck	185
Stewardship of Wild Game Resources	189
My First Strange Deer from the Kodiak Archipelago	193
Finding the First Undescended Testis	199
Dry Ice and Messenger RNA	203
The Sample Collection Procedure	205
Collecting fetuses	211
Deer "Horns"	217
Cryptorchid Bucks: Common Myths and Misconceptions	221
Attempting to Generate Interest	227
Various Considerations	247
Government Reluctance to Investigate	255
References	261
Photos	267

Admission to Heaven

Several years ago a deer hunting guest of ours told the story of the smartly dressed fellow who approached Saint Peter at the Pearly Gates, asking to be granted entry.

Saint Peter asked the man what his I.Q. was.
The man said it was 165.

Saint Peter asked if he had received his PhD.
The man answered in the affirmative.
Saint Peter said "Well, come on in, then."

Soon thereafter another applicant came to the gate, also praying for admission.

Saint Peter asked about his I.Q.
The fellow replied it was 137.
Saint Peter asked if he had a master's degree.
The man said he did hold a Master's in engineering.
Saint Peter replied, "Well, come on in, then."

It was't long before a disheveled, grizzled man shuffled up to the gate and requested entry.

Saint Peter, following protocol, asked for his I.Q.
The man said, "Wull ... it's 'bout sebenty, I reckon.
Saint Peter asked "Did you get your deer?"

Well, when my turn comes, if I am asked if I got my deer I will have to say,
"No, sir, I'm still hunting for him."

I Wish I Had Taken More Photographs

I never owned a camera until I bought a used Brownie Box for two dollars when I was in high school. In those days the cost of film developing, even for black and white prints, was enough to keep me from taking many photographs that I now wish I had.

As I grew older I began to carry a cheap film camera. Then, after a few years in Alaska I added a movie camera. As technology progressed and prices declined, eventually I acquired a better quality film camera and a video camera. The cameras were included on most of my trips, along with binoculars and other hunting gear. I came to realize that some of the things I was seeing and doing might never be repeated, except in my memories.

For me, and I suspect for most people, photographs incite far more vivid memories than mere human recollection can do. Objects in the photographs remain the same over time. Ground shrinkage and imaginary magnification are eliminated.

So, I really wish I had taken more photographs.

My labrador dogs, especially Zeke and Max, were as close to me as any dog could be to a man. Every lab I had loved to hunt -anything—and each one was always on the alert and ready for whatever might come. My labs did show signs of boredom when not hunting. We shared that and many other things.

The other day I was straightening things up in the office and a picture fell out of a book. It sent me back. There, smiling at me still after so many years, was my dog Max, pleased at the nice Sitka Blacktail buck we had taken together after an exceptional day of hunting so many years ago.

Max had passed on to the ultimate hunting grounds a quarter of a century before, but he came back to life in the photograph, and sweet memories of that fine dog filled my consciousness.

That day began with us up before sunrise in preparation for a hunt with a friend using his boat to access one of the less hunted areas on an island near Kodiak town. As I flipped the sausage and eggs out of the skillet, the phone rang. My friend called to inform me that the trip was cancelled. His spouse insisted that he attend a school bazaar sale featuring local arts and crafts. He asked if I would care to join them? Well, Max and I were thinking of hunting, not shopping for things we didn't need. So many such shows are full of truly bizarre items, most of which held no fascination for me. I thanked him and said Max and I would take a rain check on the boat trip.

But there was no rain that day and from the hang-dog look on Max's face, I figured he must have understood every word I had spoken on the phone.

The few miles of the road system of Kodiak get hunted more than any other area of the archipelago of course. But any hunting opportunity is better than none at all. We loaded the gear, Max jumped on the seat next to me and we were off in our old pick-up.

Frost was forming on the grass and brush as we drove down the road, and the sun was threatening to rise above the horizon. I counted about a half dozen cars parked along the dirt road leading to Antone Larsen Bay. We were late for those choice areas, but they were the most popular spots, and it was late in the season, so they would not necessarily be the best places to hunt anyway.

We drove on. Max kept his nose to the window, searching the surroundings for game. A doe and her fawn crossed the road in front of us. Max moved over and jabbed me in the ribs with his nose.

"Yes, buddy. I saw them," I assured him.

We arrived at the top of the pass and started down the grade toward the bay when I noticed a likely looking pocket on a hillside to the south. A large basin midway up the far mountain had long grass with spotty spruce trees and minimal alder brush. There were some open patches which might provide me with an opportunity to see any deer that moved through the area. Most road hunters would not care to walk that far. I glassed the area and decided we would try that place. It would be our first time in that section of hills.

I had to go back a quarter of a mile to find a suitable spot in the road which was wide enough to leave the truck. Actually, it was probably just as well to not park directly in front of the basin as that might draw other hunters' attention to the inviting area I had decided to visit.

With the truck in a safe place, Max and I started back down the road, then dropped off into the bush. We had a steep downhill incline to travel before reaching the creek. We crossed the clear, knee-deep water and began to labor up the opposite side. The water on Max's hair immediately froze into little balls that tinkled like tiny bells when he shook off. We reached the basin after two strenuous hours—strenuous for me anyway. I had not kept Max at heel as we climbed, allowing him to look and sniff around, ranging twenty to thirty yards or so from me. I figured he might jump a nice buck that we would otherwise pass by. He was putting in three to five times the amount of travel that I was, yet he was bursting with enthusiasm. I was feeling a bit tuckered.

Once at the lower end of the basin, it was time to have a sandwich and gaze about. I seldom carried lunch for Max, but his looks always melted my heart and I never failed to share my sandwich with my best friend. Even a stingy little piece was enough to satisfy him. I guess it was the thought.

Thirty minutes was enough time in that spot. I glassed three does and a small forked horned buck. Two flocks of Willow Ptarmigan had flushed up the hill from us, but I did not see any large animal to explain their flight. I decided maybe they just felt like jumping and pumping air.

The sun warmed the day and dried out the grass and soon had me starting to sweat. I removed my jacket and tied it to my pack board. Max's tongue was extended to maximum length. I told him that he looked a bit like a happy anteater.

Plenty of sign punctuated the grass and narrow trails, which were more like tunnels in the tall grass. There was evidence of their frequent use by deer. Deer could course through this growth without being seen unless the hunter was very close.

Six more deer showed long enough for me to determine that none was a mature buck, but I figured with as many deer as used the area and left sign, there might be a taker buck in there, somewhere.

Once we were at the head of the basin we climbed toward the crest of the ridge. Halfway up, I realized that if we took a buck much later in the day and much farther from the truck, we would be faced with a return though stumble-prone terrane after sundown. We'd have to battle alders and other growth which become "witches fingers", bent on tripping hunters after dark. A new moon would give us no light and the trail was indefinite and broken by brushy patches . Then there was that extra tall grass … with the potential for a sudden bear encounter.

It was time to hunt our way back.

Max seldom disagreed with me on decisions like that.

So we began our leisurely, ever observant return, coursing a few hundred yards to the east of our outbound route.

Max found a spring seep on the hillside from which he drank, so I sat down, had a swig from my water jug, and refilled it. It's such a welcome freedom to be able to scoop up water almost anyplace in Alaska and drink it without fear of catching a loathsome parasite or disease.

Enjoying the beauty of the golden sunlight of late afternoon, I picked up faint movements in the tall grass. Several deer were browsing on the remains of dried fiddle head ferns in the long grass below us. The grass concealed them, except in a few areas near some open patches of green moss. I counted eight animals at an estimated distance of five hundred yards from us. There might be more. Our trip up the hill had been only a few hundred yards west of that very area, but either we had not disturbed the deer, or they had moved into the district in the past two hours. A gentle breeze was coming up the hill to us. Max perked up his ears, sniffed the air, and moved to my side. He couldn't see the animals, but he poked me on the leg with his nose to alert me to their presence. I whispered my thanks to him as I stroked his head. "Yeah, buddy, I know they're nearby," I told him.

That dog had an extraordinarily fine nose and proper manners.

After a few minutes of close scrutiny with my binoculars I determined that one of the deer was a three by three buck with brow tines. He could fill the bill for us if I could find an opportunity to take him.

A quick evaluation of the lay of the land revealed a route we could use for discrete cover and remain constantly up wind. We could ease into a small depression, follow it downhill to a knoll which should put us slightly above the browsing deer and within range for a shot.

Twenty minutes of slow, silent stalking put us on the knoll. One deer was within forty yards of our position, but when it raised its head, it showed

I Wish I Had Taken More Photographs

Max was pleased with the little buck we took that beautiful day.

no antlers and, lucky for us, paid us no mind. A "skin head", it was. The breeze remained the same, so standing in place, I searched for the buck. Max, unable to see above the grass, poked his nose into my leg several times. He didn't care what type of head gear the critters might carry.

"Okay, buddy, I see them," I whispered.

Max looked up at me, no doubt questioning why I didn't act.

Long minutes later, the buck lifted his head, then lowered it. I quietly chambered a round and got ready. I calculated the buck was about seventy yards from us. The grass obscured body outlines of four deer, but I was uncertain which position the buck occupied. So we waited.

When the buck looked up again, I was ready and held for the top of his neck—just behind and below the ears.

When I fired, the buck dropped out of sight, but the other deer bounced up like popcorn in a skillet. They milled around, then two went back to browsing. One old doe decided things just didn't seem right and came bounding up the knoll toward Max and me. Most spooked game animals run uphill. That doe was acting true to her nature.

Max was tense, so I dropped my left hand to his head and patted him, comforting him without needing to speak or restrain him. He looked back at me with his big almond colored eyes and I nodded.

Just as the lead doe came to within twenty yards of us, the closest deer on the left saw me and the whole mob took off across the hill, quartering away.

Max was quivering, but he remained with his body pressed against my leg.

Removing the spent hull from the barrel, I put it in my pocket for future reloading, jacked a new round into the chamber and applied the safety. We went to look for the buck.

Our deer was right where last I saw him. His neck was broken and he had dropped straight down on all fours. He died instantly and we would lose none of the delicious meat.

Max poked the carcass with his nose several times before I could get him to lie down next to the buck for the photograph.

This was years before I acquired a digital camera. I felt lucky weeks later when I got the print in the mail, and the picture turned out so well.

We still had the rest of the slope down to the creek and the steep hill back up to the road to transport the deer, but with a pack board, it was no big chore. I cut the carcass up and loaded it on the board—far easier than dragging the whole carcass. We were at the truck just after sunset.

Max and I visited about the day and life in general as we headed for home. He talked a lot with me, but only when we were alone—never in front of other people. If he had not been too shy to speak in front of other people, I think he might have made a formidable pinochle partner.

Our day could not have been more memorable if we had made the boat trip.

Maybe I ought to straighten up the office more often. My wife would like that, and who knows what wonderful memories might rise up out of the clutter?

END

Edited by Martha Stewart.
This story was published in the *MENSA BULLETIN,* January 2018

The First Deer

As I was driving to the grocery store for doughnuts one morning, I saw a young buck in the dim light of pre-dawn. He was tip-toeing out of the salmon berry bushes at the edge of our yard. He brought to my mind a pointer dog, with his neck stretched straight out and his nose wrinkled in the flehming response. This is a mammalian behavior seen in horses, cats, deer and other large animals. (I think I've seen similar behavior in men who lost their sense of discretion.) The animal inhales with the mouth open and upper lip curled to facilitate exposure of the vomeronasal organ to a scent or pheromone. This results in a strange sneering appearance. The buck was straining to catch a whiff of a receptive doe. It was a lovely sight—an ideal opener for what I anticipated was going to be a beautiful day.

My fascination for deer exceeds the keen interest of I have always held for all animals, especially the "higher" mammalian life forms. For me, deer have always been special.

Sometimes as I wait for a meeting to begin, or during a less than gripping sermon, lecture, or discussion, I've frequently lapsed into day dreaming. Often I have tried to imagine how it might have been when the first deer (always an antlered buck in my visions) emerged from the antediluvian brush in the cold light of an autumn morning. Or was it in the fading glow following a sunset? Did it take place in a tropical, jungled area, or was it in a frosty northern woodland, or might it have been someplace in between? For that matter, it could have occurred in some ecosystem entirely different from what we see today.

There have been many permutations of my recurring day dream of the first deer. And there have been innumerable variations in the evolutionary end result of gradual adaptation of the cloven hoofed members of the order known as *Artiodactyla*.

Whatever the progenitor environment may have looked like, its form should come as no surprise to us, for deer, in one species specific form or another have adapted to every available eco-type from caribou in the seemingly "never summer" Arctic to the ubiquitous whitetail deer found throughout North and South America, including the Coes deer of the high, cactus cluttered deserts of the Southwest.

Then, there are the fanged barking muntjacs of lush primeval jungles.

We all owe profound gratitude to the scientists and speculators who have compiled a wealth of information on deer from prehistoric times to the present. Their discoveries and theories are readily available to anyone with access to a good library or a computer.

Currently fifty-three cervid living species of eighteen genera are recognized, however with the advent of DNA sequencing data, no doubt more species will be identified, from both past and present times.

It is likely that more deer species are yet to be discovered. New species from the entire spectrum of life on earth are being uncovered regularly. To name a few: *Homo habilis* ("handy" man) was discovered in 1960. *Homo floresiensis* (the "hobbit") was discovered in 2003, and as recently as 2013, *Homo naledi* ("star man") was discovered in South Africa. Among the so-called "lesser" animals, in 2017 a new species of rat, measuring eighteen inches long, was discovered in the South Pacific. Also, in 2017, a new and distinctly different species of Great Ape—an orangutan—was identified in Sumatra. And the long list of new discoveries of sometimes entirely new, and sometimes slight variants of already known animals goes on and on.

Of course the fossil record of Cervids is usually brought to light as a coincidence to other paleontological pursuits. Few "digs" have been conducted with the primary focus being ancient deer.

The imperative of practicality has always been the driving force of evolution. As a result we see many differences in body size and conformation, as well as a wide range of antler sizes and forms—from the extinct Irish Elk's (*Megaloceros giganteus*) massive headgear with a spread of more than four meters (more than twelve feet), akin to that of the modern Alaskan Moose (*Alces gigas*), the antlers of which sometimes weigh in excess of one hundred pounds, to the diminutive spikes or mere nubbins of the northern Pudu (*Pudu mephistophiles*) of the Andes Mountains.

I read that Muntjacs of the genus *Muntiacus* are the elders of the deer family. They are believed to have made their world debut 15 to 35 million years ago in the Miocene epoch of Western Europe. (The paleontologists' official "guestimators" left plenty of room for error. That's playing it safe in such speculations, based as they are, on scanty fossilized evidence.)

In a departure from what we think of as "normal" rutting behavior for deer, those muntjac species living today use primarily their tusks, rather than their antlers in rutting battles.

The fossil record of the Artiodactyl deer *(Cervidae)* family includes several now extinct species of huge deer that flourished throughout the Pleistocene era, which was a time of exceptionally large mammals that began around two and a half million years in the past and endured until about eleven thousand, seven hundred years ago. The onset of the most recent Ice Age seemed to bring about the gradual disappearance of the giant deer and a proliferation of smaller species.

Foto of Bob Johnson and his Muntjac.

But the last of the five great ice ages also coincided with the appearance of mankind on earth. Well after the beginning of the the Pleistocene Epoch humanoid life forms evolved to the point of being called man—*Homo*. Mankind's residency on earth is of much shorter duration than that of the many species of deer. The fossil evidence indicates that man's evolutionary changes were much more rapid and dramatic than those of deer—the *Cervids*.

The whitetail deer is believed to be the oldest large mammal species in North America. The oldest deer fossils were found in Florida and date back a whopping three and a half million years, whereas human life forms have only been around for about two hundred thousand years or so.

We think of all ungulates, deer in particular, as being strict herbivores—true vegans—but in recent years Scottish Red Deer have been documented eating shore birds, and in North Dakota white tail deer have been recorded eating the nestlings of song birds. In Canada, deer have been filmed eating birds caught in live capture "mist nets". The deer ate the small birds alive as the hapless flyers struggled to free themselves from the confining web. Their actions were not merely the accidental munching of birds as they browsed twigs. That were deliberate acts.

These are not behaviors of strict herbivores.

Deer of most species tend to show large variations in their population numbers, going from scarcity to over abundance, then crashing, and rebounding in a short time. This population resilience is due to several factors: their overall hardiness, their adaptability, and the fact that the females of most deer species—except Caribou *(Rangifer tarandus)*—produce two fawns each year from the time they are as young as six months throughout their normal life span of 6 to 14 years in the case of white-tailed deer *(Odocoileus virginianus)*. Elk *(Cervus canadensis)* normally live from 10 to 13 years, while Moose *(Alces alces)*, the largest member of the deer family, has a life expectancy of 15 to 25 years. The females normally produce two young each year.

Of course other factors such as condition of the range, amount of predation, climatic events, and adequate numbers of fertile adults of both sexes, influence any species ability to reproduce, especially after a crash in the population.

To say that deer have tremendous reproductive potential is an understatement.

But enough musing on my favorite wild critter, let's get to the history of deer.

Prehistoric Giant Deer

Has anyone ever seen an article describing a dig devoted to the discovery of a *Cervidosaurus antiguas* or *Artiodactyl prehistoricalensis*?

Well, I haven't seen one either. Occasionally we see stories about discoveries of what appear to be new hominids which may prove to be "missing links" in the human evolutionary tree. We are entertained by descriptions of the excavation and restoration of yet another *Tyrannosaurus rex*, but I have never read a story about a discovery primarily based on a research project to dig for an ancient precursor of deer.

Arguably an exception might be digs for the *Megalocerus giganteus*, the extinct "Irish Elk", also referred to as the giant deer or Irish giant deer, which were first recovered from bogs and lake sediments in Ireland.

Talk about the ultimate in charismatic megafauna !

Most deer fossils are found by pure accident in the course of industrial work or paleontological digs for other species.

But back to *Megalocerus*. That extinct species of deer is one of the largest cervids that ever occupied the earth. Their remains have been found from Ireland to China, with slight regional variations (Paleo subspecies).

However, with any member of the deer family, individual variations in antler form is common, so one must wonder if the sub-classifications of these ancient ruminants are truly valid, or are they merely based on dissimilarities of individual antler form, which are normally found within any branch antlered deer species. See the following two photos.

Interestingly enough, *Megalocerus* was first described in the seventeenth century—before the time of Darwin and the concepts of evolutionary biology. Initially, leading scientists believed that some representatives of *Megalocerus* must be living somewhere on earth at the time. The idea of extinction came later. The happenstance Irish elk discovery was a key moment in the developing studies of extinction and evolution.

Taxonomists tell us that *Megalocerus giganteus* derived from *Megalocerus antecedens*, but M.g was not closely related to either European elk *(Alces alces)* known in North America as the moose, or to the North American elk or wapiti *(Cervus canadensis)*. Studies suggest that the Irish elk was more closely related to the Red deer *(Cervus elaphus)* or the fallow deer *(Dama dama)*.

This *Megalocerus antecedens* skull shows more complex, compact antlers, but could be within the norm of species variation.

Initially, some research people thought the giant deer was identical to modern reindeer, but that proved to be erroneous.

It is estimated that Megalocerus stood nearly seven feet tall at the shoulder, with antlers up to twelve feet wide which weighed close to ninety pounds. The widest moose antlers spread up to eighty inches or a bit over six and a half feet. I have a moose rack only sixty-six inches wide that, with the skull, weighed right at one hundred pounds when the bull was killed. Officially the giant deer is believed to have weighed close to sixteen hundred pounds, which is comparable to a large Alaskan bull moose.

Upon his return from the great exploration of the Louisiana Territory, which he led with Meriweather Lewis, William Clark, at the request of President Thomas Jefferson, visited the Big Bone Lick in northern Kentucky. There, along with mammoth and other fossils, he discovered the first remains of a *Megalocerus* relative, *Cervalces scotti*, which It is the only known North American member of the genus *Cervalces*. Also known as the stag-moose it is believed to have become extinct approximately 11,500 years ago, near the end of the most recent ice age, as part of the mass extinction of large North American mammals

Stag-moose skeleton displayed at the Royal Ontario Museum

A mounted *Megalocerus* skeleton in Bremen, Germany. This is similar in appearance to the Ballaugh Elk skeleton discovered in 1819 in a marl pit at Ballaugh, Isle-of-Man.

We must keep in mind that the widest known moose racks are the very largest of the thousands on record, so I wonder if the few huge Irish elk racks that have been discovered are likely just average for their kind.

Stephen Jay Gould's important 1974 essay on *Megaloceros* "concluded that the large antler size and their position on the skull was very much maintained by sexual selection: they were morphologically ill-suited for combat between males, but their position was ideal to present them to intimidate rivals or impress females." (I have witnessed and filmed this display behavior in Alaskan moose, but I have repeatedly seen that if two large bulls are equipped with similar sized antlers, they usually do clash. Sometimes their fights result in fatal injuries to one or both combatants. So whether or not the massive deer fought rival males might be determined by the number of broken antler tips of recovered racks.) I once watched two huge moose bulls battle intermittently for more than four hours. The press of current duties kept me from witnessing the final outcome of the contest.

Annual growth of a set of antlers imposes extreme metabolic demands on the animal. Zoologists theorize that such expenditures of time and effort are not made without a specific purpose. Such expenditures are made in response to a biological demand. The potential gain must justify the pain.

Most scientists believe that sexual selection was the driving force behind the large antlers.

Regarding the cause of the disappearance and extinction of the Irish elk, several factors could have come into play. Possibly the large racks made the animals more subject to human or other predation in that movement through dense vegetation may have been impeded.

A change in the nutritional qualities of the animals' forage might have doomed the browsers. A significant decrease in calcium and phosphate, both necessary for antler growth, may have resulted from vegetation changes as glaciers receded and the climate warmed. A reduced availability of critical nutritional elements can result in the lowering of the female reproduction output by up to fifty percent.

This nutritional theory is supported by the fact that the most recent specimen of *M. giganteus* in northern Siberia, dated to approximately 7,700 years ago—well after the end of the last glacial period—shows no sign of nutrient stress. They come from a region with a continental climate where the proposed vegetation changes had not yet occurred.

"New radiocarbon dates from specimens in stratified contexts suggest that giant deer still existed 1,400 years after their supposed extinction. Giant deer fossils found on the Isle of Man at Ballaugh confirm the survival of the species into early Holocene in at least this area. The Ballaugh Elk skeleton is smaller than most Irish elk skeletons, but it has a relatively large skull and the antlers are well-sized for an adult male. This suggests that size decreased into the Holocene period".

With such scant evidence the cause of extinction cannot be definitely stated, however whatever the cause or causes, disappearance of the species was likely due to several factors which had different impacts and timing in different parts of the animals range.

The last few million years of the Glacial Periods, specifically the Pleistocene Epoch (2,588,000 to 11,700 years ago), saw the emergence and specialization of Irish elk and other cervid species, including the white tailed deer in North America.

In summation, we hunters are fortunate that through all the trials and tribulations of history, today we are blessed with many cervids to enyoy. And the populations of most are not threatened with extinction.

References:

1. Geist, Valerius (1998). *"Megaloceros: The Ice Age Giant and Its Living Relatives.* Deer of the World: Their Evolution, Behaviour, and Ecology. Stackpole Books. ISBN0-8117-0496-3.

2. Lister, A.M. (1987). *Megaceros or Megaloceros? The nomenclature of the giant deer.* Quaternary Newsletter 52: 14-16.

3. Gould, S.J. *The misnamed, mistreated, and misunderstood Irish elk. Ever Since Darwin.* W.W. Norton. pp. 79–90.

4. Stuart, A.J.; Kosintsev, P.A.; Higham, T.F.G. & Lister, A.M. (2004). *Pleistocene to Holocene extinction dynamics in giant deer and woolly mammoth.* Nature 431(7009): 684-689. PMID 15470427 doi:10.1038/nature02890 PDF fulltext[permanent dead link] Supplementary information. Erratum in Nature 434(7031): 413, doi:10.1038/nature03413

5. Vislobokova, I. A. (2010), *Giant Deer: Origin, Evolution, Role in the Biosphere*, Paleontological Journal. vol. 46 no. 7 pg. 643-775

6. Bro-Jorgensen, J. (2014), *Will their armaments be their downfall? Large horn size increases extinction risk in bovids*, Animal Conservation. vol. 17 no. 1 pg. 80-87

7. Lemaitre, J. F. (2014), *The allometry between secondary sexual traits and body size is nonlinear among cervids*, Biology Letter. vol. 10 no. 3

8. https://en.wikipedia.org/wiki/Irish_elk

Characteristics and Origins of Deer

Odocoileus hemionus sitkensis, or Sitka Blacktail Deer were first transplanted to Kodiak in 1924 when fourteen deer were captured near Sitka and released on Long Island, near the town of Kodiak. One report, which I have not been able to substantiate, claims that some Sitka deer were brought to Kodiak in 1887, (U.S. Fish and Wildlife Service—McCrea Cobb). The Alaska Department of Fish and Game file contains a letter from the U.S.Marshal's office to the Territorial Governor, dated March 15,1919, stating "The Alaska Commercial Company planted some deer on Kodak Island some twenty years ago, and up to the time of the Katmai eruption (1912) they were increasing very nicely…" Hunters and ash from the eruption decimated the Kodiak deer population.

We should use 1924 as the first introduction of deer to the Kodiak Archipelago, from which the current population grew..

In 1930, two deer from Prince of Wales Island in southeast Alaska were released on Long Island.

In 1934 five does and four bucks, captured near Petersburg, Alaska were released on Kodiak Island. Reports of deer sightings in the Kodiak Island group became more detailed and verifiable as the years went by.

The first legal deer hunt in the Kodiak Archipelago took place in 1953 and thirty-eight bucks were reported as having been harvested.

By 1967, approximately one thousand, five hundred deer were harvested on Kodiak (I got one of them) and the average annual harvest during that decade was nine hundred and fifty animals.

By the mid 1980s the deer population of the Kodiak Archipelago was estimated to exceed one hundred thousand animals and deer had swum to adjacent islands, including Marmot, Shuyak, Afognak and even to the more distant Trinity islands which are separated by several miles of ocean with strong currents and treacherous reefs. The deer swam between land masses throughout the Kodiak Archipelago, including to Marmot Island, less distant than some islands, but subject to extreme currents. No doubt many deer were lost in these waters as they sought greener pastures on distant horizons.

In November, 1989 with an extraordinarily heavy snowpack on the main island, I personally witnessed several hundred deer carcasses floating in the currents of the Geese Channel on the southeast aspect of Kodiak Island. Seeing so many drowned deer was an emotionally difficult experience for me. But such is nature and these events must have occurred many times throughout history. Range expansion or extension can come at a high cost.

The introduction of Sitka deer to Kodiak and their expansion to adjacent islands is one of the most successful manipulations of wild animal populations in North America.

But where did deer come from in the first place?

Let's start with some basic deer information. This a collection of widely accepted facts relating to anatomy, behavior, and the general nature of deer. Though some individual species vary in some respects, these features apply to most deer of the world. If the reader is not into scientific information, this may be a bit tedious. So, if you begin to feel smothered by too much biological information, facts, and intuitive speculation, it might be best to thumb through the pages until you find a picture that holds your attention.

My understanding and appreciation of deer has been greatly aided by the written and spoken information provided by others, both professionals and amateurs.

First, all deer of the world are of the order Artiodactyla and the family Cervidae. We refer to them as cervids. All deer are ruminants, meaning they chew their food which enters a specialized part of their four compartment stomach where their relatively low calorie, natural food is fermented thanks to microbial action. Then the food is regurgitated and chewed again. There are approximately 150 species of wild and domestic animals that are classified as ruminants.

Cervids (deer) are native to every continent except Antarctica and they are classified as herbivores, but on the small island of Rum which lies on the southwestern or Atlantic side of Scotland, local red deer are known to consume birds, in addition to their normal vegetarian diet of grasses, forbs, herbs and lichens. There have been documented reports of white tail deer eating Bob White quail eggs and chicks.

I previously thought of these as rare cases—behavior aberrations, actually.

Then I read reports of White-tailed Deer in North Dakota eating the nestlings of song birds and Canadian deer eating small birds caught in live capture nets.

So one must conclude that some species of deer are not strict herbivores, though it seems a serious stretch to classify them as omnivores.

The wide variety of types of deer has gradually evolved over countless millennia resulting in the largest, Alaska moose which weigh up to 1,800 pounds and the smallest, the northern Pudu of South America which weighs in at 7 to 13 pounds.

Some of the smaller species of deer (Muntjcs) have impressive fangs, appearing like those of the extinct Saber-toothed cat, or *Smilodon*. Vestigial canine teeth may sometimes be found in any deer species. I have found small maxillary (upper jaw) canine teeth in Barren Ground Caribou and Sitka black tailed deer. Elk and Red Deer males form such canines as well. Those are referred to as "ivory", and are prized as trophies for use as jewelry.

Antlers also vary from the up to one hundred pound palmated head ornaments of Moose to small spikes or nubs found on Pudu, Brocket deer *(Mazama americana)* and other small members of the order.

Amongst members of the Cervidae, only the females, or cows, as they are called, of *Rangifer tarandus*—which includes both Caribou and Reindeer—normally carry antlers, but their antlers are much smaller than those of the males, or bulls. Thus for most deer species, only the males are subjected to the strenuous metabolic demands of growing antlers for use through the rutting season, only to be shed shortly afterwards with a brand new set of antlers to be grown the following spring.

The metabolically expensive antler growth process is an exaggerated instance of formation of male secondary sexual characteristics. It begins as antlers emerge from their buds covered by skin and downy hair, called velvet.

Velvet is an extension of the skin that covers the growing antlers. During the growing period, blood carries nutrients to the antlers via the velvet. Mineralization of antlers along with a decrease of blood supply due to rising testosterone levels trigger removal of the velvet. This process is called shedding. Testosterone is the hormone that dominates antler growth. In four or five months the antlers begin to harden into bony structures as calcification occurs, along with blockage of the blood flow to the velvet. This cessation of blood flow progresses from the tips to the base. By late August to early September in the Northern Hemisphere, the velvet dries and is soon scraped off by rubbing the antlers on brush or whatever else is available.

Deer go through two moults (loss of pelage accompanied by growth of new hair) per year, growing more dense pelage for winter which is shed and replaced with a lighter coat for summer. All deer hair is hollow, which gives the animal great bouncy and is partially responsible for their ability to swim great distances.

Deer have large livers, **but no gall bladder**. This may be due to the relatively low percentage of fats in the diets of deer.

Seven major scent glands have been identified in deer.
Field and Stream magazine showed the instructive drawing on page 37. Locations of the seven major external deer glands.

1. The metatarsal glands locked on the outside aspect of the lower leg are believed to produce an alarm scent. These glands average about one inch in length in Whitetails and are about four inches long in Mule deer. As one might expect, hybrid animals, such as Whitetail/Mule deer mixes, have metatarsal glands between one and four inches in length.

2. The tarsal glands on the inside of the hock are believed to serve for individual recognition between deer.

3. The Preputial gland is found inside the buck's penal sheath or the doe's clitoris (yes, all female mammals have clitorises, and these

miniature organs are sometimes referred to as a "deer foot") and is believed to be responsible for transmitting the individual animal's identification to other deer.

4. The Interdigital glands which lie between the toes, leave a scent trail

5. Nasal glands are located inside the nasal passage, *but little is known of their function or purpose.*

6. Deer display large lacrimal or pre-orbital glands. These exocrine glands appear as trench-like slits and are lined with sebaceous and sudoriferous glands which exude secretions containing pheromones.

Biologists attribute the presence of pheromones exuded by the glands to allow much information to be silently passed between animals such as deer. Of course predators with their keen olfactory senses key in on these signs in their pursuit of deer.

Pheromones are chemical substances produced and released into the environment by an animal, especially a mammal or an insect, affecting the behavior or physiology of other members of its species.

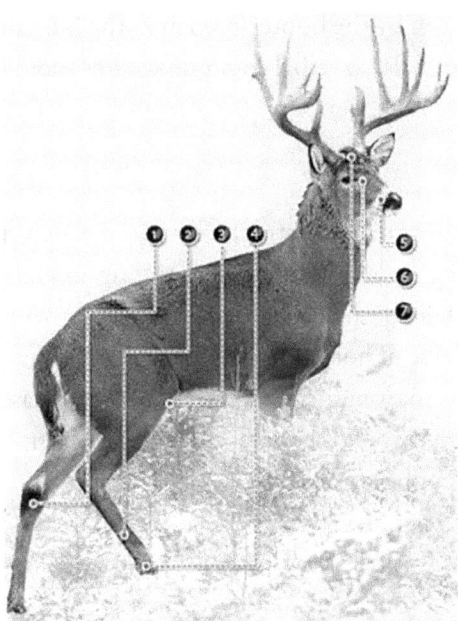

Deer often rub the pre-orbital areas on twigs or grass to leave evidence of their passing and their individual identity. Some researchers have found antimicrobial (antibiotic) compounds in secretions from these glands. This gland is most important to hunters wishing to have a taxidermist mount the dear for display and must be carefully skinned out to avoid a large hole in the skin near the inside aspect of the eye.

7. Forehead glands are tubular apocrine sudoriferous (sweat & pheromone producing) glands found in both male and female deer. These glands are larger and apparently more active during the breeding time. It is believed that testosterone levels play a dominant role in the activity of these often unnoticed glands. Testosterone is produced in both the testis and the adrenal glands, thus females have testosterone as well as do males.

Deer are born with the *tapetum lucidum* which is a biologic reflector system that is a feature found in the eyes of some vertebrates. It normally functions to provide the light-sensitive retinal cells with a second opportunity for photon-photoreceptor stimulation, thereby enhancing visual sensitivity at low light levels. This also results in the eyes of deer glowing when struck in the dark by a bright light. This is the biologic reason for that "deer in the headlights" look.

Hearing, sight and smell are well developed in all deer. Their oversized ears can be moved independently and often remind me of the deck men on an aircraft carrier using semaphore signals to bring in a landing plane. Those in pursuit of deer must pay careful attention to their position in the prevailing wind to avoid alerting the deer. Failure to do so often results in the deer departing without being seen by the hunter/predator. The human voice is very recognizable by wild animals, so verbal communications should be limited to a low whisper.

Deer Estrous

Female deer—does—go into heat (estrous, or estrus) for approximately a twenty-four hour period beginning in late October and ending in early December. It is believed that the fall equinox (September 22) along with the decreasing daylight triggers release of hormones that brings on the first estrous. A doe's cycle lasts twenty-six to twenty-eight days and is a two-phase cycle. The does are in heat only seasonally and they are "short-day breeders", being fertile for only a single day per heat cycle.

If the doe is not fertilized during her first "heat" period, she will become receptive again in about four weeks. This is especially important in situations where there are not enough fertile bucks available to impregnate the receptive does during the first heat. If the doe does not conceive until a second on third cycle the fawn will be born a month or two later than normal, and those late-born fawns will be less likely to survive the coming winter.

With the normal "rut" beginning in October and lasting through November, there is enough variance in the timing of does' fertility within any population of deer to become pregnant and give birth to their fawns over a similar period of time—a month our so—the following spring. Thus, late winters, rainy springs and other adverse climatic conditions in any single year, do not normally cause a large die-off in the fawn population. Births being spread out over a month or so insures that a significant number of the fawns will have conditions to survive birth and time enough to grow sufficiently to survive the coming winter. Furthermore, with most of the fawns born in a relatively short period of time, the predators are swamped with the huge number of newborn prey and most of the fawns survive.

Male deer, or bucks, are capable of breeding throughout the year, but only do so when stimulated by the appropriate pheromones emitted by the doe.

Sexual Maturity

White tailed deer are the most common, most frequently hunted and most studied of North American deer. Therefore, it's no surprise that most deer research has been done on white tails. However, all branches of the species Hemionus share many characteristics in appearance and anatomy as well as biological cycles. So bear in mind that most of the material published regarding sexual maturity, life spans, etc. are derived from white tail studies, but have reasonable, intuitive and practical application to Mule and Blacktail deer.

Deer reproduce early in life and throughout their average life span of up to ten years or so. The vast majority of does produce twin fawns each time they give birth. Most deer become sexually mature when they are about fifteen months old. Fawns born in May are ready to mate by autumn of the following year. However in areas of exceptionally good habitat conditions, females have their first estrous and can be successfully bred, and conceive at six months of age!

Thus it is not surprising to see a depressed deer population to recruit and repopulate rapidly, and in a few years rebound from low numbers to a robust herd, providing the habitat is favorable and other factors such as adverse climatic events, excessive predation, or over hunting do not prevent the recovery.

Sexual maturation is in large part dependent on body size and that depends on habitat quality as well as age.

Phototropism, the response of deer to the amount of sunlight which begins to wane as winter approaches, triggers the release of hormones—Follicle Stimulating Hormone (FSH), Luteinizing Hormone (LH) and Lactogenic Hormone (LH) which initiate the estrous cycle in females and the production of testosterone initiates the development of sperm cells in males. Testosterone also stimulates antler growth, body strength, and aggression in males.

The normal harmony of hormones begins in late October and peaks during the third week of November, when the majority of conception takes place. If the doe is not bred by a fertile buck, she will go into heat again in about four weeks.

Sleep

In my more than sixty-five years of hunting and observing wild animals I have often seen bears, wolves, coyotes, moose, wild sheep, and other big game animals sleeping in a wide variety of positions.

Most hunters I know report, as I do, that deer sleep with their heads in a variety of positions and with their eyes either opened or closed. They sleep wherever they bed. Their head position may be varied and changed frequently.

Most commonly I have seen them lying with legs tucked beneath their body and head held high, but I've seen them, with their front legs thrust in front and also lying on their side with all four legs extended and their chin resting on the ground. Sleep sessions seem to last about thirty minutes with dozing interrupted by frequent alert moments. It seems that every half hour or so the deer adjusts its position and frequently stand up to urinate or defecate, before lying back down.

Deer spend the majority of the time bedded and chewing their cud, in any given day, with their ears always erect and senses alert.

Vocalizations

The snort or alarm call is the most commonly heard sound, but bleats and mews can sometimes be detected. The bawl call can be heard on rare occasions when a deer is being traumatized. I have hear it only once when an injured buck was being attacked by a coyote in Arizona.

Evolutionary development of black-tailed deer.
But from where did Kodiak's Sitka Blacktail deer come long before they were captured in southeast Alaska, and how far back do we want to go, and what about Sitka blacktails and their ancient genetic kinship with other North American deer?

Odocoileus hemionus sitkensis, commonly known as the Sitka black-tailed deer is generally believed to be a subspecies of mule deer common to the western part of North America.

In my personal correspondence, telephone conversations with Dr. Valerius Geist and reading his books, he told me that he believes that mule deer derived from hybridization of black-tails and white-tailed deer *(Odocoileus virginianus)* at the end of the Pleistocene epoch—sometimes referred to as the Ice Age, which took place between twelve thousand and three thousand years ago. It appears that Mule deer may have only existed in their current form for as little as 7,000 years.

The end of the ice age occupies the same time period as the end of the Paleolithic age as described in human archaeology. We can surmise that stone age hunters may have pursued mule deer, as well as white tails.

However white-tailed deer are thought to have been around for over three million years! That makes white-tails the oldest known of the living species of North American deer and examination of ancient remains indicates they have retained essentially the same form for the entire period. Muntjacs of the old world left evidence of their appearance long before whitetails, they date back to 15 to 35 million years ago.

Whitetails adapt well to a variety of habitats, which explains their presence from Canada to South America, from mixed woods forests to high plains deserts and low altitude jungles, and from sea level to tall mountains. Their adaptability helps explain how they have been so successful for so long.

Taxonomists have subdivided the genus *(Odocoileus)* into two subspecies. They are *Odocoileus virginianus*, the white tails, and *Odocoileus hemionus*, the blacktail and mule deer. Today there are many sub-species of the two main types of deer. There are some biological reasons for the distinctions, primarily the phenotype or form of isolated or separated groups of deer. The two subspecies can interbreed and such genetic mixing may produce outstanding individual animals. The offspring of such interbreeding seem to seldom survive long in the wild. Dr. Valerius Geist theorizes that the poor success of hybrids is primarily due to the fact that they do not show the "stotting" behavior common to mule deer, which is a unique four-legged jump which gives the animal an advantage in escaping uphill.

In 1987 I measured the world record nontypical Coes deer. That was an example of one Whitetail/Mule deer hybrid that did survive—and in grand fashion—until it was harvested by a hunter. I wrote a story called World Record Non-Typical Coes Deer which was published in Petersen's Hunting in the November, 1989 issue.

Dr. Geist suggests that during the ice age some populations of white tail deer became separated from the main group and began to evolve differently due to their isolated, localized survival requirements. When the glaciers began to dramatically recede about 12,000 years ago, the formerly separate deer populations were once again able to interact and interbreed, which gave rise to the mule deer subspecies, but mule deer were not firmly established until about 7,000 years ago.

Evolution takes time—eons for more advanced animals—with many side trips up wrong alleys before a species is firmly established. This is especially true in animals as complex, large, and long-lived as deer. Even longer—much longer—for humans. In house flies, a new generation occurs every month or so. In deer it takes many years. Basically one can gage the time required for significant evolutionary change to be based on the average life span of the animal in question. So, I suppose, elephants and whales must be the slowest of the great mammals to demonstrate evolutionary changes—theoretically even slower to change than humans.

The most rapid evolutionary changes occur in viruses, which is due to them having only a single strand of DNA, whereas "higher animals", including humans and deer, have a double strand of DNA. A mutation in viruses results in immediate expression of the new trait, but in the case of more complex organisms, a mutation on one chromosome must be matched by a similar mutation on its allele (the same gene of the second of the pair of chromosomes). This explains why we see new flu viruses requiring a new vaccination each year, as well as why "higher" animals seem to change little over time.

Humans transitioned from hunter-gatherers to agricultural societies within the last 10,000 years, and archaeological evidence indicates dogs were domesticated as far back as 27,000 years ago—long before mule deer as we know them even existed! So, the really old-time hounds did not have opportunities to chase mule deer.

Among other noticeable changes, the mule deer grew larger and more robust than white tails and their tails became shorter and showed a black tip.

DNA is an immense boon to the study of evolution, as well as in criminal investigations. White-tailed deer and mule deer have nearly the same mtDNA (mitochondrial DNA), which is primarily a record of the female ancestral line of the animal being investigated. However, the mtDNA of black-tailed deer is quite different from the other two major species. These studies indicate that most interbreeding was between black-tail bucks and white-tailed does.

Careful scrutiny of mtDNA indicates we should consider black tails as a unique species, rather than a subspecies of mule deer. In fact evidence seems to indicate that blackmails existed before mule deer.

Two Types of Black-tailed Deer

While attending the University of Oregon Dental School in Portland, I hunted the local deer—*Odocoileus hemionus columbianus*. These deer occupy coastal woodlands from northern California to British Columbia.

From somewhere south of the Alaska border and throughout Alaska, the coastal deer are referred to as Sitka blacktails—*Odocoileus hemionus sitkensis*—but no distinct geographic line or characteristic differentiates the Sitka from the Columbia black-tail. However some easily seen, phenotypic differences are apparent, the most notable of which is the "rose' or coronet at the base of the antler. The rose of Columbia black-tails is similar to that of white-tails, with a neat, close-nit appearance, while the rose of Stika black-tails often has the appearance of a splotched or melted mass of pearling.

All North American deer are primarily browsers, selecting mostly leaves which are easier to digest than grasses and twigs, with approximately fifteen percent of their food being a mixture of grasses, sedges, and lichens. Fiddlehead ferns are a favorite fodder of Kodiak deer.

Rutting normally takes place between late October and early December in the Kodiak Archipelago. The first full moon of November normally sees the bucks in full rut mode. They drop their antlers anytime after Thanksgiving, but I observed a large mature buck still carrying both antlers in early February in 2017 and a saw three bucks (a forked horn, a three by three and a four by four) inside the Kodiak city limits in January, 2018.

New antlers begin to emerge from their buds in April and the growing head gear normally carries velvet until sometime in late August or September.

After a successful breeding, the does normally carry the fetus for close to seven months—about 200 to 205 days. Most fawns are born in late May. Twinning is the norm for healthy, mature females in good habitat. Interestingly, fawns have no scent for the first week or so. This provides some protection from predators, though predation of deer on Kodiak by other than humans, is not high.

In the Kodiak Archipelago, the deer on Afognak, Shuyak and adjacent Islands as well as the northern, more heavily wooded parts of Kodiak Island are reported by the Alaska Department of Fish and Game to average 90 to 110 pounds, with larger animals occasionally taken. Noticeably deer with larger body size come from the less forested, open country on the south end of the island group. I have personally weighed whole, un-gutted deer carcasses taken near the beach around Alitak Bay. Using an accurate scale, I recorded several large bucks at 235 pounds and one was a bit over 260 pounds.

Of interest to this discussion, desert white tailed deer, or Coues deer, were named by a U.S.Army surgeon, Elliot Coues. These high desert whitetails differ greatly from other deer in the timing of their rut, which takes place in January. The fawns are usually dropped in July or August to coincide with the rains that produced new nutritious growth that time of year, which augments the doe's ability to produce milk for the fawns. The bucks carry their antlers until April or May.

Mature Coes bucks weigh up to 125 pounds while most does register 80 pounds on the scales.

So much for a run down of deer of North America.

My First Sitka Blacktail Hunt, December, 1967

Hunting has always been a driving force for me, and pursuit of wild game runs the gamut of critters from Earthworms to Elephants, which is the title of my first book.

Some of the exotic species I have pursued, including African Cape Buffalo, Greater Kudu, other plains game and Lion, the Giant Rusa deer of New Caledonia, the Red, Fallow and Roe deer of Europe, all bears of North America and many other species have certainly left their indelible marks in my membrane (is that the recollection folds of one's brain?), but the more commonplace species readily available to most Americans have been my favorites. I'm referring to North American deer of all species and bunnies—both rabbits and hares.

For my first year in Alaska I would remain legally classified as a non-Resident which translated to my need of a more costly nonresident hunting and fishing license which was twenty dollars then, and an additional tag or permit fee for hunting each species of big game. I splurged on a Black bear tag and a deer tag at ten bucks each. Some of the big game species, such as Brown/Grizzly Bear and Dall sheep required that I employ the services of a Registered Guide, which would have been completely out of my financial reach and not worthy of serious consideration.

I was anxious to hunt every species available, but figured that for the first year I could easily keep fully occupied in my spare time with hunting big game that did not require a guide, and for which the tag did not set me back too much. Deer and black bear tags at ten dollars each I could afford.

Early on I got licensed and bought federal Waterfowl Stamps to allow me to get after ducks and geese.

Snowshoe hares, called rabbits by most of the local folk, and ptarmigan were included on the bag list at no extra charge beyond the price of the hunting license.

Alaska's only native deer, the Sitka Blacktail *(Odocoileus hemionus sitkensis)*, is common only to the South East Panhandle, Prince William Sound and, thanks to some introductions in the nineteen twenties and thirties, Kodiak Island. Today such a farsighted introduction of any specie would be unlikely due to overly restrictive regulations.

Having been transferred to the Alaska Native Medical Center in Anchorage from the Marine Hospital on the east coast, I was assigned the position of Itinerant Dentist, the only such job in the state at the time. My duties would take me to many villages from the Southeast Panhandle to the Arctic and westward out the Aleutian chain of islands. My first trip was to the village of Tatitlek, in Prince William Sound. I had studied the geography and natural history of the Great Land and figured I just might get an opportunity to hunt deer and or black bear while on that trip, so I purchased a tag for each species. The black bear tag got filled before I even reached the village, but I found no opportunity to use the deer tag.

However, I scheduled my next trip to Kodiak Island and each of its six remote villages. The trip would last from mid-October until the middle of December. This would coincide with the deer rutting season and hunting should be at its best. I carried my non-resident deer tag along.

My itinerary took me clockwise around the island from Kodiak to Old Harbor to Ahkiok and then up the west side adjacent to Shelikof Strait.

As always, I carried my spinning rod and reel, my 30:06 rifle and my twelve gage shotgun along with the dental freight. I could not resist the temptation to shoot some Emperor Geese at Ahkiok, along with some beautifully marked Harlequin ducks. I had only seen pictures of these magnificent birds prior to this trip.

The plucked and baked geese provided my assistant, the local school teachers and me with a most memorable, delicious Thanksgiving dinner. I was especially thankful that at last, I had reached Alaska and was able to dine on the bountiful wild game food that it offered.

Deer had gradually been expanding their occupancy of the archipelago for the past thirty-five years, but had not yet reached Old Harbor on the

My First Sitka Blacktail Hunt, December, 1967

east side of the main island, however they were numerous on the west side as far south as Larsen Bay.

In Larsen Bay I hunted one weekend with the school teacher as he harvested a doe. Sunday morning as I headed for the outhouse with rifle in hand I shot a beautiful silver fox (I always keep a few hand loaded solids in my shell box for fur bearers), but I saw no buck to shoot at on that two day trip. With that ten dollar tag, by golly, I wanted to hold out for a deer with a nice rack!

That school teacher was a man after my own heart. When we got back to the village, he and his wife set about canning some of the fresh venison. It turned out delicious and he sent two quart jars with me when I departed.

The last village on my trip around the island was Ouzinkie. I worked full days and long nights to allow me to take

Emperor geese were abundant and legal to hunt in 1967.

Thanksgiving and a few more dinners.

Sunday off. Actually the weekends and evenings were officially "off" times, but I felt obliged to work as much as possible, as the local people had only one chance each year to receive dental services delivered in their own village. No one ever begrudged me the time I took to hunt or fish on Sunday. On the last Sunday in Ouzinkie (situated on Spruce Island, a short distance from Kodiak Island) before I was scheduled to fly back to Kodiak, I arranged with a fellow for whom I had performed some dental services to take me across the narrows to the main Kodiak island. He dropped me off in the morning and said he would return to the same beach to pick me up just before dark.

From the beach I walked up the steep slope only a short distance before I encountered dense alder tangles—more like jungles, they were. I had read some books on plants of Alaska and read that four species of alders were native to the state. I reckoned that these must be either Sitka Alder or Red Alder, more likely the latter. But whatever type they were, they were hideously frustrating to fight through.

Alders grow up from the slope pretty much toward the sky, but they also send long branches out which tend to

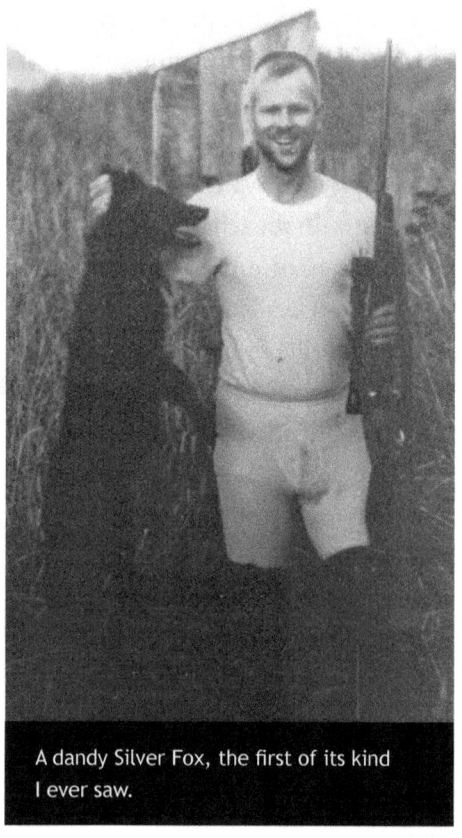

A dandy Silver Fox, the first of its kind I ever saw.

hug the ground, then turn up at the end. These branches can be over twenty feet long and are very tough and springy. It may be that gusty storm force winds played a part, but it appeared that a crew of malevolent forest demons had put in a lot of overtime weaving the alder branches together to make passage all the more difficult. In some places they are so dense, with criss-cross branches, it's like walking through a large net with variable meshes. The walker's temptation is often to step on a low hanging branch, but the tough growths tend to spring up as one lifts a foot which can lead to an ignominious tripping.

Then, there are downward growing branches from higher on the main trunk through which the person must contort his body, with the back pack in place and the rifle in hand. For me, it takes both hands, thoughtful caution, and a lot of time to negotiate such a tangle. Passing downhill through such a maze is only slightly less miserable than going up. To describe the passage through dense alder thickets as being extremely frustrating is inadequate.

"Packing through the alders" soon became a uniquely descriptive phrase in my vocabulary. I often apply it to dealing with government agencies and politicians, which can be even more frustrating than the actual physical activity of battling brainless plants.

It's not uncommon to stumble or fall in a patch of dense alders. Early on I figured "witches fingers" must be responsible for my spills.

Some game trails were evident in the tangle, but they were of little help to me, though most did show signs of frequent and recent use. Fecal pellets and tracks were abundant.

In retrospect, it probably took only three quarters of an hour to battle through the alders before I reached the primary Sitka spruce forest, but it seemed to take half of forever at the time I did it. I was anxious to get into deer country that provided some decent visibility. Snow was deeper at just a few hundred feet above sea level and the white stuff held a profusion of deer tracks and droppings which were quite fresh as a new snowfall had graced the hills the night before.

The higher I climbed the more and larger open areas I found. The larger clear spaces were dotted with stumble- causing hummocks and grass, which were barely discernible under the snow. A considerable amount of fiddle head fern—now bent over from snow load and turned a dark brown, and berries added to the vegetation, all of which looked like potential prime deer fodder to me.

As I topped out and was about to descend the opposite side of the crest I looked back at Spruce Island and could see some of the Ouzinkie houses. As long as a heavy fog did not envelope the area, I was sure I could easily navigate my way back to my pick-up point. The wind was offshore, coming from the Southwest, but considering the mountainous terrane, I suspected that local effects were directing the wind, rather than a weather system. Rogue gusts are not welcome when hunting and I was getting plenty of those.

A doe with two robust fawns rose from her bed to watch me from a nob only fifty yards away. They seemed curious, rather than alarmed, and remained motionless as I slowly walked out of sight. In all, I observed sixteen deer, including one small forked horn buck before I sat down on a prominence to glass across a large draw. Traveling was easy once I gained the high ground and I figured I could go at least another mile before I had to be judicious about killing a buck, which would have to be packed or dragged out by myself—hopefully well before dark.

As I chewed my Spam sandwich I sighted five more deer, two of which were bucks across the draw. The larger of the two was a dandy three by three with brow tines—that would be an eight point by eastern count. If I were hunting Coes deer in Arizona, he would be a taker for sure. I decided that was a good first big game animal for me in Alaska. I felt a warming rush of adrenaline.

Easing off of my perch, I threw on my back pack and skirted around some large Spruce trees to get closer to the good buck, which was still standing in the same place, turning his head from side to side as he searched, most likely, for a doe. The rut was in full swing. I was forced to take my eyes off the target as I went around the broadly spread lower branches of a large Sitka Spruce. When I emerged on the other side, I could not find the deer. So I waited, motionless.

Just less than a minute before the deer had been standing in the clear, separated from cover by several yards in each direction, but he had vanished! I kept searching, using my eyeballs, rather than my binoculars, to give me a broader field of view, hoping and expecting to see a movement.

Then, just below me I glimpsed the top points of a set of antlers. I turned away and, as silently as possible, jacked a shell into the chamber of my rifle.

There it was again! I saw the antler tips come up and disappear. The buck was coming up the hill toward me. As he took a step up he lifted his head and as he put weight on his front feet, his head went down into the long grass and ferns, and momentarily out of sight.

Bringing my rifle to my shoulder, I flipped off the piece of rubber inner tube that I used as a scope cover. When the deer drew closer, the scope revealed that it was not the buck I had selected. This deer was a three by three, but its antlers were spindly. I was tempted, but decided that going back without a buck was better than botching a chance at a really decent one. I pushed the safety back on. The young buck continued up the hill, passed about seventy yards to my right and continued into the spruce trees. As his rump disappeared I caught a movement below and to my left.

It was the heavy antlered buck, and he was coming up the slope, directly toward me.

When the larger buck was in the middle of the open spot between me and the nearest cover, I held on the animal's throat, but did not fire. This was indeed a worthy trophy, but just as I was ready to squeeze the trigger, I heard some noise below and wanted to see if an even bigger buck would materialize and offer me a shot.

With strong reservations, I let the big boy walk past me and disappear into the trees. I hadn't seen enough of these deer to know for sure how good he really was.

Soon I heard the rattle of antlers below me. I had to see what was making that delightful music. I eased to the brink of a steep drop off and saw two small forked horn bucks going at it. Neither was the equal of the one I had just allowed to pass free.

Slowly I retraced my tracks in the snow to my former location, then quietly followed the tracks of the big buck. He had gone beneath some low hanging spruce branches, which were now bare of snow due to his passage. I spent ten minutes getting through the stand of trees before I saw him

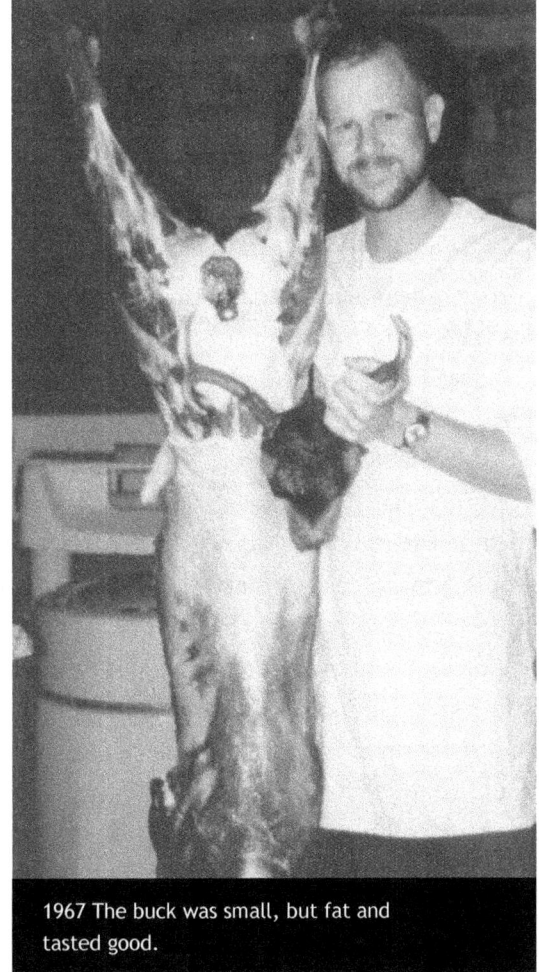

1967 The buck was small, but fat and tasted good.

running up an adjacent hillside in pursuit of a doe. There was no time for a shot. I'd blown my opportunity at that dandy deer.

But, I was hungry for fresh meat and the thought of prime venison had me in its grip, so I went back to the edge of the drop off and encountered the two smaller bucks looking straight at me from only forty yards away. Time was running short and this was my only day to hunt, so I took the slightly larger one. My Lee Loader bullet passed through his throat and entered the chest cavity, collapsing the pugilistic little buck in his tracks.

That young critter had saved me the work of crossing the deep draw, lined on both sides with alders, and of course, then packing him back to the side where he now laid.

With plenty of time to reach the Narrows well before dark, I decided to slide the intact deer down to the beach after gutting him. The meat would remain cleaner this way. I removed the lower legs but left the heart and liver attached inside the chest cavity to avoid loosing them.

Feeling light on my feet, no doubt due to the joy of at least taking such a fine meat animal, I made it back to where I could see the village houses in a short time. I made a mental note that if I hunted that area again, I could go much further back and still have an easy pack to the beach.

Much of the way down through the alders I spent sliding on my bum, but still had to kick, squirm and fight to get past the pestiferous branches. The slope was steep and snowy enough to make pulling the carcass an easy chore.

Well ahead of dark, I sat on the beach, ate my second sandwich, and reflected on that fine day, before my skiff ride arrived.

This was my second big game animal taken in Alaska and, considering all, it was well worthy of that distinction. In addition, Grandma would get a beautiful silver fox skin from my first season of hunting on Kodiak Island.

Return to Kodiak for a Sitka Buck

In 1968 I returned to Kodiak to once again make the annual "rounds" of village dental trips. The previous year's timing had been about right, so I scheduled the trips for the same this year—almost to the day.

This time I sort of "knew" the country and the people, and the people knew me. That promised to open some special opportunities for hunting that I had not been offered before.

During my week-long visit to the southernmost village, Ahkiok, I got in some Emperor goose hunting by walking out from the school in time to catch the rising sun and moving geese, as I had done in 1967. I spent the evenings holding clinics for adults and pre-school children, so the only opportunity to hunt was before most of the people of the village were awake. It worked well for me, but not so great for the geese.

One of the elders offered me an overnight trip to Portage Bay to hunt seals. We used a cannery owned fishing boat. We saw several massive Brown bears on that trip, but we harvested only some earless pinnipeds, known locally as hair seals, spotted seals or harbor seals (*Phoca vitulina* or a similar species). We encountered some of the eared pinnipeds—those were Steller sea lions *(Eumetopias jubatus)*—also, but we had no opportunity to harvest any of them. I had eaten meat from both harbor seals and sea lions the previous year while in the Aleutians, and I preferred sea lions, as their flesh is somewhat milder to my taste than that of the smaller seals.

The main means of travel between the villages in the Kodiak Archipelago was by small boat, but as time was of the essence, and government regulations required that we travel by licensed transportation providers, we usually jumped from one village to the next on scheduled mail plane trips. The passenger fares and freight charges on the mail runs were much less expensive than the cost of a charter and I was determined to spread my ten thousand dollar annual travel budget to include as many villages in my several areas of responsibility as possible. (In addition to the Kodiak Archipelago, I was to provide a once per year visit to villages in Prince William Sound, Cook Inlet, Kenai Peninsula, the Lake Iliana area, and the Aleutian chain.)

Most of the Kodiak villages claim to an "airport" was the ocean adjacent to the community. A Grumman Goose or Widgeon flown by Bob Hall, owner of Kodiak Airways, or one of his pilots, would land in the water, lower the wheels and taxi up onto the beach, then do an abrupt power turn (normally to the left) and be ready to taxi back into the water for the departing take-off after rapidly unloading passengers and freight.

This year the trip was complicated by adverse weather and rough seas which kept me more village clinic-bound that had been the case in 1967. The fall equinoctial storms came in with a focused vengeance and persisted well into winter. I took no time off for hunting other than the one weekend seine boat trip to Portage Bay, and a few early mornings gunning for waterfowl. As wind and water conditions remained mostly unfavorable for travel, I tried to complete each village and move on as soon as possible, which meant whenever the weather permitted.

Learning the benefits of the steam baths, locally called a banya, and practicing up on my Schottish dancing were new experiences for me. I read a lot, as well.

Village people were very hospitable and acquainted me with special foods from the beach, including chitons and sea urchins, or as they called them, ooducs and ooheeducs. They tasted good.

I was hoping for a day or two of unmitigated nice weather to hunt deer on the northern end of Kodiak.

The extra hours and weekend work, along with some brief, but fortuitously timed breaks in the stormy weather, put my assistant and me into Port Lions a few days before Thanksgiving. I was at least three days ahead of my projected travel schedule, so when the big weekend came, I planned to spend at least two full days hunting deer. This was different country than I had hunted the year before, but that made it all the more appealing to me.

One of the school teachers in Port Lions was an especially keen hunter, so he and I set off on foot before daylight one morning for Viekoda Bay,

Return to Kodiak for a Sitka Buck

which was reputed to provide some of the best deer hunting on the island. We'd planned to walk the several miles over, but after about a half hour of foot slogging in fresh, wet snow, another teacher came along with a six-wheeled Catagator or some such all terrane vehicle and offered us a ride, so we gratefully jumped on.

We made much better time on the machine and in spite of the lurching, spine jamming, kidney traumatizing ride over a barely discernible trail, we arrived at the crest of the ridge overlooking Viekoda Bay. Most of the journey had been along a small stream, then over a low divide and down another small drainage. The seldom used and poorly marked trail turned sharply up hill, so we lurched up toward the stand of Sitka Spruce trees near the ridge line.

The moon was waxing and only a few days remained before it would be full. Heavy overcast conditions all week made the deer hunting conditions ideal. There was little wind and a fresh four inch coat of snow covered all we could see. Tracking was ideal and the bucks would still be looking for love. It had been cold enough for long enough that most of the bears would be asleep in their dens. With a sharpened rifle, an adequate lunch and a pocket full of shells, what more could one ask for, I wondered? To top all that off, we had a ride back to town, or at least a means of sending our meat back, if we shot more than we cared to pack on our backs.

The Catigator owner parked his vehicle on an open ridge that would be easy to find when it was time to head back. From there we three went in separate directions.

Both my companions spotted several deer browsing on the slope directly below where we stood and struck off in that direction. I decided to cruise the ridge line in a southeasterly direction which lead toward the head of the bay. As I moved slowly along I was never out of sight of fresh tracks of multiple deer. I glassed several small bucks and antlerless deer below me. As is so often the case, the animals did not look up and remained unaware of my presence.

About a half mile from the machine I noticed an unusually large set of deer tracks. These prints were much larger and wider spaced and they seemed to sink further into the snow than the other tracks, that I decided I should spend some time following them in hopes of seeing the animal that made them. As the trail descended toward some heavy patches of alders I slowed down, not wanting to push my quarry into the tangled alder jungle below.

As I stood watching the small swale below me I saw what I assumed must be the maker of the large tracks. This typical three by three buck seemed half again as big in body size as the other bucks I had seen and he was looking directly at me. His rack looked heavy and symmetrical, like the one I did not shoot at the year before. I estimated him to be just over one hundred yards away. I stripped the rubber inner tube section off my scope, put a shell in the chamber and brought my rifle to my shoulder. It was an easy shot and the big buck collapsed where he stood when the 165 grain hand loaded bullet struck him in the neck just below his chin and penetrated through to crush his spine.

With that shot, five more deer, including two small bucks, seemed to blossom out of the grass near the downed buck. All briefly gazed in my direction, then began to move away and were slowly swallowed by the alder maze.

This was the most impressive Sitka Blacktail buck that I had seen in my two seasons of hunting them. His antlers were heavy and beautifully symmetrical. What a fine way to notch my first deer tag as a resident of Alaska. This was the type of buck I had been dreaming about the previous year. I was elated!

As I made my way to the deer I heard shooting from the direction my companions had gone, so not wanting to be the last to the machine I quickly gutted the buck, leaving the heart and liver suspended inside the chest cavity. I removed the lower legs at the knees and attached a short piece of halibut ground line I had picked up on the beach to the antlers. There was plenty of time, and with the lubrication from the snow, the dragging would be easy, so I decided to drag him to the vehicle intact and with the hide on, thereby keeping the meat as clean as possible.

When I was within sight of the vehicle I saw a smaller three by three buck come running up the hill toward me. I debated shooting it, but when it stopped just sixty yards from me, I shot it in the neck. It wasn't nearly as large or impressively antlered as the first buck, but this would add to my winter meat. It was a gift, and I accepted it.

Return to Kodiak for a Sitka Buck

The buck in my right hand was a good twenty to thirty percent larger in body than the other.

I quickly gutted and removed the lower legs from the second buck, took the first to the vehicle and returned for the other. I was sitting on the seat enjoying a sandwich when my companions came up the hill. Each had taken a buck similar to my second deer.

We loaded the vehicle with the four deer and headed back toward Port Lions. It was crowded, and we had to avoid being punctured by antlers of the dead deer. In some places two of us would have to walk and push, but after what seemed like no time at all we were hanging the deer in the school shop. It was a good thing we had all scored as a fresh storm moved in that night and raged for the next two days.

In Alaska and elsewhere, one must appreciate and take advantage of good weather conditions when blessed with same.

A Kodiak Skiff Hunt

One might think that being prepared for any venture, especially an outdoor trip "goes without saying", as is so often said. But it needs to be said, and emphasized.—BE PREPARED! I've been on too many excursions for which the participants, or perpetrators if you will, were not properly prepared. The consequences ranged from mild discomfort to potentially life threatening circumstances.

One damp and dismal day in Kodiak as we were enjoying deep fried fish, my friend, DeVoe Friend—yes, that was his last name—mentioned that he would like to go hunting in the southwestern part of our country for a winter break. I did some telephone calling. Dean and Ricardo, a couple of buddies in Arizona were anxious to swap deer hunts with us. We agreed to the exchange and invited them to come to Kodiak that fall. In Alaska nonresidents could then—and still can—purchase their deer tags over the counter, without going through the hassle and hoping for luck in a drawing. To hunt in Arizona, DeVoe and I would have to apply for a permit in the drawing and then get lucky if we were to hunt the next year.

My friends arrived in late October, full of enthusiasm with luggage overburdened by extra clothes and what-nots. Regulations allowed for a harvest of five deer per person. A non-resident tag would have to be purchased for each deer. This was unbelievable to those fellows who were accustomed to nervously awaiting their state's drawing announcement that, if they were successful, gave them the privilege of taking a single deer. They told us that they felt like they had arrived in the happy hunting grounds while still alive.

DeVoe was engaged with some sport fishermen and duck hunters for a few days, so at first I took our guests hunting by foot on the road system, which included wrestling my pick-up over the road to Saltery Cove and back. We saw twenty to thirty deer each day but neither guest took a shot. We did some clam digging and stream fishing for late run Silver salmon. They collected some exotic sea ducks, like the Harlequin and Old Squaw quackers. This was all great stuff to the Arizonan's way of thinking. And it was to me, too. If I live another thousand years, I will never lose my appreciation of the wonderful outdoors and natural bounty we find throughout Alaska. I thank God every day for these blessings.

After a couple of days, DeVoe said he was ready to take his twenty-two foot open skiff to Uganik Island, on the West side of Kodiak, which, in reasonable weather and sea conditions, was about a two and a half hour ride from Kodiak town. The sea was relatively calm and the weather nice. It looked like an ideal day. We hooked up the trailer and drove over the pass to Anton Larsen Bay to launch.

The four of us set out early that morning for Uganik with DeVoe's yellow Labrador, Billy, posed at the bow of the skiff. It's always colder on the water than ashore and that mourning with thirty-two degrees, our Arizona friends were experiencing bouts of shivering. I heard their teeth chattering an irregular cadence.

As we motored through Whale Pass I asked Ricardo, if he was cold. Ricardo was originally from Mexico and spoke with a thick accent. He was bundled up in a heavy coat with hood pulled close to his face and was wearing a knit balaclava face covering. He looked semi-mummified.

"Aye, Jake, I am cold, but okay. Can you tell who I yam?"

"Not until you talk, Ricardo," I replied.

With a only a gentle swell and no wind we sped through Kupreanoff Strait and rounded Outlet Cape with the skiff on the step. When we got close to Uganik Island, DeVoe throttled back as we glassed the beaches and hills for deer.

Contrary to the normal situation for that time of the year, we saw few deer with the binoculars, so DeVoe put us ashore to access one of his "honey holes". He guaranteed the guests that they would find deer a'plenty once they reached the top of the nearest ridge and entered a small valley just beyond. I looked forward to the exertion of the climb as a means of warming up. I removed my deck suit and advised the guests to leave their heavy coats

A Kodiak Skiff Hunt

Skipper DeVoe and first mate Billy.

stored on the beach along with my stuff above the high tide line, but they opted to wear all their heavy clothes as they brought their back packs and lunches up the hill. It was a form of non-resident insecurity, I guess.

Once atop the ridge we began seeing deer as DeVoe had promised. Just past the crest we stopped to scrutinize the area with binoculars which produced a count of seventeen deer within a half mile. Within half an hour each guest had shot a buck. As we finished taking photographs, Dean spotted a bigger buck further down the ridge and said he wanted to try to get it. I told him to go ahead while Ricardo and I quartered and boned the two slain deer to put in our packs.

We heard one shot from below and I rose to see Dean standing over a nice buck. As I watched I saw three bears coming toward him from below. The bruins were coming on separate routes—like spokes of a wheel with Dean standing at the hub. As things were developing the bears would be on the kill site within a few minutes. I hollered at Dean to hurry as several bears had a fix on him.

"Oh yeah, Jake. SEVERAL bears, no less," he cynically answered.

"I'm serious, Dean, there are at least three bears zeroed in on you, take a quick look downhill," I replied.

Somewhat impatiently Dean interrupted his butchering to stand up and look below.

"Darn, keep an eye on them … and me, will you, Jake?", Dean yelled. He was suddenly a true believer.

Ricardo with the first two bucks.

The shouting seemed to spur the bears on. Well, at least it certainly did not appear to intimidate them. Dean gutted and boned his buck as fast as he could.

With binoculars stuck to my eyes, I kept track of the advancing bears until they were within one hundred yards, but still downhill from Dean when I told him to knock it off, bring what he could and leave the kill site—Right Now!

Within a minute he was struggling back up the hill toward me, pack on his back and stuffed with hind quarters, rifle in one hand, dragging the front half of the deer by one antler with his other hand. Before he made it to me, the bears were squabbling over the gut pile he had just left.

As I helped him cut and load the front half, he voiced his surprise at so many bears.

Ricardo sprained his ankle on the trip uphill, so I sent him down toward the breach with the hind quarters of his deer before Dean and I were ready to depart. I tied the rest of Ricardo's deer and some of Dean's meat on my pack board. As we turned to follow Ricardo, two of the bears were coming up the ridge. It looked like each bear would soon have a gut pile all to itself.

A Kodiak Skiff Hunt

As was his usual practice, DeVoe had been fishing while we hunted. He had boated a couple of halibut of about forty pounds each. It was nearly dark, and a heavy fog had moved in when we loaded the deer and ourselves back into the skiff. Everyone but DeVoe had worked up a sweat and I advised the guests to strip off their wet undershirts or they would surely suffer from bone penetrating chills on the long cold ride back to Antone Larsen Bay.

Our guests told me that they would be fine and left their soaked t-shirts on. Yeah, right, I figured.

For seating, DeVoe used rough sawed twelve inch spruce planks placed between rails a foot below the gunnels on each side. When not being held in place by the weight of a passenger, those planks usually bounced free and wound up on the bottom of the skiff. The planks were slick and green with fish slime—making them not the most desirable or secure seats. They were "good enough for who they were for", as DeVoe used to say. As people slipped around the skiff positioning their deer and packs to balance the load, DeVoe started the engine and the skiff moved into the fog.

Suddenly the thought struck DeVoe that the guests might be dehydrated, so with the skiff running at half throttle he moved away from the control transom to retrieve some cans of Pepsi from the mess in the bottom of the skiff. Visibility was reduced to fifty yards. I asked if maybe I should look for the soda pop while he ran the boat.

"Don't worry about a thing, Jake. I know this area like the back of my hand," DeVoe assured me in his thick Arkansawyer accent.

As he spoke the skiff ran straight into a large rock which protruded at least eight feet above the surface of the water. Everyone was knocked into the slimy, stinky bottom of the boat as the vessel veered off toward another large rock. We were all anointed with halibut slime.

DeVoe lurched his way to the throttle and cut it to idle speed. Initially no one said a word.

"How's your hand, DeVoe?" I asked.

"Whaddu mean, Jake?"

"I was wondering if your hand was as well know to you as the rocks hereabouts?"

DeVoe said nothing. He just glared at me.

After resettling ourselves, our skipper again headed his somewhat less than noble vessel into the dense fog. We had about nine miles of open water to cross Viekoda Bay before reaching Outlet Cape, then another six miles through Shelikoff Strait before turning east into Kupreanof Strait. The wind was taking a break that night, allowing the thick fog to obscure all landmarks. The sea was calm, but for a slight, ever present swell.

With me in the bow trying to see any potential obstructions, and Billy, the Labrador, pressing his body close alongside me to reduce his chill, we bored along at full throttle for fifteen minutes until I glimpsed a dark shadow and hollered, "ROCK, DeVoe, ROCK !"

We had arrived at the same rock that we had struck at the onset of our trip, but we did not hit it this time—thanks only to me being on watch in the bow. The momentum carried us past the point of throttle shut down. The right gunnel of the skiff passed within eight feet of the huge rock. The dog, the ever devoted Billy, went bounding back over the people, deer and packs to nuzzle DeVoe. This was pure dog devoe-tion. (Pun intended).

Our shivering guests had a few pointed questions about continuing on in the fog, but DeVoe, ever confident, told us that he would get us home safe and this time I was to stand near him in the stern watching our wake to make sure he did not deviate from a straight course.

Yeah, right.

Another high speed run lasted less than ten minutes before Dean in the bow shouted "Rock, Again !" We found ourselves at the same rock, once again.

Having been out with my friend DeVoe lots of times, I was aware that he seldom carried extra fuel. I was concerned that we would run out of gas before we reached the sheltered Antone Larsen Bay, which could result in our drifting into Shelikof Straits or Marmot Bay and from there, maybe the Gulf of Alaska and who knows where. But I was overruled by DeVoe. He insisted that we strike out again and somehow, after thirty minutes we could actually hear the surf pounding on rocks ahead. Our skipper said he recognized the sound of Outlet Cape. I wondered how that sound could be distinguished from any other rocks, but I kept my thoughts to myself.

A small break in the fog confirmed a large headland on our starboard side as we continued on a northerly course. After several minutes a change of heading to the ESE (thank God the compass was more-or-less accurate) brought us within sight of the lights of the old cannery at Port Bailey. I suggested stopping there until conditions improved, but DeVoe insisted we continue on home.

"We got 'er made now, boys," DeVoe assured us all.

Visibility had improved to a half mile, at times, but when we entered Whale Pass, the fog thickened again. It seemed we were now in a nebulous cotton-filled environment. We had previously used an old dilapidated cabin nearby on Whale Island in a situation like this, and at my insistence DeVoe reluctantly ran the skiff to the beach. We debarked and I set the anchor high on the beach to accommodate the incoming tide. As we walked toward the cabin, our guests mentioned through shivering lips—with chattering teeth sounding like Spanish castanets—how nice it was to walk enough to warm up a little bit. Their wet under shirts must have felt like ice.

Then, the skies opened enough to reveal a single star.

"That's all I need, a single star to guide me and I can get us home," DeVoe trumpeted. I had serious doubts about DeVoe's ability to navigate by celestial reckoning. Furthermore he had no sextant and I doubted he knew how to use one, anyway.

"DeVoe, we're unloaded and have a safe, relatively comfortable place to stay until morning, so let's not push it anymore, we're worn out, cold, and hungry, plus we're too low on fuel to chance crossing Marmot Bay in the fog and dark," was my prudent suggestion.

"Well, you guys can stay here if you want, but I'm for going home. Them folks back in Kodiak will be worried if we don't show up tonight," was DeVoe's counter argument.

By then it was two o'clock in the morning and I did not feel comfortable with going on.

"They'll be a lot more worried if we don't ever show up, buddy" I replied.

But my friend was determined and I saw that he would go alone if we did not join him, so we all loaded back into the skiff and began what we hoped would be the last leg of the trip. It was against my better judgement.

Visibility continued to slowly improve as we crossed the big stretch of open water making up Marmot Bay, and DeVoe hit Kizhuyak Point at the northern entrance to Anton Larsen Bay rather than Craig Point further south which gave us less to travel. Ten minutes inside the sheltered bay we

Dean with his second buck.

ran out of gas. I had been dreading such a development for the past hour and a half.

I asked DeVoe where his reserve gas was, knowing that he never carried any.

"Don't normally need none, so I ain't got any, Jake", was his reply.

I asked DeVoe where the oars were located, but he said there were none and no paddles either. I knew that. At least we were not in rough water or at risk of drifting out to sea.

DeVoe had a spare fifteen horsepower outboard, but I had never seen him start it, so I doubted that it would function and there was no spare gas anyway.

We used the slimy, slippery seat planks to row toward the landing. Manipulating a twelve inch plank for use as an oar or paddle is frustrating, inefficient, and very tiring. The lone clam shovel was quickly seized by Ricardo who used it as a tiny paddle, DeVoe found a smaller piece of wood, but Dean and I were stuck with big planks. When we coordinated our strokes we actually saw the skiff move in the direction we intended. We spent over three hours paddling the last two miles to the launch site, arriving as dawn peeked over the mountains. It was the least efficient, most demanding paddling that I have ever experienced. We were blessed with calm winds or we would have had to beach the skiff at the nearest point of land. But the paddling had warmed everyone up nicely, except for our feet, which were cold. The southern boys discovered, perhaps for the first time, that numbness does not substitute for insulation.

We got the skiff loaded and drove over the pass to Kodiak in time to meet the early morning traffic rush. We must have seen thirty vehicles on the road—and that's heavy traffic for the area! After getting the deer meat hung and a good breakfast I taped up Ricardo's ankle which had swollen considerably from the sprain, followed by the exertion of getting off the mountain and returning in the skiff. We all dozed off until nearly supper time. We got the most important thing on that trip—we got BACK.

Our guests from the desert had another unique experience while they waited to leave the north country. The day before their departure, Kodiak got a record rainfall,—ten inches in twelve hours as I recall. It was enough to cause mud slides that destroyed several houses on the hill overlooking the harbor and a massive rock slide closed the road to the airport, so we got them to the plane via DeVoe's skiff. It was a memorable end to their first hunt in Alaska.

Windage and My Longest Shot

Whatever the circumstances, super long range shots are subject to so many variables that I rarely try to make a shot much over 300 yards, and then only if I have a solid rest and plenty of time.

But some rare and extenuating situations sometimes call for a try.

No doubt my longest successful shot was at a deer.

My partner, Tom Dooley, sister Pat, and I were on a hillside on the south end of Kodiak several years ago when we spotted a heavily antlered Sitka Blacktail Deer *(Odocoileus hemionus sitkensis)* with three points on one antler and four on the other. It had a decent brow tine on each side, and it was moving up toward us. We waited.

Then we saw a fellow from Kodiak, a known jerk he was—we called him Jude, he was so low he had even tried to steal a nice deer rack from a high school kid, among the numerous other infamies of his. Our misanthropic acquaintance seemed to have also spotted the same deer from his skiff in the bay.

The objectionable fellow or a friend of his, got dropped off on the beach by the skiff operator and was obviously coming in a rush, in pursuit of the same buck. He was in such a hurry he fell down twice as we watched.

Dooley's favorite movie is "Quigley Down Under" and he likes to relate instances of some long shots that he has made. Buddy or not, I've wondered at some of the distances and details, but so it is with hunters. This was going to be a "Quigley shot" for sure.

For years, we'd been taking super long shots on calm days at floating driftwood in bays—just to see how effectively we could "walk in" shots until we hit the inanimate object. Actually, it's amazing how far you can reach out and touch a target with a good steady rest using modern ammunition. Once a person has practiced such long range shooting, the need and time for walking in a shot is greatly reduced. After a few sessions we could often hit objects at well over five hundred yards on the first, if not the second try. There are no serious negatory consequences if you don't get a good hit on a chunk of wood. In the case of hairy targets, at long range you run the very real risk—maybe thirty percent or greater—of hitting the animal in the guts, which may lead to loosing the critter and condemning the wounded animal to suffering a long time before finally succumbing.

I have almost always limited my shots at game to not much over my estimate of 300 yards.

"Partner, do you think we ought to long cock Jude on that buck?" Dooley suggested. He was itching for a try at that buck and sorely tempted by the prospect of taking it under the circumstances in which we found ourselves.

"I can't think of a better candidate for having a buck shot out from under him, Tom. You get ready and I'll try to spot for you," I encouraged.

Dooley was using his home modified Remington .300 Weatherby Mag, with it's sawed off sixteen and three quarter inch (or so) barrel. The end cut on the barrel was uneven and purely amateurish looking, but that rifle shot very dependably. I had named it "Old Kindling", as it looked like he'd been shaving wood off the ancient, weathered stock for starting fires.

The buck was looking right up the hill, toward us, but I was convinced he didn't know we were there. There was no wind where we were, nor did there appear to be any breeze at the deer's location.

Dooley fired three times, carefully, and with a rest, but the buck never twitched or changed position. He just kept staring up our way. Dooley fired three more shots and was getting noticeably frustrated. He said, "Partner, why don't you try one?" I was reminded of state game wardens that use fake deer to catch pouchers.

By that time, my blood was up, so I asked him where he was holding. He said, he had held about eight inches high and just at the middle of the rack.

The buck was standing in short grass with little else within a hundred yards or so, so I reasoned that even a less than optimal hit would give us a good chance of recovering the wounded deer. And if he got hit at all, I expected him to go downhill. Unfortunately there was no open ground or anything nearby that would reveal where the shots had been hitting.

Dooley is a very good shot. I'd seen him make some remarkable offhand shots at running game. For him to miss six times when using a rest was extraordinary. I had to try to figure out why. With no need to rush, I studied the scene and looked for signs of wind. I figured the range was a bit over five hundred yards and the wind seemed calm.

The buck just kept standing there looking up toward us, as the downhill hunter struggled to get closer.

I was using my Ruger .300 Winchester Magnum and decided to give it a little more elevation, maybe hold for about the top of the antlers. I haven't hazarded a shot like that at a live target more than three times in my entire life. But this situation was extra special—urgent, even.

To both Tom and me the thought of our disliked neighbor seeing that we had taken the buck he was after was just too tempting to resist.

I took my coat off and laid it on top of my pack board, got a good rest and just as I squeezed off, the buck turned 90 degrees to it's right, giving me a broadside view, but I had already touched the shot off.

The buck dropped, as if it had been poleaxed!

I looked at Dooley, whose face flashed up raspberry red or maybe like a piece of raw liver, and by reflex, I said "Hey, I'm sorry, Tom!"

"Jim Dandy shot, partner! Do you want me to help you get him?" Tom said after he had regained his composure.

"Naw, Tom, he's stone dead, I can see him clearly and he's not even twitching," I told my buddy.

So I went for the buck, as Dooley and my sister headed up country to find more deer. We all watched as the man coming up from the beach stomped his foot angrily and turned around, heading back down the hill. That just made our day! I doubt he knew who we were, but he would get word and that would upset him even more.

As I picked my way down the grassy slope, considering how the deer dropped so suddenly, I expected to see the skull destroyed by the bullet.

When I got to the dead buck, I was surprised to see that my shot had broken it's pelvis, causing the deer to bleed out quickly. If the deer had twitched or kicked at all after being hit, we must have missed seeing it at such a long distance. Normally an animal so stricken would struggle a bit,

The bullet broke his pelvis at about 650 yards.

trying to regain its feet, but this one had simply dropped to the ground and remained motionless.

The wind was blowing from the Left about twelve to fifteen miles per hour where the buck had been standing, which was enough to drift the projectile considerably, especially over a long distance. The short grass had given us no sign of the breeze, which was less right at ground level. The bullet impacted a good three feet to the right and eighteen inches lower than the target.

When I met Dooley and Pat, he was full of wonder at my report and wanted to verify the distance as accurately as possible.

That evening we moved the boat and dropped anchor just offshore from where the buck had been standing. Using radar, we pegged the range at about 650 yards.

Dooley had figured the elevation pretty well, but his bullets were all being blown to the right. Dumb luck had given me the buck and the longest measured range shot in my life!

That will likely remain the longest shot I will ever make.

An Unusually Wide Rack

I've never, in my recollection, willingly passed up a chance to get out to see and hunt new areas. And I still don't.

In 1989 I got invited to go on a large commercial fishing boat to circumnavigate the Archipelago. We would be hunting along the route as we went. We would begin with Afognak Island for which two in our group of six hunters had elk permits. The permitted men each took an elk and we all got to help in packing the meat out. Bears are thick on brushy Afognak and if all the meat is not removed the same day, the bears will quickly enjoy whatever is left at the kill site. We got back to the boat with the meat and antlers of both elk the same day the animals were shot, so things were getting off to a good start.

We cruised down through Shelikof Strait, hunting different bays on the west side of the Archipelago. At a place called the Green Banks, some impressive bucks were harvested, but I found none that took my fancy. With plenty of moose, caribou, and sheep meat in the freezer from a successful season in the Arctic, I was holding out for something special, or nothing at all.

The weather got colder, much colder. Deer began to bunch up. We were seeing massive herds numbering in the hundreds, even thousands, of deer as they left the higher elevations and headed for lower meadows close to the ocean. The deer looked like armies on the march.

The air temperature was well below freezing and the big boat began to accumulate a dangerous coating of ice. With each splash and spray of the large waves, the ice layers thickened, similar to the manner in which aufis glaciers build in the braided channels of Trail Creek, where our lodge is located. The skipper on the boat kept a good supply of wooden ball bats

Huge accumulations of deer began showing on the beaches.

handy, with which we all took turns at pounding the ice from the rails and rigging. The pounded ice eventually turned loose and dropped overboard. Too much superstructure ice can lead to dangerous imbalance of the boat and in extreme cases, it can cause the boat to roll over or capsize. So, out of concerns for self-preservation we were diligent with the ball bats.

We enjoyed the stories of commercial fishing in the Barents Sea as told by a fisherman named Sig who had been born a Norwegian, then migrated to Alaska and became a naturalized American citizen.

The Barents Sea lies north and east of Norway and is bordered by Finland and Russia. This wild, Arctic water is known for huge waves and dangerous weather, especially in the commonly sub-zero air temperatures, but it's abundant fish stocks draw fishermen, despite the threatening conditions. In a way, it was a bit like Kodiak—however it sounded like its bad weather potential was significantly amplified over that at Kodiak.

Sig had seen and endured some really horrendous storms, so the memorably adverse conditions that visited us on that trip were of little concern to him. He had seen much worse stuff.

We sat at anchor for a couple of days, occupied with reading, playing cards and visiting, as we waited for conditions to improve.

After a day at anchor in Rodmans Reach—a part of Lazy Bay—on the distant southeast end of Kodiak Island, we had an opportunity to go ashore to hunt deer.

An Unusually Wide Rack

Sig and I had become hunting partners, but he was having little success with hitting what he aimed at with his new rifle. So I spent some beach time with him sighting in his firearm. In the Barents Sea, fishermen get no opportunity to go ashore and hunt.

With the scope adjusted Sig showed more confidence. We went inland from the beach, looking for bucks.

From a promontory I glassed a gang of five deer. Two were bucks but neither was especially outstanding, however Sig wanted to take one. We took advantage of the local terrane features and closed to within a bit over one hundred yards from the browsing deer. I noticed two more deer coming toward the group, but at first glance, neither looked larger than the bucks we had stalked so I suggested to Sig that he go ahead and take the one he fancied.

Sig fired and down went the buck. Sig's smile extended from ear to ear. This was his first deer and the single killing shot bolstered Sig's confidence. The wind was from the deer to us and after the shot, the other animals went back to their browsing, unconcerned.

We just watched as the two incoming deer approached. One was a small buck with unimpressive antlers, but for the fact that they were extremely wide and seemed to lay flat out from the top of his head. The deer kept coming, walked past the dead buck without noticing it, and continued on toward our location.

I became intrigued with the wide antlered buck. It had only two points on the right antler and three on the left, with a small brow tine on each. It was not at all remarkable in antler development. But there was that unusual spread! We had time enough for another, more distant stalk but I decided to take the wide one, primarily to satisfy my curiosity. The deer appeared to be healthy and fat.

At about seventy yards I held for midway on the neck and squeezed off the shot. The deer nosed into the tundra and never twitched again. The companion buck raced away toward the original group of deer. Now there would be five in that gang again.

The head of my buck was unlike any that I had seen before. A palpably sharp ridge ran along the center of the skull between the antlers. I suspected a drastic sagittal suture malformation of some sort to be the cause. I could sort that out once we were back at the boat, so I removed the head at the

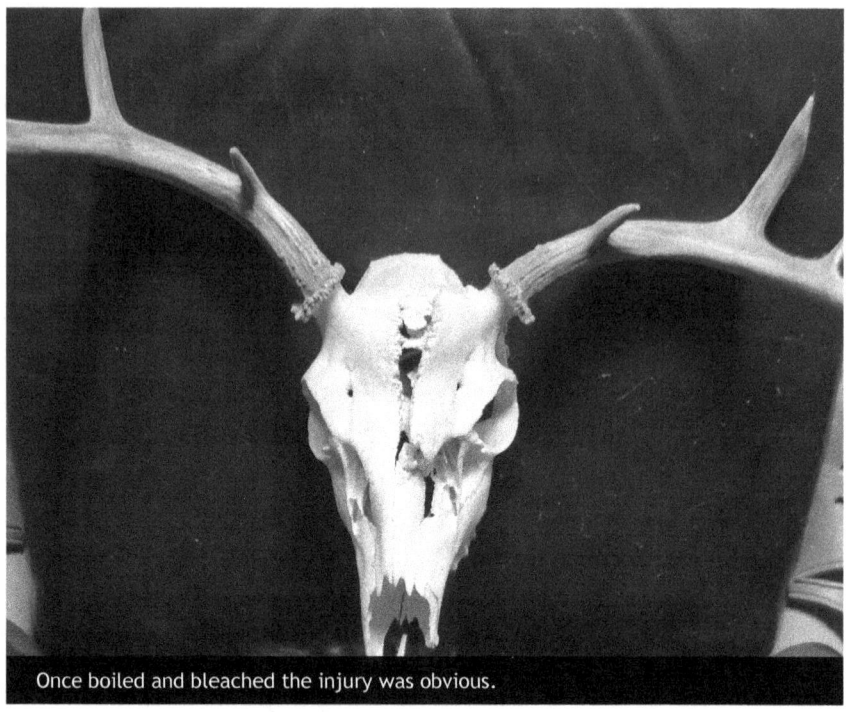
Once boiled and bleached the injury was obvious.

foramen magnum and went about butchering the deer. This rutty buck had the normal two testicles in the scrotum. Sig helped and he was a quick study. He did his deer the same way and in good time.

We packed our loads back to the beach and were aboard the big boat well before dark.

I carefully skinned the hide away from the skull and realized that a serious injury had befallen the buck some time long before I shot it. The sagittal or midline skull suture had been torn apart, leaving only the intact skin between the animal's brain and the rest of the world. Furthermore, about five eights of an inch of reparative bone had formed. If left alive, it appeared that this buck would have formed new bone to cover the entire defect and its life span would not be shortened by this unusual injury.

Abnormal, asymmetric antlers most commonly form on the side opposite the side of the animal which has been injured—this is the contra-lateral manifestation of antler asymmetry due to injury. The most common injuries of this nature involve the foot or leg.

An Unusually Wide Rack

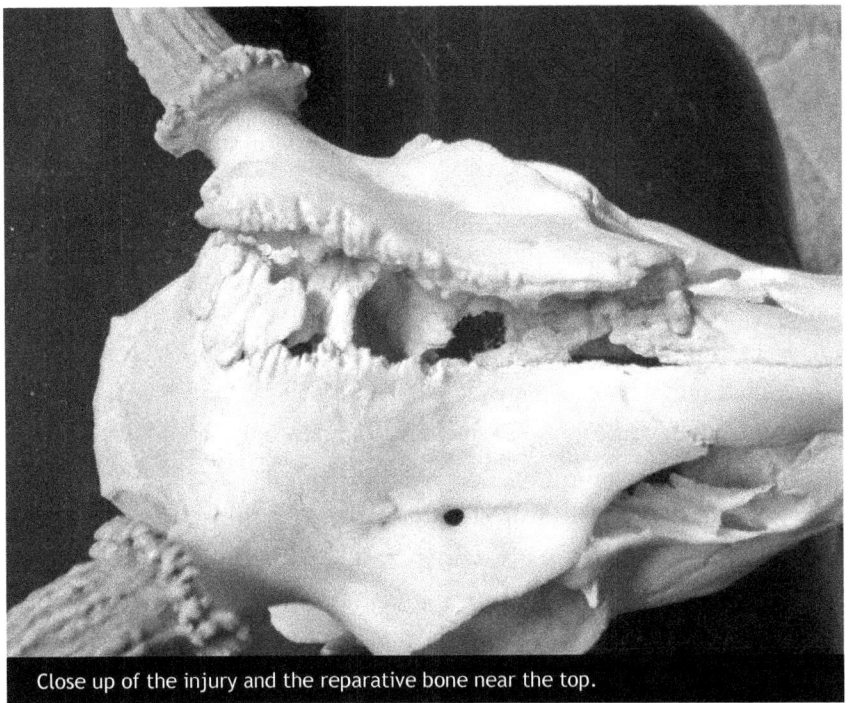

Close up of the injury and the reparative bone near the top.

But this bucks antlers did not show such contra-literalism. It had no apparent leg or foot injury and had not been limping. The only discernible injury was the drastically opened saggital suture.

I believe the buck got its antlers locked in a mating battle with another deer. There is enough spring in antlers to result in them locking after a forceful clash. But to escape from the locked antlers, no extreme force such as that resulting from a rush is possible, so the unfortunate deer twist and thrash. Often their struggles are to no avail and both the deer slowly perish due to starvation, locked together, for eternity.

In this case, the buck's twisting separated the saggital suture and he and his opponent were free—but with a heck of a headache no doubt. No injury to the skin was apparent, so the risk of infection was minimized, and the animal went on its way to recovery.

The reparative bone must have formed in a matter of four to six weeks or less, I believe. It was a remarkable thing to find.

The following summer, my long time friend and veteran Arctic guest of a dozen hunting trips with me, Ulrich Herbst, came from Germany to visit, fish, and make photographs. When he saw the strange skull, he concurred with what I had figured about the origin and cause of the suture separation. The points of which are:

1. The injury took place during a rutting battle.
2. The suture separated after being subjected to extreme lateral torque.
3. With no interruption in the skin cover, infection was averted.
4. The rapid formation of reparative bone took place in a few weeks.
5. Had the buck not been shot this injury should not have prevented the deer from having a complete recovery and new bone would have formed to fill in the gap.

As Forst Verwaltung (forest manager and administrator) of a large section of northern Germany, Ulrich checked hundreds of red, roe and fallow deer each year. He had seen similar cases on a few occasions in his forty years a chief forester of his area.

The amazing reparative, regenerative abilities of this buck still give me cause to sit back and reflect on the tenacity of life forces as I try to understand the wonders of life on earth. All organisms are subliminally programed

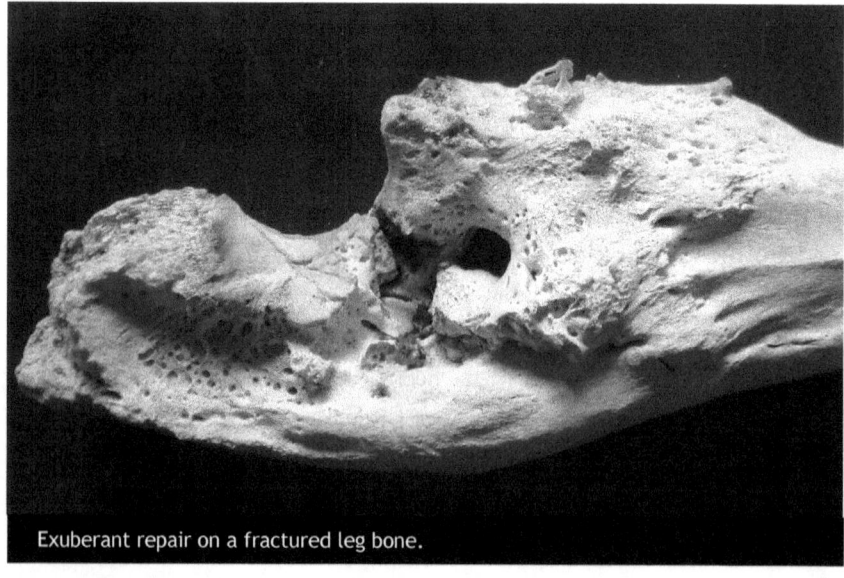
Exuberant repair on a fractured leg bone.

An Unusually Wide Rack

to cling to life as their primary motivation and perhaps only in humans do conscious decisions, such as giving up, play a part.

A few years later I picked up the remains of a deer tibia (the larger of the two bones of the lower hind leg) which showed an extraordinary bony repair. Due to the somewhat moth-eaten appearance, I suspect that a bacterial infection, along with continued use of the leg, may have complicated the healing.

We humans, among the other life forms are designed to endure and survive truly incredible insults and injuries. Too often these attributes in other species fail to catch our attention.

That little split-skull buck was the only animal I took on that long trip, but it was a top trophy for me.

From 1994 onward, Tom Dooley and I Transported deer hunters to the area around the location which had produced the first cryptorchid buck for me. We harvested more and more of the sterile bucks and began to appreciate that any type of antler formation from completely normal and typical in appearance to wildly non-typical racks might be carried by a cryptorchid. Retained velvet was found in about thirty percent of the sterile bucks.

One of cryptorchids I harvested in November, 2001 was unremarkable except for sharp antler tips and a telltale sharp ridge on the skull between the antlers. When I boiled the skull, it was apparent that this buck had suffered a separation of the sagittal suture, which had been completely repaired.

But, unlike the buck with a similar injury that I took in

Complete repair of the sagittal suture separation in a cryptorchid buck.

1989, this buck was a bilateral cryptorchid. So, what led this sterile buck to engage in such a fierce mating battle that resulted in locking his antlers with those of another buck? Maybe it was just very bad luck.

I have often witnessed bilateral cryptorchid bucks mounting does during the rut, however I have never seen a serious mating battle between a cryptorchid and a normal buck, but cryptorchids can sometimes be mistaken for normal deer, so maybe some of the fights between what appeared to be normal bucks actually involved one or more sterile cryptorchids.

Questions like this may never be satisfactorily answered. But they lead us to healthy speculation, some of which may be fanciful or contrary to intuitive thinking, but at least they do produce brain exercise and they focus people's attention on the problem.

King Crab Fishing and Deer Hunting

In 1989 or so I took a position as deck hand on a local king crab boat. The glory days of making big money in the winter crab fishery were long since past, but I saw this as an opportunity to do something useful with my free time, which otherwise would be spent reading, playing racquetball and whatever else I could find to do to try to keep fit. I seldom had a very long period of time with not enough to do.

We were to begin with prospecting for King Crab, which required the boat to travel to areas expected to be opened for commercial fishing. We went out prior to the opening of the crab season in hopes of knowing where to be when the short period of legal fishing came about. We had to bait and drop enough pots to give us an accurate idea of what to expect if the skipper/owner decided to seriously engage in the effort. Some areas produced so few crab they were marked off as being not worth fishing when season opened. All this took considerable expense as bait, fuel and overall boat operations were not cheap. And there was no guarantee that the time, effort and expenses would prove to be worthwhile. It was a gamble, as is all fishing and hunting.

To minimize the cost of crewmen ... and to avoid workmen compensation costs, etc., we crewmen were promised that we would each receive the legal maximum number of King Crab for our personal use, and we were doing this as friends, not employees.

Additionally we would be provided access to, and time enough to pursue deer hunting in some of the more remote, and theoretically best deer hunting areas in the entire Archipelago. The prospecting trip was planned for November or December. With deer season open until December 31 and a limit of five deer per hunter, the timing was ideal. We could hunt during the day, while the pots soaked in various areas. The pots were to be set and pulled after dark. That convinced me to sign on. Some things, like deer hunting, are more important than the wages one might receive from actually working.

Having not been on a commercial crab boat since my brief stint of two weeks fishing near Akutan in 1969, these survey trips should provide a low stress reintroduction to the operation

In 1989 in the Kodiak waters, the season was short, the crab less abundant, and the boats were many. Once season opened the activities would be hectic and often sustained "round the clock". During the long dark hours of night pot hawling, I learned to appreciate munching on a "deck steak" which was a candy bar washed down with strong coffee.

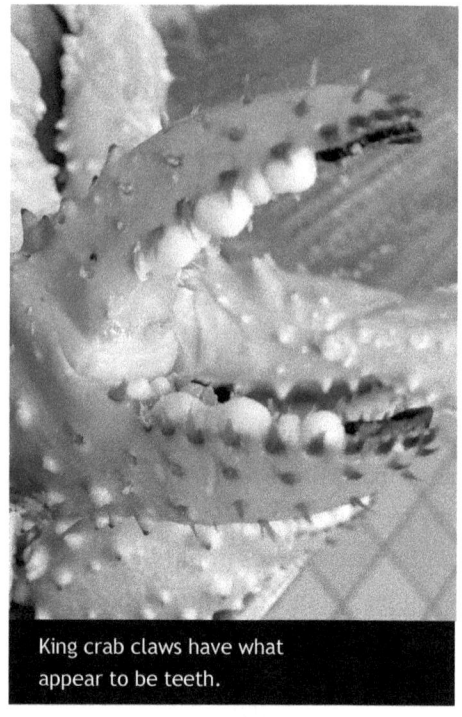
King crab claws have what appear to be teeth.

Large orange or green inflatable numbered buoys were attached to the line which ran from the crab pot to the surface. The inflatable buoy had a short line leading to a styrofoam, or "sea lion buoy" to insure that the pot was not lost, as sea lions often slap and puncture the inflatable buoys which causes them to sink.

The crab pots most often used were seven feet by seven feet square or "pyramid pots". The pyramid pots could be staked inside each other, allowing more pots to be carried in the same deck space.

The crabbing operation was essentially the same in Kodiak as I had seen in the Bering Sea. The boat would approach a buoy, a crewman would throw a grapple hook with light line attached, such that it landed between the inflatable and the styrofoam bouy. Then the line was yanked aboard by hand to the big boat. Not many tosses of the grapple were unsuccessful.

King Crab Fishing and Deer Hunting

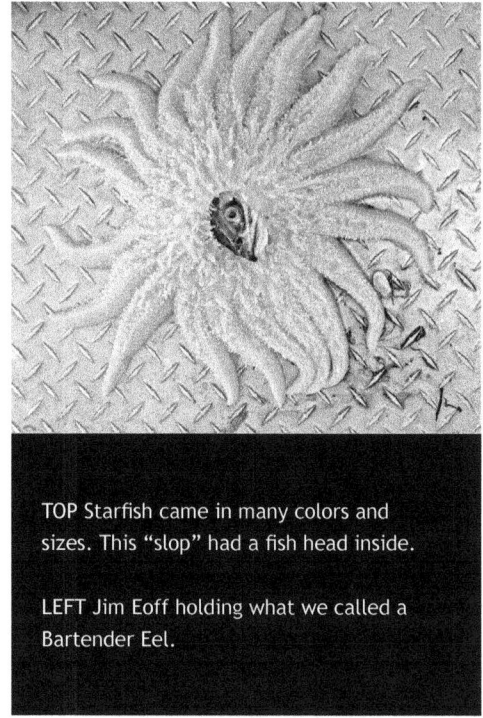

TOP Starfish came in many colors and sizes. This "slop" had a fish head inside.

LEFT Jim Eoff holding what we called a Bartender Eel.

The small bouy would be hooked by a crewman on the deck and the main crab line was put in the power block. The block would begin bringing up the crab pot. The big seven by seven footers weighed about six to eight hundred pounds—empty. As the pot came up, a crewman coiled the heavy line carefully to avoid a tangle when it was tossed back overboard with the next setting of the pot.

Once the pot was on the deck, or in the pot launcher cradle, a large door was opened and the contents spilled out. The crab were measured, undersized ones and females were tossed overboard and the "keepers" were put in the live tank. Often other interesting critters came up in the pot. There were weird looking eels and many strange invertebrates, most of which were tossed overboard uninjured. Sometimes really spooky things come up in a crab pot on a dark night.

To keep live octopus from oozing out of a tub and escaping, we would turn the siphon inside out. That seemed to confuse and immobilize the octopus. It remained alive until we could boil it up for consumption. The

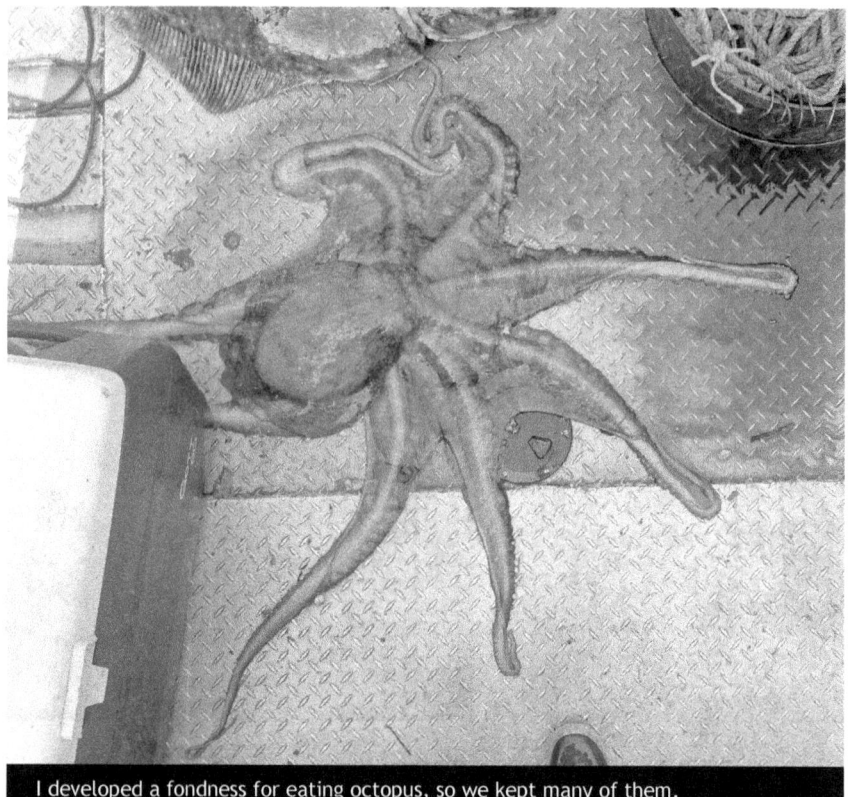

I developed a fondness for eating octopus, so we kept many of them.

mantels were delicious—fresh boiled and dipped in teriyaki sauce. I preferred to grind up the arms for making chowder.

If the fishing was productive enough, a new bait can or hanging bait was placed in the pot, the door was lashed closed, and it was launched again. As it sank the coiled shot of line was tossed overboard along with the top buoys and the boat went on to the next pot. Usually the pots were set in a straight line, referred to as a "string", for easier retrieval the next time. This was in the days prior to the Global Positioning System or GPS, so locating the pots was sometimes difficult—especially in high seas or foggy conditions. Depending on the size of the boat, dozens or hundreds of pots might be set in one location.

Prior to departure, it took a few days to check over the pots, re-coil some of the shots of line, repair torn web, replace leaky buoys and make the gear and boat ready.

King Crab Fishing and Deer Hunting

Deer hunting while crab fishing.

This buck had a swollen neck and was fully into the rut.

So, finally, off we went one dark night, headed for the south end of Kodiak. The boat I was on did not have a large deck, so the big 7X7 pots were stacked one on top of the other—five pots high. Even with the live tank pumped full of water, or "tanked down", the vessel felt top-heavy. As we turned hard right to depart the channel a gust of wind hit us and, in spite of heavy lines and tightened chains securing it, the stack of pots shifted and one of the top pots came loose and went overboard.

The skipper turned the boat around and headed back to port. The pots would have to be re-stacked and secured. It was a simple, and relatively easy lesson. The lost pot was worth several hundred dollars, but that was cheap compared with losing the whole load, the boat ... or the crew.

Several years later I dropped the anchor for my little twenty-four foot skiff, the *Sasquatch*, and when I began to retrieve it, it felt like it was hung up in something that had some "give" to it—like the web of a crab pot. I remembered that windy night years before and thought I just might have found the long lost pot. Unable to retrieve my anchor, I tied a couple of buoys to it and motored to port. The next day I returned with a larger boat which had a good hydraulic wench and we retrieved my anchor with the lost pot. After several years of soaking submerged, it had an interesting growth of sea anemones and other critters decorating the web.

With the pots re-stacked we set off again for the south end.

After running at eight knots for sixteen hours we began setting crab pots.

We got a few hours sleep, then went ashore to do some serious deer hunting. Immediately we found plenty of deer tracks on the beach, as well as in the well worn bear trails which held fresh tracks of the giant Kodiak bears.

The weather was plenty cool to keep meat from spoiling, and we had time enough to be picky about the deer we took.

As usual, I was hunting alone. Late one afternoon, after passing up some mature bucks I took a decent three pointer near the entrance to Jap Bay. The outside beach there had too many rocks and too much surf to attempt a skiff landing. It was going to be a laborious pack along the brushy sidehill, to get the meat back to an inside beach for pick up by the skiff, but just as I had the deer's guts spilled, the skiff man came along and hollered to me to catch the buoy he had tossed into the surf which was attached to a line leading to the skiff. The onshore wind and incoming tide drifted the buoy within reach, so I was able to reach it without getting too wet. That made getting the deer out an easy task. I secured the carcass to the buoy and signaled for the skiff man to back off. He drew the carcass up close, then towed it to the big boat where the picking boom deposited the deer on the deck. This was a large bodied buck, so not having to carry it was nice.

The November full moon was near and the bucks were fully in the rut. This one had a swollen neck and smelly hocks—the odor of which by the way, is attractive to me. I've considered using the rutty buck essence as a male cologne, but maybe the ladies would not be affected the same way I was. Women can be strange.

So far, after fifty seasons of hunting deer in the Kodiak Archipelago, and taking dozens of bucks heavily into the rut, I have yet to find one with anything but wonderful meat.

A worthwhile side benefit of this trip was our share of King Crab.

This trip proved to be well worthwhile and we "crewmen" brought home fresh venison and some prime King crab.

The Daughters' Deer

One December we got a message from Colorado State University. The cryptorchid study could use some data from deer collected late in the year. This gave Tom and me an excuse to make a hunt during Christmas vacation. We had no booked hunters, making this a perfect time to get our daughters on a hunt. We had talked about this for years. Neither of the young ladies had yet taken a deer. They were keen on joining the trip.

We had only a few days free for us all, so we took the boat to Afognak Island. Snow was heavy, as was ice in some of the bays, but the girls were willing. We cruised the beaches where deer were beginning to collect to escape the difficulties of life in deep snow and to dine on fresh kelp.

Amy Dooley and Bess Jacobson with their first deer on a brutally cold day.

Bundled up we began to search for bucks still carrying antlers. The first afternoon we found a pair and each girl took one. When Bess's buck hit the ground, the antlers popped off.

Three hours in the open skiff at below freezing temperatures were enough. The frazil ice hissed against the hull of the skiff as we returned to the *REBEL*.

We had the samples we needed and the deep satisfaction that our kids had opportunities to put some meat on the table for the winter.

A Grandson's Visit to Kodiak

November, 2005. I remember the time well. While collecting samples for the sterility research I allowed a huge brown bear to come within touching distance of me as I stood next to a fresh deer gut pile. My action could only be viewed as negligent. That story appears in my first book: *ALASKA HUNTING: Earthworms to Elephants*.

A week later my oldest grandson, Spencer Shroyer came to hunt deer. We visited the site of my close encounter and measured the distances from my first sighting of the bear to the gut pile. It was less than fifteen yards. As the bear came closer I resolved to brain shoot it, if it looked directly at me. The bear did not make eye contact, nor did it increase its slow deliberate pace. I did not shoot. It was a win-win situation for both of us.

Snow came early that year and in spite of intermittent heavy rains, remained throughout the season. Deer were at an all time population high and we picked over dozens of bucks, searching for a good first deer for Spencer.

In spite of the heavier than normal snow cover bears were out in force everywhere, aggressively looking for anything to add to their winter fat stores. The bruins were more actively moving about later than usual for this time of the year. This was probably due to the poor humpy salmon run.

Dooley and I had three new guests that trip that preferred to hunt as a trio which reduced my concerns for them with so many bears about.

This was Spencer's first trip as an adult to Kodiak, so every evening he had a line in the water, hoping to catch a halibut. Between helping with deck work, cleaning the galley and washing dishes, Spencer was as active as the bears.

The last and third from last deer on the right are decent bucks.

A side benefit of hunting deer from a boat is the opportunity to catch tasty fish. Most of our guests were not familiar with the salt water critters we found, making this a special treat for them.

A series of small low pressure systems kept the area wet with greatly reduced visibility for the first part of the week, so we had plenty of time while sitting at anchor to tell stories, play pinochle and read, but Spencer preferred to fish.

A favorable weather break came with cooling breezes and more snow. The improved visibility revealed grey/brown deer standing out in contrast to the white surroundings. Only three days remained before a new

Spencer's first halibut came before his first deer.

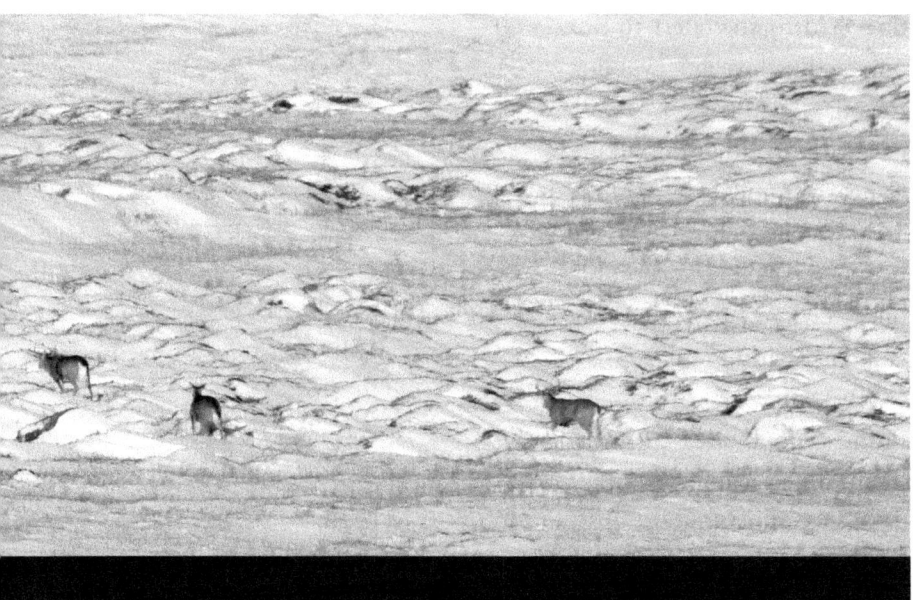

A Pacific Cod.

group of guests would arrive, but with the new conditions, that should be plenty of time to lay up some winter venison. I wanted a good three by three or better buck for Spencer. We turned down several that had "crab claw" antlers, holding out for a better rack.

Our summer camouflage clothes were of no help to us in the snow covered hills. With clear conditions after so much rain and snow, the deer were more twitchy than usual. The bears were out scratching around, which no doubt kept the deer nervous. With the once per year rut on, both bucks and does had to stay alert to not only finding love, but avoiding the big predators.

Cover to aid us in stalking is nearly nonexistent in the area we were hunting. We watched several acceptable bucks charge away before we could get within range.

By mid afternoon we found a good 3X3 that was intent on courting a group of does. As the band of deer meandered toward the foothills, we stayed far enough away to not spook them. Finally they moved over a small ridge and out of sight. We closed the distance as rapidly as we could manage over the slippery ground. We spent more than an hour maneuvering to get a shot within one hundred yards. When the opportunity came, Spencer was right on with his rifle.

Spencer with a better than average Kodiak buck.

Walking Out

My friend Rob Coyle and I were on an eight day deer hunt in the Kodiak Archipelago.

Weather had been typical for the area and season—which means very windy most of the days and nights, with the wind occasionally slackening to a mere fifteen to twenty mile per hour blows.

It had been uncharacteristically dry for the area and warmer than usual.

Finally on day five, it began to freeze up, making some areas, especially the wet, slick, muddy slopes which ooze small springs continuously, much more accessible. Some of the hillsides in the area weep continuously, even in dry weather.

We both had already harvested three good bucks on Federal land but we had Designated Hunter permits from the U.S. Fish and Wildlife Service, allowing us to fill as many tags for family members and friends as we had in our possession. We decided to scout a new area, keeping our last tags handy, in case we found a real monster buck. On day seven we decided to investigate a remote area we'd not visited before which required passage down a very steep hill.

Access to most of the Archipelago is by foot only, but there was an old road system in this area, traversable by an all terrane vehicle, if conditions permit. The freeze-up suggested that traveling down, then back up the hill would be manageable. So we used the machine to go further than we'd gone before, including going down that last extremely steep mile-long hill which certainly taxed my judgment, especially when it became apparent that the slope was beginning to thaw out after the short period of freezing. But once we began the descent with the vehicle, turning back was not an option.

It was a gnarly trip down the increasingly slippery, muddy slope with the machine occasionally slipping sideways in the mud and icy spots. The closer we got to the bottom, the warmer the air and slicker the route was becoming. I realized we should have walked, or not come here at all.

The machine slipped, slewed and crabbed most of the final half mile to the bottom of the grade and our thoughts were on how we were going to get it back to the top of the pass and on to our camping spot. We had no winch or other means of augmenting the ascent. I mentioned that I'd dread having to walk out, and worse yet, leaving the machine behind. My partner shared my concern.

As we were seeing far fewer deer and less deer sign in this near area than we'd seen each of the preceding six days, I commented that I didn't want to waste the whole day in this area, thinking that if we had trouble getting up the hill, it was better to tackle that chore with plenty of daylight and time left. Again, Robb, my partner, concurred.

Our plan was to each check out a valley to the West of our machine, and return within a couple of hours, which would have put us back together about an hour after noon.

So off we went.

Seeing only a lone doe in my valley, I was back at the entrance in an hour, so I went up another drainage. This valley also had little sign and I located only a single doe there, as well. I'd become accustomed to much better hunting than I was finding in this area.

I returned to the machine about one-thirty that afternoon, expecting to find my buddy restlessly waiting to get the ATV up that miserable slope, which by now, glistened as rivulets flowed over the sticky mud that marked our route.

The wind had increased to about 30 mph and the thermometer indicated plus thirty-seven degrees fahrenheit which accelerated the deterioration in the trail's traversability.

As I waited I ate my sandwich.

By 3:00 pm I reflected on my situation and that of my hunting partner. He was one of the three most competent and dependable hunting buddies that I have enjoyed in more than sixty years of wilderness hunting and

Walking Out

fishing. He was also one of the two most physically fit of my partners. But bad things happen to good, fit, competent people.

I began to wonder if the thaw had released a mud slide that might have caught him.

Several fresh slides were visible from were I sat. This area has brown bears, too, not many,—but there are bears. A twisted ankle or knee, or God only knows what else, might have incapacitated him. If I sat here until dark, then, if he did show up, how much help could I be?

For sure, I would not take the machine without him. If I sat all night and he had not showed up, I would be walking out to get help first thing in the morning. If, on the other hand, I walked out now, and he did not show up in camp by morning with the machine, I could use my camp satellite phone to call for help. But I needed to get through a half mile of tall grass with enough light to see the trail leading to the correct slope and get over the pass. Also, I needed to leave word for him that I was O.K. and walking out, or he would be sitting, waiting on me—maybe all night.

Normally I carry a pencil and paper, but I had not put them in the pocket of the fresh shirt I used that morning. Ratz! Checking all my pockets, I found a part of an envelope, but no pen or pencil !

I'd been using the last of some Hornady 200 grain hollow points that I'd loaded up a few years ago, but I had some Sierra 200 grain hand loads with lead tips in my pack, and a lead tipped bullet will write on white paper. So I carefully scratched "WALKING OUT", and laid the paper under a flat rock on the seat of the ATV, along with a piece of orange surveyors tape to catch my partner's attention.

I started off just before 5:00 pm, hoping to make it to the pass by dark. We were just a day away from a full moon, but a heavy, dark overcast had moved in that morning and the light, which had been dim all day, was quickly fading. No moonlight would show through the cloud cover that night.

Since my bilateral complete knee replacement in March, 2007, I've intentionally traveled much slower, watching every step, but this time I hustled through the long grass, found the correct spine to take me to the pass, then slipped and sloshed my way to the top. Using my newly acquired "Backtracker" GPS, I ascertained that I had covered nearly a mile of rough, steep, slippery terrane in just over twenty minutes. And that was done while carrying my thirty pound pack and a load of gumbo packed mud and grass on my boots, which I had to stop to scrape off several times.

Since grade school, I've used the butt of my rifle as a walking stick and this trip was no exception, it was an invaluable aid in keeping me upright in the slippery conditions.

The top of the pass was now engulfed by a heavy, damp fog, making the trail far less than obvious. I was wringing wet from sweat, but determined to get down the other side of the pass before I stopped to shed some clothes and locate my flashlight which was stronger than my headlight. I wanted to find a mini candy bar, too.

The downslope was less sloppy than the other side, as the wind had less force and the temperature had dropped at least ten degrees since sundown, so the mud was freezing up again. Those changes were in my favor.

With the freeze-up, the creeks had solidified, but in the past two days the water levels had dropped by up to two feet, leaving the surface ice suspended above flowing water. As I came to the largest of the several creeks I had to cross, I remembered seeing fresh silver salmon there that morning in some holes that appeared to be at least four feet deep. The surface ice on this creek was broken in some places, but the small light on the bill of my cap was insufficient to give me a clear view of the bottom.

I needed my stronger MagLite.

Being extremely thirsty, I refilled my quart bottle and drank it all, then refilled the bottle again to carry along. I swallowed a mini candy bar and removed my vest and jacket liner.

I groped through my backpack, but did not locate the flashlight. I knew it must be there, but a second search did not turn it up. I could well imagine starting over the ice, only to break through and wind up in the swift, cold current, perhaps waist deep in the icy water—with about ten more miles to walk to camp. As I began my third search for the light, I saw it's glow in one of the pack's compartments! Wow, wonderfully, my rummaging had twisted the head of the light enough to engage the contacts, making it light up, and allowing me to find it! Now I could see how deep the water was in the areas where the surface ice had broken. I crossed with the water just below my boot tops.

Refreshed and relieved (yeah, I did that, too) now I was re-energized and making much better time on the trail. I figured I pretty well had it made. As I rounded a small hill, something went crashing through a patch of wind-bent willows a few yards in front of me. I saw only the dark form of a beast in motion. A bear, maybe, but more likely not, nevertheless I slowed down a bit when approaching brushy areas and hollered to broadcast my presence. No use stumbling onto any bear in the dark, especially a sow with cubs.

I was nearly half way to camp and everything was great, except for my concern for Rob. I was sweaty, but my knees were fine, so I kept pushing myself, as I headed toward our shelter. After about another mile I looked back toward the pass, which was now completely fogged-in, and saw a pair of lights coming erratically down the slippery slope. My buddy, no doubt, was headed my way with the all terrain vehicle.

As we rode back to our camp he told me his story.

He had gone to the head of his valley, saw only a couple of does, then topped out and came down another ridge, expecting to wind up near the machine. But after getting out of the higher terrane, he realized that he was on the opposite side of the range. Figuring he would skirt the range and soon be in the correct drainage, he had to walk about eight miles before arriving at the ATV. It was well after dark when he reached the machine.

He was shocked to not see me there waiting for him, but he found the note, or he would have still been there, waiting for me. I told him that I knew that's what he would do. It was a good ending to what had started out to be an easy day of scouting, then became somewhat gnarly. Unforeseen complication do arise while hunting, especially in unfamiliar country.

The most important thing to get on any outing is BACK!

Hunting Solo—
Not Always the Best Idea

It's always best to hunt with a reliable partner. Whether one is hunting in wild remote locations or closer to home, accidents can happen to anyone and often they occur in what one assumes to be a routine, relatively risk-free situation. They tend to take place at the end of the day.

The Kodiak Archipelago has a maritime climate. The island group sits in the North Pacific Ocean, bathed by waters of the Gulf of Alaska. In November the temperatures typically range from a high of 39 down to a low of 20 degrees fahrenheit, with similar conditions throughout the fall hunting season. Rainfall averages about six inches per month. Most days are overcast, and wet days far outnumber those with no rain or snow. From November through April the precipitation remains mostly in liquid form, but can turn to snow anytime.

With daily temperatures hovering around freezing and night time lows a bit cooler, ice prevails at ground level for most of the winter months. Lakes, rivers and creeks typically freeze over, as do some of the bays and inlets, especially those with a large fresh water input from rivers and creeks.

Iliamna Lake is known by many as the "mother of the wind" but Kodiak typically generates wind which often reaches gale or storm force. Wind accelerates the changes imposed by temperature variations.

The conditions of near freezing weather, wind and moisture make the risk of hypothermia on Kodiak high. Add some sweaty underclothes from outdoor exertion and the threat is magnified.

In the fall months one often finds a sudden cooling after a period of heavy rainfall. The surface water freezes. The cooler temperature leads to a drop in water level. The creeks may show a solid ice cover with the water surface a foot or more beneath the bottom of the ice. This unsupported ice is more apt to fracture than ice directly over and supported by water.

On one November hunt I was accompanied by two companions, but, as usual, we hunted individually, hiking up different drainages. We all knew the country well and each of us was capable of packing out a deer. We had plenty of time to select desirable bucks and with so much country to cover, we could do it most effectively by hunting separately, then rendezvousing near the end of the day.

The snow that year had accumulated up to a depth of a foot or so in the flats and half again that, or deeper, in the canyons, making walking up the frozen creeks preferable to high-stepping through the riparian brush and snow drifts. The surface ice had matured from shiny black to dull white in color which normally indicates a thickness sufficient to hold the weight of an average man—even with a pack loaded with deer meat.

The drainage I selected that day changed from a twenty foot wide and four foot deep gut in the muskeg and low brush to a gradually narrowing canyon with steep sides. Visibility was very good as I proceeded slowly up the ice on the stream. All but my head was hidden by the sides of the creek as I proceeded, watching deer up ahead. The rut was in full swing and most of the bucks were actively cruising and looking for love. The does seemed fascinated by the posturing bucks, but most remained stationary.

By the time I reached the more abrupt side walls of the canyon I had counted over fifty deer, however none of the bucks looked appropriate for shooting that early in the day, so I crept along, hoping that an impressive stag would reveal himself. I still had more than three hours before dark.

About a mile into the narrowing canyon I saw a buck on the right side that looked like a taker. He was over five hundred yards from me, lying on a ridge about a hundred yards from the bottom of the canyon as he surveyed the ground below. I never got the impression that he had seen me. As I drew closer I was able to see less and less of the resting buck as the intervening terrane erased a bit more of my sight picture with each step I took.

Finally, at two hundred yards I could only see his head and the top of his neck. One option for me would be to cross the creek and proceed up the opposite side until I was closer, then shoot him from about one hundred fifty yards. But seeing me move up the drainage in the open might spook

Hunting Solo— Not Always the Best Idea

The best buck I saw that day.

the complacent buck. My intended target was moving his head around as he watched other deer and he might well decide that I was something he should avoid. If he walked over the side of the ridge he was resting on, my opportunity to take him might go with him.

So I elected to try to shoot him from where I was. I removed my back pack to use it as a rest, but when I knelt down to do so, I could see only the top of the buck's antlers. It was going to be a stand-up, offhand shot or none at all.

The snow on top of long grass and low sedges made for an unsteady pose, so I stamped down the area and was able to get a steady hold on the top of his neck. When I squeezed the trigger I saw his head jerk out of sight. I was sure I had him.

Reaching the deer proved to be a struggle. I put my boot chains on. The snow overlaid rocks, hummocks, dead ferns and grass that made the ascent slippery. I stumbled and fell several times before reaching the ridge, but there my buck was with his head downhill, draining blood from a wound at the top of his neck. He was dead before his head hit the ground.

My right knee was bothering a bit. I had wrenched it in one of my tumbles and it felt swollen. I had total replacement of both knees a couple years before and I tried to not abuse them, that day the right one reminded me that I had pushed it too far.

The slope was steep, so I attached a piece of line to the antlers and pulled the carcass over the snow behind me as I headed for the creek bottom. The drag served as an anchor for me as I went down the slippery slope, twice keeping me from falling forward. Butchering was much safer and more comfortable on the level ground.

This buck was normal with two scrotal testes. He was fat, but less so than the one I shot the day before which was a bilateral cryptorchid. This one's rutting activity had already depleted some of his fat reserves. Old bucks are the most vulnerable to winter kill due to loss of fat and seldom eating during the rut. This old boy was a candidate for winter kill before I shot him.

Deer moved calmly past me within forty yards as I worked on the buck. They were headed out of the canyon for the more open terrane below. I wondered if this was an indication of more snow coming?

Time had flown by that afternoon and I decided I should hurry to avoid walking back in the dark. The heavy overcast would yield no moon light. I hurriedly secured the meat on my pack board.

When I reached the broadening of the stream, the ice looked good. Since my right knee was becoming more noticeable with the load of meat on my back, I elected to go down the frozen river In the path I used coming up to avoid the lumpy muskeg and give my strained joint a break. The ice was chalk white and looked safe. My boot chains served as a counter measure to the slippery ice.

About eighty yards down the river I felt the ice crack and before I could dodge to either side I fell through. The added weight of the deer on my back was too much. The ice was suspended about twenty inches over the water, but the flowing water was only a little over a foot deep, so I did not get soaked. I only got water in one boot.

But I was standing on the bottom of the stream with the top of the ice now at the level of my navel. Getting out with the heavy pack on my back was problematic, so I took it off, gouging myself on one antler tip in the process. I pushed the pack ahead of me on the ice. As I broke my way closer to the bank, the ice kept giving way and a deeper channel near the bank had the effect of raising the ice level to near the top of my chest. Next thing, the water was over my boot tops, so now both were full of cold water. An alder branch offered me a purchase with my free hand (the other held my rifle) which allowed me to slide my body up onto the edge ice. I rested belly down on the ice for a moment, then rolled into the bank and did a push up to regain my footing and walk away from the creek. Without the traction provided by the chains getting back on my feet would have been much more difficult.

It could have been serious if the water had been deep enough to soak my lower body. I've heard of people who were unable to get back up on top of the ice in situations like this.

Finding myself on the wrong side of the stream, I busted a trail through the alders and tussocks for a quarter of a mile until I found a much wider, braided place in the river where I crossed without difficulty.

The remainder of the return was unremarkable, other than the sloshing of water in my boots. I had forgotten about my sore knee.

My partners each had a small buck and reported seeing about what I had.

That evening after draining the water, I stuffed wadded newspaper pages and paper towels in my boots to soak up the moisture and propped the boots near our Coleman stove. I hung my pants over the stove, which had soon nearly dripped dry. The boots were clammy and damp in the morning, but two pairs of fresh, dry socks took away the chilly bite and would allow me to hunt comfortably that day.

At sunrise a new snowfall began with strong wind and we decided to stay in camp. I was doubly pleased that I had taken that buck the day before.

The Big One Got Away

Tom Dooley and I have hunted together for over thirty years. We never missed a season for the first seventeen years and spent up to six weeks hunting deer full time, some years. We began transporting hunters, which gave us ample excuse to spend more time in the field in the fall months. October, November, and sometimes part of December on the south end of Kodiak were my favorite times of the year.

Early on in our friendship we began Transporting guest deer hunters to the most remote parts of the Kodiak Archipelago. We only took American citizens, as the law required fully guided hunts for aliens. As Transporters, we could access the entire island group and we discovered and annually returned to areas that offered clearly the best deer hunting in the world. My guest and friend, Craig Boddington proclaimed it so after a hunt with me in 1993. The limit was initially seven deer per hunter, then due to some heavy winter kills, the limit was reduced to three. We handled up to sixty deer carcasses in a good season for our guest hunters and ourselves, but most years we did not see any typical, four by four heads (ten pointers by the Eastern count). Antlers of that configuration are rare in Sitka Blacktails. Most commonly seen bucks of this species show a "forked horn", or two point, set of head gear, with or without brow tines.

As Transporters, once our guests were placed on the beach, we could go hunting for ourselves. It was wonderful that we were privileged to have access to such a place, and I looked forward to that magical time each year.

Always sad to see the season end, I could never get enough hunting, especially deer hunting.

It's hard to come up with an explanation of just why deer have appealed to me so much. I've been extraordinarily blessed with being able to enjoy multiple hunting opportunities for just about every game and feral animal in North America, as well as dozens of African species, with some critters from South America, Europe and the South Pacific thrown in. But North American deer hunting has always reigned supreme in my hunting psyche.

As much as I enjoy hunting in general and deer hunting in particular, it probably sounds strange that I did not do much traveling away from my home area to hunt the hairy venison as a boy. Since I was in grade school I've been hearing tales of super hot spots, but in my younger years none were ever close enough to permit us, with our limited family budget, to go check them out. In the 1950s, a drive of more than a few miles seemed an unnecessary and therefore, unjustifiable, extra expense. And I have been content to hunt the animals close to home. Less time traveling makes for more time to be in the field hunting, or so I've always figured.

In thinking it over, all these years, I am convinced that most people can learn the ins and outs of their local game and terrane and once that is done, they can spend more time, sacrifice less money and enjoy greater success and satisfaction, by hunting close to home, as long as it has healthy game populations. And they are hunting an animal with which they can become intimately familiar—not a strange beast in a foreign land.

If I hadn't lived in Alaska for most of my life, I probably would have come north to pursue the uniquely charismatic species here, especially caribou, moose and Sitka blacktail deer. Of course the Dall sheep, mountain goats and three species of bears would have been a draw for me as well, but first and foremost I have always preferred to hunt the antlered animals.

With Sitka blacktail deer, native to the Southeastern Panhandle and introduced to the Kodiak Archipelago in the late 1920s and early 1930s, a four by four buck with brow tines is considered the ultimate trophy, comparable to a six by six Rocky Mountain or Roosevelt Elk. However, after now over fifty-two years of hunting the Sitka deer, I am convinced that the likelihood of taking a four by four with brow tines (ten total points) is far less than that of collecting a big six by six elk, no matter where one chooses to hunt.

While still officially a non-resident, in 1967 I purchased a tag for ten dollars to allow me to hunt a Sitka deer. It was my first and one of the few non-resident tags I have ever splurged on. The hunt was memorable and after one weekend of being skunked while hunting with a local fellow, I got out another time, had a full winter day to hunt by myself and I harvested a small forked horned buck.

But the second year on Kodiak Island, as a resident I took three bucks, the first of which was a heavy antlered, beautiful buck, the like of which I had dreamed of for years. Having long since been solidly hooked on deer hunting and eating, I swallowed the lure even deeper into my soul the day I took that big 3X3.

Over the ensuing years I found many reasons to return to Kodiak and never failed to hunt deer each time. Under a variety of circumstances, all of which included good luck, I managed to collect four or five nice four by fours, but most years I never even so much as laid eyes or binoculars on one of such high quality and so many points.

Since 1988 I have made Kodiak my permanent winter home which gave me many more and much better opportunities to pursue deer. Still, I seldom see an ideal buck with the total of ten normal points.

In this coastal species, the most common antler configuration is a forked horn—a two by two, with or without one or two brow tines. I've seen some very old, gnarly antlered bucks that were just big forked horns and probably never had, or would have had, more points. It's the nature of this particular beast.

In November of 2005 we had some Transported guest hunters on the south end of Kodiak. The hunting was excellent, with most hunters seeing over one hundred deer each day. We would drop anchor and hunt one area, then move on to a different bay the next day. No single area was over hunted or heavily harvested and the deer were much less twitchy than those that are accustomed to being hotly pursued by humans.

On our Transporting trips we usually took care of four hunters per week, then exchanged that group for another. With few exceptions our guests harvested at least two deer each. Some added a fox or two to their bag.

One year, of the twenty-four bucks taken, which included those collected by Dooley and I, only three had been normal, with two testes in the scrotum. All the others were cryptorchids, either bilateral with no scrotal testis or unilaterally cryptorchid, showing one scrotal testis and one undescended testicle.

Some good bucks, but no typical four by fours, note the second from the right, an outstanding non-typical.

The deer taken included some outstanding trophies, about half of which still carried the velvet and showed non-typical points.

But no one had reported seeing a typical four by four buck.

Our next group of four guests were all from the Seattle area and among them was my long time friend, Bruce Moe, with his wife Lori. Bruce first hunted with me in the Arctic in 1978 and since that memorable experience we had hunted together more than a dozen times, including one trip to Africa, which was his first excursion to the dark continent. Bruce is an excellent shot and knows his game. This was his second trip with us for Sitka deer.

Having taken some dandy Sitka bucks on his previous trip, Bruce was primarily interested in giving Lori a chance to harvest some really good trophies. He deferred shooting at every opportunity, allowing his wife to drop some fine animals. He, knowing the culinary qualities of these deer, took two fine, but lesser animals, which, once in the pan, taste just as good as the ones with more impressive head gear.

On their last day to hunt, we dropped anchor in the same bay that had produced the monster three by three shot by Craig Boddington twelve years earlier.

More than twenty-five years later, Boddington still says that is the highest quality deer he has ever taken. That story appears in my first book: *ALASKA HUNTING: Earthworms to Elephants.*

We were on the beach and went our separate ways early that morning. Bruce gave the other two hunters their choice of which area to hunt, while he and Lori went in a different direction. With so much prime country, I set off for yet another area and did not see any of our guests until we met on the beach at the end of the day.

Soon after separating on the beach I heard some shooting from the direction where I assumed Bruce and Lori would be.

Remembering the giant buck killed by Boddington, I carefully glassed over dozens of deer that day, in hope, more than expectation, of finding a comparable monster.

Over the years, I've come to realize that the general area or even the exact rock or tree where an exceptional trophy is taken is a prime spot to look in the future for a big one. Some areas just have appeal to big old deer, it seems.

That day I also saw eight bears. The presence of the bruins helped me decide where I traveled—and where I did not. I wanted to avoid any close encounters with the true monarchs of that wild country.

By mid afternoon I settled on a taker with lesser antlers than I had in mind, but once again, I was reminded of how nutritious and flavorful the meat was once we had it ready to put on the dinner plate. I was further encouraged to take that deer, which appeared to be a normal buck, for the value of its samples for our cryptorchid study. We desperately needed normal samples as a control for the study. Furthermore, I was comfortable in knowing that if I encountered an irresistibly large buck on the way back to the beach, I could add it to my load. In those days, at the age of only sixty-three years, several times each season I would place the meat of two bucks on my pack board. It made a heavy load, but it was not that much more noticeable than the meat of a single deer.

When I reached the beach, the four other hunters were gathered near a small fire. Each had taken their third buck and Bruce was telling his story of the day's events.

Within half an hour of leaving the beach, he glassed a huge four by four with two long brow tines and a three inch drop tine on the left antler. The antlers were heavy, wide, large in girth and long in length. The antler points were all long—there were no "crab claw" points on this buck. He told his wife that was the buck for her and they made a discrete stalk to within two hundred yards of the deer.

That remarkable buck was moving in an alder thicket directly uphill from Bruce and Lori. It was precisely the spot where Boddington and I had jumped his huge buck years before. The excitement of the moment did not rob Bruce of his better judgement. He maneuvered up the slope and managed to get above the buck without alarming the animal. When the object of their concentration stepped out into an opening in the alders, Lori fired. The buck did not move. She fired again. The deer ran along the crest of the ridge, this time followed by lead from both Bruce and Lori's rifles. It did not appear to be hit. At the end of the ridge it turned downhill and was lost from sight in the heavy alder brush.

A spooked buck's turning downhill often is a sign that it has been wounded, and most often, wounded in the chest.

Bruce and Lori searched in vain for the deer and blood, but found neither. He was sure they were on the trail of the deer of their desires as confirmed by the fresh hoof marks, but no blood was found in the snow. They saw no more of that great buck.

Later that afternoon they each harvested another mature buck.

Knowing Bruce as well as I did, I had no doubt that he had seen a truly enormous buck. I felt nearly as sorry as he, that the deer had not fallen to their shots.

We pulled the anchor that evening and as we motored toward the village where the charter plane would bring in new hunters and take this group to Kodiak, I prepared the blood and tissue samples from deer taken that day. I heard Bruce's story all over again and questioned him about landmarks, thinking that I might have a chance to visit the area sometime soon.

We replenished our water supply on the boat from a creek that evening. The next day was sunny and calm and the charter plane arrived early. We departed the village with our new guests and crossed the large bay toward the place we had been the day before. Tom asked me if I wanted to look for that big deer. Of course I did.

We were back at anchor shortly after noon. A solid five hours of daylight remained, so we went ashore. I had informed our new hunters of the previous day's events and they too, wanted to seek the giant. Tom and I would hunt in a different area after out guests selected theirs. When we were all on the beach, the new hunters saw several deer on the skyline showing their racks against the blue sky. This was too much for them to resist and they all struck off in that direction.

So Tom and I were left to search the area where Bruce and Lori last saw the monster. We began walking for the spot. As we began to climb the hill, I glassed a huge buck with four does on a lower level hill further up the valley. It was about a mile from where Bruce found it the day before. I told Tom that it looked like the deer Bruce had described, so we changed course and headed for the group of five deer.

Gregg took this nontypical cryptorchid buck.

Fifteen minutes later we were on a nob just above the big buck and his four does. The range was less than two hundred yards. The deer were strung out single file as they crossed a flat berry bog with the buck at the rear. They were walking toward our right, offering a clear broadside shot.

Our usual argument began. Who's going to shoot? I insisted that Tom shoot, but my contrary buddy was adamant that I be the one to put lead in the air. I told Tom that the deer would be out of range before we resolved this common, though ridiculous dispute. And I had shot more deer that year than he had. I laid my rifle on the tundra and folded my arms across my chest.

"Well, okay, pordner," Tom reluctantly drawled.

By then the deer were at two hundred yards, not moving fast, but walking steady and putting more yardage between us and them.

Tom took a careful rest on the moss and squeezed off a shot.

The deer did not react at all.

Tom shot two more times, with the same non-effect.

"You shoot, partner," Tom urged me.

"Nope, that's your buck, Tom," I insisted.

Normally in circumstances like this I automatically hand my rifle to the shooter and reload his, but that action just never occurred to me that day. Honestly, I never thought to do it.

Tom reloaded and shot three more times, but the deer kept moving in line until they were out of sight.

I told Tom that I would go left and he should follow up behind the band of deer. They did not act spooked and one or the other of us would likely get another crack at the big fellow.

By then I was resolved to shoot at the buck if I could locate it.

Without a doubt, that was the biggest typical Sitka deer I have ever seen—to this day, more than fifteen years later.

Nearly an hour passed without seeing the deer when I heard Tom shoot. I was certain he had the deer on the ground. Then I heard another shot, then another. In all I counted fifteen shots.

This was not a good sign and certainly not what I expected or wanted to be hearing.

Normally I carry three shells in the magazine, four in my pocket and a full box of twenty in my pack. Tom usually packed fewer rounds. I knew he must be out, or nearly out of ammo. I'd seen eight single bears in the area the day before, so I hustled to locate my buddy.

Gunfire is a magnet for bears in the Kodiak Archipelago. Some hunters have been killed and others mauled in situations like this.

Soon, I spotted Tom at the edge of a large alder patch and he had a deer at his feet, but less than one hundred yards above him on the hill was a large, dark bear.

An old gentleman boar, waiting for his dinner of deer guts.

Wasting no time, I got to Tom as soon as I could, expecting to see the giant buck at his feet.

It wasn't the one we were after. It fell on a bear skull.

Tom had a dandy big three by three, but it was not the object of our attention. He told me he never saw the huge deer again, he knew this was not the one, but he wanted to take it, so he tried. His rifle was shooting off center. He had one bullet left.

From my reserve box I handed Tom ten rounds and reminded him to load so that his remaining bullet was in the top of his magazine, as it should

The Big One Got Away

Old boar patiently awaiting dinner.

Dooley's buck fell on a bear skull.

shoot more true than the hand loaded rounds of mine would in his rifle. Sometimes other shells do not perform so well as those for which a rifle is sighted, and I reload with two hundred grain bullets for all Alaskan big game, which is a heavier bullet than most hunters use for deer. We both reloaded.

The big bear looked old and was well mannered. He patiently edged closer, then remained lying on his belly until we vacated the area. As we departed the big brownie moved right in to enjoy a feast of fresh, warm venison guts.

Once on the beach, Tom shot again and his bullet impacted the sod a foot from the target. He was lucky to have finally hit the deer at all.

Remorse for not thinking to pass my rifle to Tom hit me hard.

Our four new hunters had scored on three mature bucks and were ecstatic. We all agreed to change our schedule and hunt that area again the next day. Normally we did not hunt any bay two days in a row. But this was a worthy exception to our rule.

Early the following morning Tom retired his favorite rifle that I called "Old Kindling" due to the appearance of the wooden stock, and used a new .300 Winchester Magnum that he had purchased from one of the previous hunters.

Our guests paired off and returned to the area they had visited the day before, while Tom and I separately went back where we had lost the big buck.

In mid afternoon I spotted an obviously non-typical buck that had shed the velvet. It was far less desirable than the giant one I was looking for, but it was good enough for me that day. I spooked the animal from beneath me and watched it run across a broad valley, accompanied by a buck with normal looking, velvet free antlers.

It was a good time to eat my sandwich and to let the animals settle down. I still hoped to find the big one. An hour later, after carefully scrutinizing the area with my binoculars, I could see the buck lying near a patch of alders. After a bit of position shifting I found an avenue free of branches for my shot. It was a so-so, narrow, non-typical, cryptochid buck.

Dooley scored with his new rifle and our guest hunters came back with four mature bucks.

The remainder of the week we hunted other bays in the general area and enjoyed good success, but that did not include a typical four by four buck.

Some of the non-typical cryptrochids shed their velvet.

We returned to that same bay five days later and saw plenty of deer, but we never saw the giant again. I suspect ... and hope that he got to sire a lot of fawns that season. Maybe, someday I will encounter one of his progeny.

Dandy Buck, Bad Company on Kodiak Island

In November one year I was invited to make a trip on a purse seiner boat that would carry us around the west side of the island, across the bottom, or south end, then back up the east side. The owner, who I will call Jude, said that he wanted to hunt every bit of the route—as much as wind and sea conditions would permit. It sounded like it had the makings of a wonderful trip. He invited me to his home and proudly led me to a room that was jammed full of deer racks. It appeared that he had hunted deer a lot!

As we were loading the boat for departure from Saint Paul harbor in downtown Kodiak, one of the three invitees came by to tell Jude that he could not go, after all. An objection from his wife prompted him to back out at the last minute. That seems to be the most common cause of last minute cancellations of hunting trips—a wife's objections.

As the skipper of a sister boat was walking along the float, Jude hollered at him, asking if he wanted to go hunting.

"Well, sure. When are you leaving?"

"In about thirty minutes, and we'll be out for ten days or maybe two weeks," was the reply. I thought Jude really didn't believe that his invitation would be accepted. He was merely making a perfunctory gesture to the other fellow.

"Well, I got my rifle, sleeping bag, and stuff on my boat, so I'll be here in less than thirty minutes," was the surprise reply. Not many men could manage that, especially if they have a wife to consult.

When the new guy returned with his rifle and gear I took a close look at him. He was a giant, standing over six and a half feet tall. His hands were the biggest clamps I had ever seen on a human life form.

He had a set of feet to match those hands! Those size sixteens of his stuck out from the lower end of his legs and seemed to just kept on going.

When he jumped from the dock to the deck I walked up to him and extended my hand. When we shook, it seemed that my hand and arm—all the way up to my elbow—was enveloped by those massive mitts he wore at the end of his wrists. He was grinning from ear to ear and seemed harmless.

Figuring I could take a chance, I held eye contact, raised one foot and stomped it down just off the end of his big toe. I missed, as I intended to do.

"Oooo, don't do that, pordner, he soothingly warned."

"I just wanted to see if those things were live all the way out to the end." I smiled as I said it and everybody laughed.

I was convinced that he was good natured. His name was Tom.

We had a good first day's run around the north end of Kodiak and down Shelikof Strait, then the boat turned into Uyak Bay. We saw a few deer from the deck of the boat, but we also saw several other boats hunting in the area, so we motored further south.

Each morning, before every meal, and again before retiring Jude would get out his bible, pray, and then read us some passages. He gave one the impression of being a very devout Christian.

Jude soon proved to be one who avoided walking. He liked to shoot deer from the boat. He was not much of a marksman. On a beach south of Karluk he shot at a run-of-the-mill young forked horn, as it stood broadside about one hundred thirty yards away. He hit it in the guts. He shot several times as it ran down the beach, but did not connect with another round. The guy suggested that I use the skiff to run the big man, Tom, and the other fellow to the beach so they could chase down his wounded buck for him. I did that and returned to the mother ship while the others dutifully dogged after the stricken deer.

As we sat at idle waiting for the others, Jude saw a small doe watching us from high on a bluff overlooking our position. He lined up, braced against the widow sill, and shot. The deer tumbled off the bluff and hung up in an alder bush about a third of the way to the beach. It remained hanging there, dangling over the steep drop-off. I was hoping it would have a kick or two left in it, to dislodge it from the bush that arrested its fall, but the lifeless carcass did not move. Jude suggested I should go get that one for him. I told him that I could manage the big boat if he wanted to retrieve his deer for himself, but I would not attempt to go where the deer was. It was in a worse than hazardous place. Jude frowned at me, picked up this binoculars and began looking for another deer to shoot. The dead doe was left hanging in the bush and I was left with a bad feeling about the guy.

When Tom and the other invitee appeared on the beach about a half mile below were I had dropped them off, they were dragging a deer. I took the skiff to pick them up. When I saw the deer I remarked that it was not the same buck that the skipper had gut shot. This deer was not gut shot. They cautioned me not to tell Jude. The deer they had taken was an average forked horn, but it was not the little forky that escaped with a bullet in his gut. I wondered why they wanted to spare the skipper from the truth.

Beginning to dread what might be coming next, I held my tongue.

We made landfall off Halibut Bay, Gurney Bay, and Bumble Bay. Jude went ashore at Bumble Bay, but he did not walk far, and he shot nothing. He was grumpy when he returned to the boat. In all three areas I saw plenty of deer, but found nothing worthy of shooting.

Tom returned with an admirable, old, gnarly antlered buck. It was only a 2X2 (2 points on each antler, regardless of brow tines), but the heavy, wrinkled rack gave it a distinctive, appealing character.

We went around the south end of Kodiak and entered Alitak Bay.

We were spending too much time looking for shootable deer from the wheelhouse of the boat. It was akin to road hunting. We spent three entire days cruising, watching the skipper shoot at deer from the wheelhouse, and watching them run away, fortunately unscathed.

I quietly hoped, prayed actually, that the guy would miss clean with every shot he took. Maybe that jinxed him. I hoped so.

Each morning and evening Jude would make a huge display of bringing out his Bible and reading from it. His hypocrisy was disgusting. As an invited guest, I held my tongue, but I had a hard time doing that.

One morning as we were cruising close to Hepburn Peninsula Tom told the skipper that he wanted to stretch his legs and suggested that the third fellow drop Tom and me off on the beach, then return to pick us up just before dark. The skipper held Tom in great respect and agreed to the proposal.

For the first time in nearly a week of fine weather and sea conditions, we were going to spend a day doing what we came for—hunting deer.

Tom and I had gone only a few hundred yards from the beach when I noticed a dandy three by four buck coming toward us. He was fully in the rut and oblivious to our presence. I pulled out my video camera and told Tom to shoot the deer. He protested, I insisted. He shot it. I got the footage. As we walked toward the fallen buck a large 3X3 buck appeared across a small swale less than one hundred yards from us. Tom told me to shoot it, but I still had the camera in hand and told him that if he didn't take it, it would get away. I was already filming. Reluctantly, Tom shot the second buck. I told my new friend that I would gut the first one if he wanted to do the second. As Tom began to cross the swale, it looked like his second buck stood up, so he shot it again. I had a funny feeling about that, as my brief glimpse of the deer gave me the impression that it was not the same animal. I'd seen that sort of thing happen before.

Sure enough, Tom hollered that he had two bucks across the swale. But the annual limit was five deer, so everything was legal.

When I completed gutting the first deer, leaving the heart, lungs, and liver in the gut cavity I hollered that I was going up the mountain to hunt and would see Tom on the beach before dark.

"Ya gonna give me a hand with these deer, partner?" Tom asked.

Clapping my hands in applause, I waved as I turned right and walked toward higher ground. Tom was a big, strong man, and I wanted to go hunting. Besides, we were not too far from the beach and we had at least six hours of daylight before it would be too dark to see well.

As I hunted my way up country I got some good footage of several rutty bucks. I had yet to shoot my first deer on that trip. I would be satisfied if I shot nothing but video tape.

One young 3X3 buck spotted me, then came from upwind to check me out. He seemed to be looking for love—in the wrong place. I filmed the inquisitive, amorous, young deer as he came to within ten yards of me. He seemed a bit unsure, often lowering his head to try to pick up a scent on the ground. Finally, he diverted off the trail and cautiously worked his way around and through the brush to come up downwind of me. When he got a whiff of me he seemed unwilling to believe his nose. Instead of pheromones of an ovulating female, he detected my offensive fragrance. There was no harmony of hormones. He stared at me, sniffed the ground three or four more times, snorted, and reluctantly trotted away.

As I enjoyed the walk into the mountains I kept count of the deer I saw that fine day. When I came to a deep canyon I stopped to glass what appeared to be a much larger bodied deer with an impressive rack. It was near a mob of fourteen animals. That brought the count to fifty-three bucks and sixty-one does—and it was just a bit past noon! I spotted what no one could mistake for anything but an outstanding buck!

Having hunted deer throughout the Kodiak Archipelago for over twenty years, I'd seen thousands of deer and had a good idea of what a really good rack looked like. I'd even taken a few bucks with outstanding racks.

If one happens upon a super buck, there will be no doubt in you mind that it is indeed a giant of its kind.

More than a mile and a deep canyon separated me from the bunch of deer on the hillside. The biggest buck was intermittently sparring with two other large bucks, but it was not difficult for me to keep track of the best one. At least a dozen does were watching the action, fascinated by the conflicts.

The terrain contours required me to loose sight of the deer as I dropped into the canyon to come up on the side of the slope and downwind from where the deer were milling around. Knowing that these deer, especially while in the rut, are not as twitchy as elk or caribou, I was reasonably confident that I would be able to locate the buck when I came over the hill, but a tinge of anxiety spurred me up the icy slope with as much haste as I could muster. I had been in similar situations before, only to discover that the object of my attention had vacated the area and was lost to me forever.

Near the crest I slowed my pace and concentrated my vision on the country that was slowly being revealed with each step I took. I selected a dead alder snag as a landmark. When I neared that snag, the deer were not where I expected them to be. I continued my now much slower and more stealthy creep up the hillside. The contour was more pronounced that it appeared from below. I kept going up the slope, but saw no deer. I wondered if somehow the whole bunch had spooked and run off. After much too long, in my estimation, I saw first one, then finally, six of the does. It was the same bunch. They did not appear to be alarmed. I stopped and scrutinized the area, then I took a few steps forward and spotted the rest of the deer. In the eighteen minutes since I lost sight of them, the group had moved another three hundred yards upslope.

There was the giant, standing and looking to my right. One of his recently intimidated bucks was walking back up for another round with the dominant one. The does' attention seemed fixed on the master buck, expecting another pugilistic display. Another dead snag offered the only concealment I could use, so I slowly made my way toward it.

In the meantime, a contender buck had paused downhill and well away from the big one. The big buck was carefully watching down hill and eventually zeroed in on my position.

The alder snag prevented him from seeing me clearly. In his rutty condition, had he seen me, I expect he would have figured I was just another buck to subdue, or possibly a doe, ripe for seduction.

Subdue or seduce is the way of bucks during the rut.

Certainly I was seduced by the sight of that extraordinary buck.

But I decided to take no chances. The range was about two hundred and fifty yards.

Kneeling at the base of the alder snag, I removed my pack board and rested my rifle on top of the frame. I held for the base of the deer's throat and lovingly squeezed the trigger. The regal buck collapsed where he stood.

The band of deer did not notice the sound of my rifle. I watched for several minutes and saw no motion from the area my deer had fallen. When I stood up and began walking toward the spot, the other deer drifted slowly away. I watched two other large bucks square off and clash antlers briefly, before falling in behind the soon-to-be fecund does.

When I came to the fallen buck, he was all that I expected. He had one non-typical point on the right antler that had recently been broken. He also had a small projection on the inside of a slight palmation on the right antler. I'd not noticed those features before I fired, but had I seen them, it would not have changed my decision to shoot.

This was the most outstanding Sitka Blacktail that I had taken, though he was only a 3X3 with bilateral brow tines. He was about as good as they get.

There was no need to rush, with less than a couple miles of easy going to the beach. I savored the special moment before eating my sandwich and

The big buck where he fell.

On the hillside with the route to the beach in the background.

beginning to butcher the deer. No cape was necessary as I planned to boil and bleach the skull in the European style.

The old buck had been engaged in his annual fertility rituals, and his flat belly indicated he had not been feeding much for some time. But he was a large bodied deer and the meat would make a full load. With my spirits so high and most of the trip downhill to the beach, I would not notice the weight.

Most Kodiak deer hunters drag out the whole carcass of their deer after gutting it, but I had long ago found it easier to butcher the animal, then tie the meat on a pack board. This is the most reasonable way to get the meat out if you are well away from the beach. The four quarters, ribs and two long back straps, taken from the base of the ears to the rump fit nicely on my military board. The heart, tenderloins and liver were placed in a plastic bag and tied on top. Then I secured my pack sack on top of the load of meat. The head was tied on top of the pack sack.

As I made my way down the big hill and through the rolling countryside I was in easy shooting distance of antlered deer during the entire journey. I saw two single bears ambling through the open areas, scarfing up berries as they moved. The bears did not see me, though I made no point of concealing myself.

When I reached the area of Tom's three kills, he was just starting for the beach with the third deer. I fell in behind and we enjoyed our recounting of the day's events as we took our time going to the beach.

The boat was late coming to retrieve us, so we built a small fire and ate our last mini candy bars as we waited in the cool evening breeze. It had been a super fine day for both of us.

When we unloaded the skiff at the big boat, Jude took one look at the four deer, briefly focused on mine, and angrily declared that my buck would no doubt be the largest taken on Kodiak that year. His comments were not cheerful. He abruptly turned and entered the galley. I thought he was forcing himself away, to keep from making a more negative comment. I figured I was dealing with a rogue in camouflage clothing that could not hide his miserable nature.

His was a strange reaction, however I had seen other hunters become angry at the good luck of another person. I figure those people are upset

Bleached and ready for the wall.

at the realization that someone else bagged an animal that they desired and might possibly have taken for themselves. This is a twisted form of schadenfreude.

Dinner in the galley was not as animated as usual. No jokes were cracked. The skipper dished up his grub and went up to the wheelhouse to consume it alone. Tom went topside to try to console the skipper. I stayed below and washed the dishes.

That night we anchored nearby, but first thing the next morning we pulled up and ran to another bay. The skipper put on some new ostrich skin cowboy boots and proudly showed them to us all. Jude's preening about with his fancy boots and bragging about his shooting ability made me nauseous. The other guests made complimentary remarks on his foot gear and marksmanship. They treated Jude like a spoiled little kid, but I ignored his attempts to draw attention to those boots and himself. It was just too disgustingly childish.

Jude had some serious ego and personality problems. One could say that he was a guy who makes the boast of any situation.

The next day was spent with the skipper glassing from the wheelhouse windows, shooting and missing. We saw plenty of deer near the beaches and bluffs we passed, but no one went ashore, even though each area potentially held huge bucks. Jude brooded. He was unhappy.

For the next two days without leaving the boat, time dragged along. On the way home we nosed into a small bay and glassed several big bucks from the boat. Jude said I should drop Tom and the other fellow off. I had the impression that the skipper didn't want me to hunt anymore. When we got to the beach, conditions were right for me to secure the skiff and go ashore too, so I did.

Tom and the other fellow took off after bucks up the valley. I hung back until I saw where they were headed. Then I went to the opposite end of the beach and cut back into a stand of cottonwoods. Soon I came to some grassy knolls. Near the top of the first knoll a good buck stood up about one hundred fifty yards from me and I shot it in the neck. It was a far better than average Sitka deer and carried a 3X4 rack. It was the second biggest buck taken on the trip. I was sure the skipper would be livid when he saw this deer—especially since I had taken it. But, oh well. In fact, I might bloody well be amused by his ire.

Tom came by after I dumped my second buck and snapped a picture of me with the deer.

"Jim-dandy buck, porder," was Tom's comment.

We arrived at Kodiak harbor well after dark the next day. The skipper was adamant that no one should take their deer off the boat until morning, as he wanted to make pictures, he said. But we had already made photographs of the many deer on the boat.

Smelling a rat, I placed the head of my biggest buck in my sea bag. I thought it would be apt to disappear if I left it on the boat.

The next morning I brought the head back, but left it in my pick-up. When I arrived at the boat, Jude was extremely angry and screamed that I had removed my deer.

Unable to pass up an opportunity to irk the fellow, I said if mine is not there, did he think maybe someone stole it? Then I said that I had taken it to avoid it being stolen. I told him that I had it in my truck if he wanted to take pictures.

His face was about the color and texture of liver, his uncontrolled anger showed through like a soured wound. His lips quivered as he spoke. He

With a limit of five deer per person, some hunts brought in a lot of fresh venison.

did not mention pictures. I was sure he had intended to steal the big head. I did not see the head of the second buck I harvested, nor the gnarly two by two that Tom had taken.

We three guests cleaned up the boat and paid our share of the cost of the trip, which were heavily padded. The food bill was for far more than we had consumed, so the boat's can locker got filled at the cost of a few hundred bucks extra. No one complained.

One wonders how Jude, as he read the bible, could rationalize his sleazy behavior, which was so transparent.

As I was the only one who had quartered the deer in the field, and I had killed only two, the meat was easy to identify. I took the pieces to my truck and helped the others get their whole carcasses up the ramp and into their vehicles.

When we returned to pick up the heads and racks, Tom's big, gnarly two by two and my three by four, along with some other racks, were not to be found. I was quite angry about that and mentioned it to Tom, who said we should just let it go. If not for Tom, I would have confronted Jude. I might have slugged him.

I would have preferred to take my second head away from him and I would have let the community know what a jerk he was.

Now I understood how it was that Jude had a room full of deer racks.

In chance encounters with Jude in the next few months, he was cordial, but I was cool and minimized the time I spent with him.

That twisted soul, who always clumsily attempted to make the boast of any situation, was so transparently juvenile and spoiled, I could not understand how anyone, once they knew him, could tolerate his presence.

Since I had a big buck to enter in the contest, I told the shop owner that I would not score for the competition that year.

Jude and a sycophant of his were friends of the sport shop owner and they volunteered to score for the contest. Neither were official SCI measurers. When I saw the scores, they had underscored my antlers by over eight points, making it third place. When the shop owner offered me third prize I refused to accept it and said we should refer the issue to the head Master Measurer of Safari Club International.

A week later we got the determination from SCI and my buck placed first, but the shop had awarded the prize to someone else. Never again did I measure any heads for that store.

The numerical scores can sometimes be deliberately distorted. This is shameful and tarnishes the image of all sport hunters.

A manageable load of fresh venison.

Care of the Meat

Many deer harvested in the Kodiak Archipelago are shot on the beaches and the whole carcasses are loaded directly into a skiff, to be skinned later.

However, most of the deer I took were from one to several miles from any beach or road. The traditional method of taking out the meat in this neck of the woods has long been to drag the gutted carcass to the place of final skinning and butchering, but I preferred to cut up the animal on site. This provided two long strips of meat from the back of the ears to the rump—"backstraps", two front quarters, two hind quarters, two slabs of ribs, and some smaller pieces including the tenderloins, heart and liver which I placed in a plastic or cloth bag. All this fits comfortably onto my pack board, or into the pack sacks which some hunters prefer. Carrying the meat out on my back has always been much more comfortable and less time consuming and joint wrenching than dragging a carcass for a long distance.

For the whole, unskinned carcasses delivered to the large boat, we made cuts on the skin the same as if we were planning to do a rug mount. Then the skin was cut around behind the antlers. The top end of the hide included the ears, which was tied to a deck rail and the antlers were lifted by a hydraulic boom winch. The winch was operated in slow speed, allowing the skin to separate from the carcass as the body was raised. This produced a clean, skinned carcass with much less hair contamination than usually is seen after knife skinning, and it was much quicker. We would then dip the freshly skinned carcass in the salt water over the rail of the boat. This not only rinsed off blood in the abdominal cavity, it seemed to cause the exterior to set up quicker, even in relatively warm temperatures. The brine rinse was handy and free.

For lack of a winch one can tie the antlers to most anything solid, then tie the top end of the skin to a motor vehicle and pull slowly, or one can even pull the skin free by hand.

One note of caution, if the carcass is frozen, this method does not work so well.

All meat keeps and ages better in larger pieces as cut edges dry out quickly and tend to pick up dirt, etc.

In the Kodiak area from October through January we were not bothered by blowflies or other insects, but sometimes we sprinkled ground pepper liberally on the meat before it set up. There is no need to pepper the fat.

On one August hunt blowflies were especially pestiferous and black pepper was insufficient to keep the insects away, so I used poles to build a tripod from which I suspended the meat. I covered the tripod with a blue tarp and built a small smudge fire below the meat. Cottonwood or alders are preferable for smoking, but only spruce was available for the fire. Surprisingly, the spruce smoke gave the meat a delicious flavor.

Some guests have brought citric acid to treat their meat with to frustrate flies, but I have not found it necessary.

Care of the Meat

Using a tractor to pull the skin off a deer carcass.

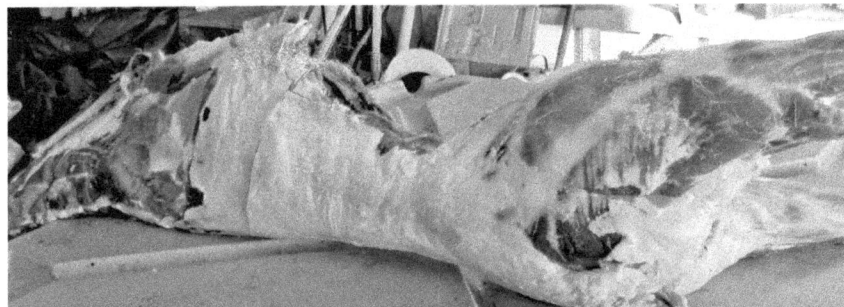
Kodiak deer taken between August and January usually carry a heavy layer of sweet tallow.

Note bundles of field-butchered venison hanging next to whole carcasses.

Heavy Buck Near the Beach

When hunting and fishing, one never know what to expect—and that uncertainty is part of the magical allure of those outdoor activities. We all anticipate and dream of successful hunts, perhaps collecting an outstanding animal, but along with that is the possibility of coming home empty handed. Without the potential for lack of success, the endeavor is not worthy of being called a hunt, in my view. Some hunts wind up being extremely demanding physically, sometimes dangerous and all is endured for the sake of the pursuit of wild and free game.

Taking game on high fenced farms or ranches does not qualify as a hunt for me. Those experiences are "shoots", similar to diving for cultured pearls or catching fish from a tank at a fish farm.

For years I have seen photographs of incredible heads, most often of White-tailed Deer, but some European Red Deer are pen raised, too. Those pictures of game with a blizzard of points on their heads have become repellant to me. I seldom even look at advertisements that show cultured trophies.

This is not to say that I begrudge people from raising such animals with abnormally outstanding racks, or people from paying huge fees to collect them, but I have always questioned the validity of such "trophies" being entered in the record books. The next year a hunter could arrange to buy a higher scoring head, if the shooter has enough money, similar to purchasing a new designer gown for a debutante.

It was just prior to Thanksgiving one year. We were done with booked hunters for that season. Terrorist attacks, tornados, hurricanes and a late season typhoon in the Philipeans, as well as a variety of domestic problems, had caused several guests to cancel. Tom Dooley and I wanted to check out a nearby island—one which had been widely reported for years to have no deer. We had glassed it from afar for several years and noticed that it had very little brush and no timber, but its beaches looked wide and inviting for an all terrane vehicle excursion. Tom loved ATVs and he had two four wheelers. Another friend, Scott, and his new wife wanted to join us, so we borrowed another four wheeler from our buddy, PlumbBob.

We loaded the ATVs on the deck of the *F/V REBEL* and set out for the new hunting country. It was going to be an eighteen to twenty hour trip in the fifty foot seiner. Ah … the irresistible lure of virgin hunting territory!

Weather forecasts are pretty accurate most of the time and for this period, it looked like we could make our destination with a few hours to spare before a big storm was due to hit the Kodiak Archipelago. It was advancing from the southwest as do most of our big storms. We'd been hunting in the general area for several years and twice Tom had been forced to run the boat onto the beach when the anchor did not hold, but we only took such drastic measures on well known beaches and only at a low tide with an offshore wind. The idea was that an incoming high tide would re-float the boat and we would not be marooned for long. Not knowing the beaches of the new area, we optimistically assumed that the anchor would hold.

We departed Kodiak about mid-afternoon to catch the ebb tide on the way out of Chiniak Bay and around the cape. We ran all night with Tom and me alternating two or three hour shifts at the wheel. By noon the next day we were offshore of the new island studying the line of breakers which indicated a reef or shoal which was about three hundred yards offshore from the beach. Tom figured we could get around the breakers on their southwest end, then run parallel to the beach until we came to the mouth of a large lagoon which had a stretch with no breakers. There, a hard a'starboard turn should slip the boat into sheltered water. The breakers were standing about three to four feet high when we skirted them. Not knowing the depth of the entrance channel, we timed our entry into the lagoon at high tide, which was a nine footer that day.

We got in after a few tense minutes of wondering if the keel would find the channel too shallow, but we cleared the bottom with maybe a foot to spare. Once inside the lagoon the depth increased and we powered up toward the foothills at the head of the lagoon. We all breathed easier.

Deer were out feeding as they often do before and after a storm.

The marine forecast remained the same with the storm now predicted to reach our part of the archipelago soon, but it was calm and plenty nice where we dropped anchor. There was time to hunt, so we used the boom to load the ATVs, one-at-a-time into the skiff and then used planks to run them off the skiff and onto the beach. When the last ATV was on the beach we decided to make a short hunt.

Scott hadn't hunted as much as Tom or me, so we told him he could take the first decent buck—if we found deer. But I had noticed deer tracks on the beach and I was certain we would find some.

After less than half an hour we spotted a decent three by three buck and Scott started blazing away, eventually hitting it. I quickly spilled the guts out, leaving the carcass belly down to pick up on the way back, and we all continued up into the foothills.

However, Scott had his wife on the back of his machine and he attempted to go downhill at too much of an angle. The center of gravity got them and the four wheeler rolled. Neither of the passengers, nor the machine suffered visible damage, but Scott surrendered his wife to ride with Dooley for the rest of the day.

Tom knocked down a bigger buck and I retrieved it, then tied it on the back of the machine I was using. We were on the lee side of a big ridge, but I noticed the lagoon was showing white caps, indicating a wind of at least fifteen miles per hour.

The wind was coming up fast and strong, so we headed back to the *REBEL*, loading Scott's buck as we drove by. We left the machines behind some large grassy dunes and were all happy to be back aboard the boat where we enjoyed a warm meal and shelter from the wind which by then was gusting about fifty miles per hour and forecast to hit seventy that night.

Dooley had a television set and a VHS tape player in the galley, so we watched a movie as the wind velocity picked up and the boat rocked and creaked. I was reminded of the old sailors mentioning "shivver my timbers" as the boat was buffeted by the howling wind, which was by then accompanied by hard rain.

The *F/V REBEL* was as comfortable as a fine motel with four bunks in the forecastle and one in the galley, plus the one in the wheelhouse that Dooley used. Scot and his wife wanted to use the one in the galley which was close to the stove, so I had the cool forecastle to myself.

About ten o'clock that night Tom interrupted a movie to go topside to take a look. He hollered that we were dragging anchor as he fired up the main engine.

This meant that I needed to go below to engage the PTO before going to the bow to pull the anchor. I hastily pulled on my boots and rain gear, then spent some wet minutes outside winching up the anchor and chain.

Dooley cruised slowly around in the lagoon looking for a better "holding bottom" but after resetting the anchor several times, followed by the boat dragging, he told me to secure the anchor for travel. We weren't going out of the lagoon, but we would have to "jog" until the wind got tired. Jogging means holding the boat in position with power and requires constant attention. Tom and I took turns at the wheel keeping the boat away from the beach the rest of the night.

As dawn approached the storm intensified and we were told later that the Coast Guard recorded top gusts at 127mph. before their anemometer blew apart. The tide was low and the next three highs would be sufficiently higher than the last, so Tom decided to "stick" the bow on the beach near the parked ATVs. That should ensure that we could back off the beach at high tide when the wind relented.

Dooley ran the boat into the beach at slow speed, but the momentum of the heavy, fifty foot vessel took the bow several feet into the sand and muck. There were no rocks.

We were headed directly into the wind and the boat was level. The last time we needed to run it aground the boat listed about thirty degrees, which was very uncomfortable during the two days we spent there. The *REBEL* creaked and groaned like an arthritic old woman. The offshore breakers were wild and seemed to have built to thirty feet high or more.

At one point Tom discussed possibly releasing the 140 pound anchor and taking it off the chain, then we could carry the anchor up over the first beach ridge, then haul the chain (which weighed more than the anchor) up, reattach it and continue to wait out the storm, but the boat seemed secure and the wind showed signs of diminishing, so the anchor remained in its bow cradle.

For that day and the next the boat creaked, shuddered, and moaned as the wind and rain continued to pound us, but peak gusts were by then only about seventy mph or so. We played pinochle, watched movies and read in safe, warm comfort. The fresh venison was wonderful.

Visibility was reduced to a quarter mile or less most of the time, so for two days we saw no birds. Sea gulls, magpies, ravens and bald eagle populations are large in that area, but, like us, they were all hunkered down in that nasty blow.

I would have not enjoyed being in the best of tents those stormy days.

So we had made good use of the last hours of day two, spent days three and four boat-bound. On the morning of day five I awoke to bird sounds, a clearing sky and only a light offshore breeze. The surface water of the lagoon showed not a single wrinkle. As sunlight beat back the darkness the birds began their displays. Gulls were swooping and squawking, eagles were chortling overhead. Sea gulls and magpies were on the deck, pooping the place up—streaking it with their own brand of whitewash as they searched for something to eat. If we had not protected the meat of the first two deer, the birds would have picked the bones clean.

It was time to go hunting!

A tide high enough to float the *REBEL* would not come before dark for the next couple of nights, so we resolved to leave her as she laid and deal with backing out later.

After a hearty breakfast of deer steak, eggs and toast we hit the beach. Dooley and I rode down the beach to the south, while Scott and his wife went inland. Tom reminded Scott to not drive sideways on the hills. Scot glumly nodded his head. The outside beach was primarily pea gravel which is tiring to walk on, but easily traversed on the four wheelers.

The boat was stuck on the lagoon side of a long spit which ran for about a mile and a half from the southern foothills to the entrance to the lagoon. The inside beach was composed of sand and loamy muck, but the outside was primarily pea gravel.

The storm had brought up all kinds of goodies. There were dozens of useable fishing buoys, one large Japanese glass ball, a medium sized whale carcass—probably a young Humpback (Megaptera novaeangliae), a life ring and wreckage from the *F/V MITROFANIA*, an eighty foot steel fishing boat that had gone down with some crewmen aboard a few years before, as I recall. Several dungeness crab pots and plenty of buckets, jugs and other garbage that had been lost from passing boats were everywhere. Several types of kelp and sponges were piled all over the shore and some large flotsam had been blown up to a hundred yards off the beach.

The birds—seagulls, magpies, ravens and bald eagles were everywhere, and in noisy disputations, especially on the beaches. They were checking for edible wash-ups and squabbling with every other bird. The whale carcass was the biggest single attraction to all species of birds and several foxes which quarreled and fought over pecking rights. We saw seven foxes scurrying along through the beach detritus that day. It seemed they too, had been shelter-bound for the past two days and were trying to fill their empty bellies.

We saw deer creeping through the washed up logs and visiting the beach to snack on fresh kelp and who knows what all else. The bright, calm conditions made it a coming out day for all critters.

Way up ahead I glassed a mob of a dozen or more deer. One buck stood out as having extra heavy antlers. We parked the machines and I trotted up the lagoon side of the spit and out of sight until I was approximately opposite to the herd of deer. I chambered a round and eased up over the bank. It was easy to locate the one I wanted. It was a dandy three by three with two brow tines and extra heavy antlers. The ninety yard shot put the beautiful buck in the grass. It turned out to be the best buck I took that season.

The good salvage material was a continuous distraction, but we were there to hunt deer, so we ignored most of the attractive goodies that normally we would have taken—at least we planned to put it off until we were done with hunting for the day.

We rode the ATVs at slow speed down past a protruding point on the ocean side, but we came to a river that was running much too high to attempt a crossing, either with the machines or on foot. This was all new hunting ground to us and we tried to take in as much as we could, in hope of returning and being better prepared—with hip boots, for sure.

My best Sitka Blacktail buck of the season.

As we were looking the river over, Tom spotted a nice buck poking around in the tall grass near the edge of the foothills. The rut was on full strength and this fellow was looking for love. The deer was coming our way, so I bent over and hobbled around, occasionally raising my head up—as a deer might do—to draw the buck in closer. My simple ploy worked. The deer was fleming (sniffing) me from less than thirty yards away when Tom shot him. Dooley hollered, "I think I saved you from an awful fate this time, pordner!" Yes, that buck was considering mounting me, for sure.

This mature buck was a monorchid, with one scrotal testicle and one still retained in his abdomen. He would have been sexually functional and with one scrotal testis, he would have been fertile.

Before we had that deer gutted several more decent bucks offered themselves so I took another heavier than normal three by three. It was just too easy. My second buck was normal with two scrotal testes.

It was time to head back. We only had three deer carcasses to load on the machines, so then we could pay more attention to some of the washed up treasures. We piled a couple of dungeness pots on the ATV racks, put the deer carcasses on top of the pots and tied several good buoys and other useful wash-ups to the pots.

Scott and his wife were waiting on the beach next to the big boat. He had taken another buck and was talking about heading for Kodiak. He was scheduled to meet a ferry to load his truck for the trip to Homer.

I was all for staying another day or several more. Not only was the hunting as good as it gets, but the beach combing was too. Neither Tom nor I had anyone to satisfy but ourselves. The temperatures were right for hanging the meat for as long as necessary, as long as we wrapped it to keep the birds from getting at it. We had more than plenty food and fuel and might never see such opportunities again. Well, that was my usual feeling about hunting another day or not. I would always opt to hunt longer.

That evening after loading the ATVs Dooley backed the boat off the beach and into deeper water. We slipped through the channel in the dark and headed north as far as Old Kaguyak Bay where we dropped anchor for the night. I was wishing we had stayed at least one more day in the paradise we had found.

Ideal situations like we encountered that day are few and far between.

Heavy Buck Near the Beach

After the 127mph blow, Tom and I were feeling pretty good about everything.

The Massive Pestrikoff Buck

Back in the mid-1990s, on our way home to Kodiak from several productive weeks of deer hunting on the south end of Kodiak with our transported guests, storm force winds and heavy seas had pounded us for several hours—all the way from Two Headed Island until we reached the sheltered waters of Sitkalidak Strait. When we were abeam of Old Harbor, Tom decided to tie up at the village for a short spell as he wanted to visit a friend. The forecast was for more strong wind, so that indicated we would probably drop anchor and spend the night in the area.

Buddy Pestrikoff holding the massive rack.

A couple of local fellows came to the dock to greet us and commented on the collection of deer heads we had aboard. One of them mentioned that a massive set of antlers was on display in the local cafe, so I grabbed my camera and walked over to view the rack.

There on the wall was the most impressive set of Sitka Blacktail antlers that I have ever seen. The owner/hunter happened to be having a cup of coffee, so I asked him to hold the rack for me to photograph. He was happy to comply. I was happy that I had gone over to see the huge rack.

That set of deer antlers was simply unforgettable. Years later the hunter, Buddy Pestrikoff, moved to Kodiak town and I occasionally would bump into him while shopping or going about my daily downtown activities.

In February, 2018 I happened upon Buddy at the grocery store and got his telephone number. I told him I wanted to hear the story behind that outstanding deer. He said he no longer had that rack. He had another massive one he took several years ago, but a neighbor's dog had grabbed that one from his porch and he never saw it again. Two great racks lost. What a shame—and both were 4X4s with brow tines.

But he remembered some of the particulars of the day he found that giant buck in the photograph on the previous page. He said he had put a tape to the rack and it scored about 118, but no official measurer had scored it.

The day he took that deer was not going well for Buddy. He had taken his skiff to Barling Bay and among other things, dropped his rifle, delivering a solid whack to the scope. The deer was standing fairly close to the beach. When Buddy squeezed off a shot, his bullet broke a branch above the head of the buck. The alder branch collapsed and hung by a strip of bark. The deer bounced off into the brush, but did not seem overly alarmed. Obviously the rifle was shooting way off.

When Buddy beached his skiff and got ashore, a doe came bounding by, almost close enough to touch. The running doe made for a small clearing in the middle of which the big buck stood. Buddy stalked to within seventy-five yards and, knowing his rifle was not shooting true to the scope, he barrel sighted and dropped the buck in its tracks.

That set of antlers does not have great length of main beams or tines, but its massive development makes it the finest of its kind, in my view.

Skip Woodward's Surprise

So many times we hear of world class animals taken while being mistaken for a smaller representative of the species, or by sheer luck. One such trophy is the Chadwick Ram, a Stone Sheep taken in British Columbia in 1936, and thought by many to be the greatest North American trophy of all time. It is the only new world sheep with both horns measuring over fifty inches in length. The hunter, Lee Chadwick, had traveled to the headwaters of the Muskwa and Prophet Rivers in British Columbia, but the arduous backcountry horse journey had left the party hungry for meat other than the salt pork that had been sustaining them for two weeks. They sought just any sheep for fresh meat. They found three rams, but the largest one did not impress them as being of trophy quality. Chadwick spent some time filming the ram before deciding to shoot it for camp meat. His first shot was low, but eventually he put the ram to earth. Even up close the hunters were not overly enthusiastic about the animal. It's body seemed too small for the horns it carried, but those horns taped out at 52 and 50 inches! That magnificent fourteen year old ram has occupied the top position in the record book for over seventy-five years! And the hunter and guide thought it to be just a meat ram!

In 1961 Harry Swank was looking for a large ram reported to be in the area of the Wrangell Mountains he was hunting. He set out walking from camp and right off the bat, the largest Dall ram so far measured, came walking down a canyon practically into his lap. Uncommonly good luck had delivered the monster ram to Mr. Swank.

And so it goes, and so it was with my friend Skip Woodward in November, 2001. Our country was still in shock from the 911 terrorist

Skip Woodward and his second buck of the day.

attacks, but life must go on for the living and Skip had flown to Port Lions to hunt deer with his brother-in-law Bruce Nelson and his nephew Lars. Skip was the only one who had not filled his freezer with winter meat and therefore, was the only one carrying a rifle. The three men set out with two four-wheeler ATVs. Behind Barabara Mountain they found a Kodiak Electric company power line trail and followed it as they searched for bucks. Toward midday they located a large forked horn buck which was still carrying velvet. Skip shot the deer but it did not drop, however they located the carcass soon thereafter. It was a bilateral cryptorchid, meaning it had no testicles in the scrotum and was therefore sterile. That large bodied buck made it a good day already.

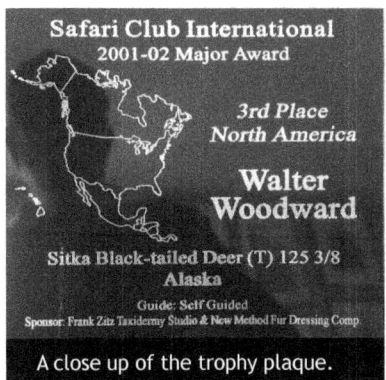

A close up of the trophy plaque.

The number one Sitka Blacktail hangs in a safe place.

A beaming Skip shows his Safari Club International Annual Trophy

On the way home they saw a large buck standing on a grassy hillside with six does. All the deer were watching the men. It looked like a good buck, Skip told me, so he ranged it at 286 yards, rested his .243 caliber rifle on the ATV and held for the top of the antlers. It was a knock-down shot. One coup de grace bullet from a pistol finished it.

Bruce and Lars remarked that it was a really big buck, bigger than any they had taken. They cut the animal up, loaded the meat and head and started back for town. Skip did not take the cape.

When Skip loaded his gear, meat and the two deer racks on the plane to return to Kodiak, the pilot gasped as he told Skip that was the biggest Sitka Blacktail rack he had ever seen.

A few days after Skip's return he called me to see if he could bring the rack over to my house for measuring. I said to come on over.

Well, it was the most outstanding Sitka Blacktail buck rack that I had ever seen, too. I scored it at 125 and 2/8 points.

After measuring it I got out the Safari Club International record book and saw that Skip's rack exactly matched the existing number one in the book.

Realizing what he had taken, Skip managed to acquire a cape and had a beautiful shoulder mount done on the magnificent buck.

Skip's buck won the Big Buck Contest in Kodiak. For that he received a hundred dollars prize and a Leatherman tool.

In January, 2002, Skip attended the Safari Club International annual convention in Reno, Nevada and accepted his award.

In addition, Skip received a beautiful plaque that reads:

> SITKA BLACK-TAILED DEER
> (TYPICAL)
> ALASKA
> NOVEMBER
> WALTER WOODWARD
> GOLD AWARD
> 125 3/8

Skip's "meat hunt" with relatives turned into one of the most memorable hunts of his life.

Unanticipated surprise events like this are almost too good to be true. The possibility of encountering such a world beater is a driving force for most hunters.

Stuck on the Beach

We used the fifty foot purse seiner *F/V REBEL* to get around the archipelago for commercial fishing and hunting, but to get ashore from the big boat we needed an adequate smaller vessel. My buddy Tom Dooley had several suitable landing skiffs, and we tried different ones, but the best was the "snag skiff" he had appropriately named *SURF*. It was a fourteen foot aluminum skiff with a self-bailing deck designed to tow the purse line when seining. It had a large outboard engine to do so. That little boat proved invaluable in rough conditions. The only draw back to *SURF* was its weight. That stout boat weighed about five thousand pounds, so once it was grounded, it would take a rising tide to float it. In some areas we would put the group of four or five guest hunters ashore, then either Dooley or I would take *SURF* back off into water deep enough to keep it floating in low tide and set the anchor. To get ashore, the last man would paddle ashore in a rubber raft which was stowed securely above high tide level. One of us would paddle back out to *SURF* to bring it in to pick up people. We always dreaded a bear coming along and destroying the raft, but that did not happen in the seventeen years we used it. We avoided putting bloody meat directly into the rubber boat, as that would surely invite serious bear damage.

When the slope of the beach and the location of rocks permitted, we could land the party with *SURF*, then set the anchor on the bow attached to a long line. Timing the launch of the *SURF* with the swells, we would push the skiff off the beach and when it reached the deeper water, the anchor was yanked off the bow with the long line and the shore end of the line was then secured to a log or rock. When we needed the *SURF* again, usually at the end of the day, we could haul the anchor in with the long

Picking up a hunter with his deer on his pack board with *SURF*.

line, load up and head back to the *REBEL*. It worked very well. With five or six hunters and as many or more deer in the *SURF*, its self bailing deck made it safe. It was, unlike the *TITANIC*, a truly unsinkable vessel.

With the shelter deck bolted to the stern of the boat, we had to tow *SURF* behind and that worked well. Depending on sea conditions *SURF* could be snubbed up tight to the stern or towed at length well behind the big boat. Spray and waves that fell into the skiff quickly drained out of the deck ports.

On one trip in the 1990s Dooley used a sort of hybrid landing vessel. It had a hard fiberglas bottom and keel with inflatable pontoons on each side. It was very stable and not so heavy as *SURF*. While using it we got stuck on one beach with a long shallow offshore area. The hybrid boat was too heavy for the three of us to drag to the deeper water but we gathered up loose buoys from the beach and tied them together in pairs with about a foot of line between them. Using three or four sets of joined buoys we could push the boat up onto a pair, then push until we had two sets under the skiff. The buoys served like wheels. We would keep pushing and add the aft pair to the to bow as we slowly moved the skiff toward the water. That kept us from having to wait so long for the incoming tide.

But, inevitably the inflatable pontoons of the hybrid skiff were damaged and we went back to using *SURF*.

Hunting in one of our favorite bays we were delayed in returning to the beach. The tide was quickly ebbing and we were going to be forced to

F/V REBEL with *SURF* snubbed up tight to the stern.

sit on the beach until it reached its low and then came back in on the next flood. We faced a long chilly night on the beach in prime bear country.

There were six of us, Dooley, me and four guests, and we each had a deer. The wind was onshore, broadcasting the smell from the deer meat inland—where the bears would detect it.

Anticipating problems in this bruin-rich area, while there was still light, we got a large fire going and stacked up plenty of extra wood before placing all the meat, except some ribs we would roast on the fire, in *SURF*, which was sitting about one hundred yards off the beach.

When bears came (not if they came, but when) we should be able to keep them from getting at our meat. With a big pile of wood, no one would have to go far from the fire to get more fuel.

Latrine use would have to be close to the fire as well, so we had to watch where we stepped.

Everyone had a good flashlight—a must on all hunts. And we all kept our rifle magazines loaded, but nothing in the chamber.

Not long after full darkness we heard the first bruin visitors. They woofed and scuffled around at the edge of the firelight. One large sow came within twenty yards of us with her two cubs, but several of us jumping up and down, shining light in their eyes, hollering and waving pieces of tarp kept her back. That area was home to one huge sow with three cubs. That quartet was especially aggressive, but luckily they did not show up that night.

This was not the only time I was alone or with a group that got caught on the beach by missing the tide, but it was the longest and one of the most memorable. We didn't have enough water to float the skiff until four o'clock the next morning. But we had water to drink and wash down the fire-roasted venison. Unfortunately we had no beer or whiskey.

When we finally began to push with poles to get to water deep enough to use the outboard, a couple adult brown bears followed us a long way into the water. Their determination was admirable, I guess, but their failure was just fine with me and the rest of our party.

Returning to the *REBEL* was delayed, but most welcome.

The Peruke

On a trip through Germany in 1978 I spent some days visiting potential hunters who had expressed interest in coming to Alaska. I was privileged to visit many trophy rooms. I saw two very strange Roe deer heads and was told that they were "Perukes". They had cauliflower-like growths on their heads that seemed to grow from the normal position of the antler buds.

The abnormal head gear intrigued me, so I began to investigate all I could learn about Perukes.

Peruke antlers, or antleromas are benign proliferations of the velvet antlers of cervids. They are believed to occur when shedding of the velvet is disrupted by hormonal disturbances. The peruke may proliferate massively over time, causing physical impairment, obvious suffering and, in some cases, even mortality.

Among cervid species, peruke antlers are most commonly reported in Roe deer *(Capreolus capreolus)* found in Europe and parts of Asia. Strangely, both males and females can show the abnormality, though female Roe deer normally do not carry antlers.

In Roe deer, almost three times as many female as male peruke cases had been documented. Figure that one out if you can! Reproduction was reported as functional in some of the affected females. Cyst formation in the pituitary gland was the most commonly noted pathologic finding that may have caused peruke antler formation, but in most cases gonads were not available for examination.

A popular theory is that the abnormal growth of Peruke antlers is due to a lack of testosterone at a time when antlers should harden and the velvet should be shed.

The young, smaller than normal, buck was emaciated and its coat was rough.

Instead, the antlers reportedly grow abnormally and never shed their velvet. Blood flow to the antlers continues, but in cold temperatures the abnormal antlers become frostbitten or completely frozen. The damaged antlers are not shed. In the spring new antlers grow from the base of the remaining antler from the previous year.

Based on what I've observed in cryptorchid Sitka blacktails, the above supposition regarding non-shedding and new growth occurring beneath the previous antler seems unlikely, but as I described in the previous paragraph, that is the current thinking.

Several causes have been suggested for what might lead to formation of Peruke antlers including cryptorchidism, an injury or birth defect affecting the testicles, or possibly a cyst of the pituitary gland could be responsible. Our research indicates that cryptorchidism is a developmental anomaly or disorder, most likely caused by exposure of the gravid doe to an endocrine interruptor or an endocrine mimic, which could be either natural or a man-made contaminant.

Perukes have been recorded in Moose *(Alces alces)* and one or two cases are reported in that species each year.

The Peruke

LEFT Boiled skull.   RIGHT left profile of the deer.

While on a deer hunting trip to one of the "hot zones" (so called due to a high frequency of cryptorchid bucks) in 2002 I was looking over several deer with my binoculars, when I noticed what appeared to me to be a Peruke. The animal was small and emaciated and seemed to be shunned by the other deer nearby. I make a successful stalk and shot the strange, pathetic appearing deer.

I noticed a fowl oder which I associated with purulence. Upon close inspection I did see pus oozing from the base of the left antler rose. I removed the head at the foramen magnum and did not salvage any of the meat. It was clear to me that this animal had a massive, generalized septicemia. I was sure the meat would be unfit for human consumption. I was on a boat and did not return to Kodiak for more than a week, but when I did, I took the head to the local hospital lab asking that a swab be taken and whatever bacteria were involved be cultured and identified, but the culture effort failed.

My usual boiling and bleaching technique revealed that the massive tumor in place of the left antler was shot through with ragged bits of bone interspersed with pus-laden soft tissue. The skull bones were greatly eroded.

To my knowledge this is the only reported case of a Peruke found amongst Sitka blacktail deer in the Kodiak Archipelago. However it is reasonable to assume that many hunters would walk away from such a deer if they killed one like this. A hunter would probably make no photographs. Most hunters would likely not file a report with the Alaska Department of Fish and Game.

This may be one more manifestation of potential adverse effects of Cryptorchidism in Sitka Blacktail deer. Or it may be entirely due to the rampant infection of the antler base. I favor the later explanation.

Hunter's First Buck

My friend Jeremiah Wagner told me this story.

It was early November, 2016 and I had decided to take my eldest son, Hunter on his first overnight hunting trip. We decided to spend a week in Kizhuyak Bay with a good friend, Mike Druckrey, at his cabin. We set out the first morning in the dark and had hiked for an hour when we spotted a decent 3 point. I had resolved that he wasn't going to shoot anything less. We tried to get in position to take a shot but Hunter, at six years of age, couldn't find a rest that allowed him to see above the alders and grass. We tried several different angles before the deer slowly walked out of sight. We were disappointed.

We kept hiking and came across another 3 point but again we were defeated by high brush and poor angles. We continued. The next deer that we spotted was a forked horn. I lowered my standards. This buck would do. Again, we ran into the same problem. The undergrowth did not allow for a clean shot. We decided to head back to camp. On the way, back we spotted a spike, but had no shot opportunity. My buddy Mike headed back to tend to chores.

Hunter and I had to change our game plan. We weren't giving up but needed more open ground. Back in the hills we found a birch tree on a knob with good viewpoints all around. I cleared four shooting lanes in hope of giving Hunter a shot. It was 1:30pm. We were going to sit it out, calling and rattling. After about three hours we decided to head to camp. As we came off the first knob we spotted a buck chasing a doe. The deer didn't see us and they were traveling. I anticipated that they were going to come out on another clearing the next knob over. As the deer went out of sight we ran to see over the hill. Once we reached the clearing I opened Hunter's bipod attached to his .223 compact rifle which was loaded with 55 grain Barnes TTSX. I placed it on the ground. Hunter got ready to shoot.

Just as Hunter was ready; the buck came into view on the next knob. I had his scope turned on 4X and asked him if he could find the buck in his scope. He replied, "Yes" so I zoomed in with 12X and again asked him if he could see the buck. He again replied, "Yes". I had him load his chamber and told him to put the crosshairs behind the front shoulder like we had discussed. I whispered when he felt comfortable he could take the shot. After about 10 seconds he fired. The deer jumped forward and ran into an alder patch. I knew that he had been hit good, but just then a buck came walking out of the alder patch exactly where our buck had gone and started walking up the hill. Now I was questioning his shot placement.

After a brief discussion we weren't sure if this was the same buck. We were fairly certain that he had hit it. It didn't make sense that it was walking uphill, apparently untouched.

We gathered up our guns and packs and took off running just as the buck crested over the hill. I didn't want the buck to get away if it was wounded. By the time that we reached the top of the hill that buck had turned around and was coming towards us. Hunter got ready again. The buck appeared about 15 feet in front of us. I could tell this buck was not wounded. Hunter's deer must be back in the alder patch. We grabbed our gear and returned to the alder patch about 100 yards away. We saw a deer lying in the alders.

Hunter began to run up to his deer but I told him to hold off a minute to make sure he wasn't just stunned. I walked up and touched its eye with my barrel. He was done.

Once we had confirmed that Hunter had gotten his deer we both were overcome with excitement. I was so proud of him. It brought back memories of my first deer. Making these memories with my own son was overwhelming, I must have given him ten hugs and told him good job twenty times. I told Hunter to give thanks to the deer for his life which is something that I always do. I finally looked down at the deer after all the excitement. I noticed that one antler was buried in the alder leaves and the exposed antler was a huge 4 point with eye guards. When Hunter raised the head the other side was just as magnificent as the first. My son at 6 years old had just

A happy young Hunter and his proud father.

Hunter's first Sitka Blacktail.

landed a dream 4x4 Sitka Black Tail buck that most hunters will never get in a lifetime. More hugs and congratulations were in order. This was the best hunting day of my life and I've had a lot of great hunting days.

The sun was starting to set and we had to get pictures and quarter the deer before dark. I put Hunter on bear watch and got to work. I didn't save the cape for fear of having my son out there on a fresh kill in bear territory. I loaded my pack with meat and put my extra gear in my son's pack. We headed down the mountain arriving at the cabin by dark.

Mike Druckrey was outside tending chores when I told him that Hunter had gotten a massive buck. My son ran up to Mike with open arms and legs and jumped onto him to give him a hug. All Hunter said is, "I got me a hogger!" as he dangled off Mike. Mike continued the congratulations in disbelief.

We continued hunting for 6 more days. Hunter took another 3 point buck a couple of days later and I continued to look for something that would beat Hunter's. Hanging in Mike's cabin is a picture of Hunter and his hogger, 4x4 buck.

2016 was a year of extraordinary antler growth for Sitka deer. Hunter's buck measured over 108 inches and placed ninth in the local Big Buck Contest. In 1989 the new number one world record won the contest and scored 101 5/8.

Luke Anderson's New Number One

The day broke clear with only a light breeze last November (1989), as Luke Anderson scanned the beautiful bay for deer. This was his last day of the season to hunt as his group planned to be back in Kodiak in time for school the next day. Primarily meat hunters, the party appreciated the big bucks, but did not consider themselves trophy hunters. But this morning was somehow different.

Some deer were spotted in a small bowl on the north side of the fjord, so Luke and his friend Chuck Ballenger went ashore in the skiff, while the big boat dropped anchor in deeper water. When the anchor chain rattled over the side, the two young hunters began to see bucks in the bowl. Antlers seemed to appear everywhere with more than 20 bucks in that one little pocket. The activity in the bay pushed the deer higher and several bucks appeared to have larger than average racks. The boys hit the beach and separated to find vantage points to check out the climbing deer. Luke saw a huge buck suddenly appear lower on the hillside. This deer had apparently been asleep, but it quickly began to close the distance between his bed and the rest of the deer. The men on the anchored boat began shouting that one of the bucks was a monster, but Luke had already settled on the buck he could see. He held for a clear shot, which came just as the big buck was nearing the top of the bushy incline.

"I knew that I'd hit him," Luke said later. "But I wasn't sure how well he'd been hit." Luke scrambled up the slope. He intended to top out above the alder patch closest to the place he'd last seen the buck, when he saw its head appear above the contour. "I sure didn't want to hit his antlers, but the buck looked like he might run, so I had to try a head shot." Before the noise of Luke's rifle reached him, the buck was tumbling down the steep,

Luke with his monster buck on the deck of the boat.

slick slope. When it stopped, one antler was missing. Luke felt sick at the loss of the antler, but he located it in the grass. Fortunately a dowel-like piece of antler and bone material attached to the shed antler made reorientation exact and simple.

This was the finest Sitka buck that anyone on the boat had ever seen but all assumed that the detached right horn would disqualify it for the Big Buck Contest at Mack's Sport Shop in Kodiak The contest was based on Safari Club International (SCI) rules and methods.

As the official scorer at Mack's, I was asked to score the Luke Anderson head. After examining the rack, it was obvious that the shed antler exactly matched the skull pedicle. I told those involved that SCI would accept this trophy for entry in the *Record Book of Trophy Animals* and that with its total of 101 5/8 points, it would be the new world record as the current number one measured 100 2/8 points. To be absolutely certain of the trophy's acceptability, I called Buzzi Cook, chairman of the SC records committee. Buzzi concurred with me.

The next day, Luke learned that his great buck not only won the Big Buck Contest, but that it was the new SCI world record.

I wrote this story and it was published in the *Petersen's HUNTING 1990 Complete Guide to Deer Hunting*.

An Outstanding Sitka Blacktail "cactus" Buck

Having been raised to expect wild game and fish to be served at home, I've always preferred to eat wild meat. I seldom notice "the gamey flavors", as described by others. It just tastes like meat to me. The prospect of putting the animals we harvested while hunting and fishing on our menu was a driving force in all our outdoor pursuits.

The horns and antlers of the critters that bear them have griped my fascination just as their meat has nourished my family. I've often heard it said that "you can't eat the horns." That is certainly true, but the mere sight of horns and antlers evoke vivid memories decades after the last belch or vapor of the best of meals as disappeared.

Some people like flowers, cars, butterflies and precious stones. I appreciate those things too, but animal head gear has a magical effect on me. Wild predators fascinated me, but lacking head ornamentation, they usually took second place on my list of preferred quarry.

Since my first hunt with my Dad, more than seventy years ago, I've always had it in my consciousness that beyond the next rise or behind the next bush may appear a capital critter—an animal of a lifetime.

And I've seen that happen several times in my hunting efforts.

I harvested my first buck in 1956 and my first non-typical buck in 1994. All objects of my hunting pursuits have been unique and special to me, but that non-typical quickly rose to near the top of the list. It was a bilaterally cryptorchid buck, meaning its testes had not descended from the gut into the scrotum. It was a "cactus buck", as they are often called, and this one sported antlers still in velvet in November.

Since then, the percentage of these non-typical bucks in the areas I frequent has increased exponentially. Since 2003, over seventy percent of the bucks taken in one "hot zone" I frequently hunt have been sterile cryptorchids.

In November 2008, my good friend and assistant guide, Rob Coyle, and I collected three Sitka blacktail bucks each and five of the six bucks were cryptorchid. We collected complete tissue and blood samples of those deer for a research study I was doing with some deer scientists. We hunted on several different parts of the Kodiak Archipelago that fall season.

On December 15, we got out for another day hunt. About mid-morning, we spotted an exceptional non-typical buck standing on a knob above and ahead of us. The antlers of this buck were still completely covered with velvet. It appeared to be sporting double main beams on both antlers. This buck was in a group of five deer that were watching us intently from about 1,200 meters. Rob had taken the last buck that season and we were in the habit of trading opportunities to balance each other's take.

"Well, Jake, it's your turn," Rob told me.

I had complete double knee replacement in March 2007, and although I've been able to hunt sheep, pack meat and generally do whatever I need or want to do, I am slower at covering ground than before. Rob, on the other hand was fit and prime, and twenty-five years younger than me.

Haste was necessary, so I told Rob that I have about three dozen non-typical racks already and he was much quicker than me. He should make the stalk on this buck. Neither of us wanted to lose this outstanding animal.

We both stepped out of sight of the alerted group of deer, then I quickly reappeared and walked around slowly in plain sight to decoy the already focused deer, while Rob maneuvered for a shot at reasonable range.

We were depending on the fact that deer and most other animals don't count. But this group sure was keeping track of me.

As I milled around, well out of range, the band of deer remained, seemingly mesmerized by my non-threatening presence.

Meanwhile, Rob was using every bit of available cover to maneuver closer to that unique trophy.

Before I heard the report of Rob's rifle, I saw the big buck drop suddenly to the ground. Immediately thereafter the four other deer turned and were gone. Our ploy had been successful.

An Outstanding Sitka Blacktail "cactus" Buck

Rob Coyle with his December, 2008 Nontypical Sitka Buck.

A close up of that unique set of antlers.

When I got to Rob and the buck, Rob told me that he was using a new .308 rifle and he had three misfires before he got a "meat seeker" off to the deer.

The deer were not aware of Rob's position and did not hear him repeatedly jacking rounds into the chamber. Rob told me that he was afraid that the deer would hear his heart beating as he anxiously kept trying to get a shot off.

When a round finally touched off and the deer dropped to earth, Rob said he felt like a fever had suddenly developed and had him in its grip.

When he walked up to his buck, he was just plain speechless. All that head ornamentation was actually antler! It was not pieces of brush that had become entangled as the buck thrashed a bush.

The velvet was firmly attached to the antler base and no hanging strips had deceived us when we glassed the amazing head from afar. This rack was breath taking!

We both knew this beautiful buck would place well in the record books. I am a master measurer for Safari Club International (SCI), and, violating my rule to never measure a head the same day it was killed, I did a quick measurement of the rack that evening and announced that it would place No. 2 in the SCI record book, even after the minimum sixty day drying period. I had previously measured the current and former No.1 and No. 2 heads, and wth a green score of a bit over 140, this rack clearly fell between those. Indeed, after the 60 days passed, I certified the buck at 139 points, placing it as the No. 2 non-typical Sitka blacktail in the SCI record book.

Racks measured with the velvet attached receive a five percent reduction, which is a bit severe, but that is the rule.

But to enter in the local Big Buck Contest, the velvet had to be removed, so Rob peeled the undamaged velvet and after some difficulties with the contest manager, he won a Winchester 300WSM, a Kershaw "blade trader" knife set, a Western Rivers jacket/pant set, and a shoulder mount of the buck.

The local shop was not using a Certified SCI Measurer and the fellow, Jude, running the tape had given the rack a typical score of 105, which was far from accurate. Had a Certified Measurer turned that head in as typical, he would likely have lost his Certification. Eventually, everything turned out as it should.

Rob planned to have the rack scored by a Boone and Crockett panel, but Boone and Crockett will not accept cryptrochid bucks. I suspect that the deer farming and cultured trophies that have become so common in the United States and a few other countries led to their decision to exclude such trophies. In spite of numerous letters and conversations between me and the B&C officials, B&C would not enter this unique trophy.

As cryptorchid deer in the Kodiak Archipelago are entirely natural, it seems a shame that they cannot be considered for entry in the non-typical category by Boone and Crockett, but the club makes the rules.

Another Outstanding Non-typical Sitka Blacktail Buck

Since 1994, when I harvested the first non-typical deer of my lifetime, I've seen an alarming increase in the frequency of sterile bucks in the Kodiak Archipelago.

These bucks are sterile due to a developmental abnormality called cryptrochidism, in which one or both of their testes fail to descend into the scrotum. Instead the testes remain in the abdominal cavity about midway between the kidneys and the pelvis. If only one testis remains in the gut (unilateral), the buck will be fertile, but if both testes remain undescended (bilateral), the buck will always be sterile.

Antler development runs the full spectrum, from wildly non-typical with some carrying velvet until the time of shedding, to polished antlers with no apparent differences from the antlers of a normal buck.

Behavior of cryptorchid bucks seems as variable as their antler development. Generally, the cryptorchids seem to be more twitchy and difficult to stalk than either normal bucks or does, but I have witnessed complacent, non-alert sterile bucks, as well. And I have observed bilateral cryptorchid bucks mounting multiple does and dominating other bucks in rutting battles. These dominant, but sterile, individuals seem as tunnel visioned and singularly focused on sex during the breeding season as normal rutty bucks, in spite of the disharmony of their hormones.

Bookings for Transported deer hunters were few in 2009, so my good friend and Assistant Guide, Rob Coyle, and I had more free time than usual. We decided to just go hunting for ourselves. Tough decision, it was not!

One day that season (2009) Rob and I decided to hunt a new area. As Rob—a full quarter of a century younger than me—moves faster and with greater ease than I do, I wanted neither to try to keep up with him, nor to slow him down. The November rut was in full swing. When we came to a ridge, I suggested we each go our own way. Rob went left toward the higher country which is generally best for bucks, but not necessarily so during the rut, so I turned right, traveling along a low peninsula with little cover. As the wind was steady at thirty to fifty miles per hour that day, with about +28 degree temperature, I cruised the terrane paying attention to the lee sides of hills, expecting to see deer hunkered out of the wind. By mid-day, after going about three and a half miles and only seeing ten does, with very little ground sign, I had decided I was glad that I had chosen that route and that I would probably not waste any time hunting in that area in the future.

Then, in a small pocket about 800 yards ahead I saw the only buck of the day. It carried velvet and had a wide spread with what appeared to be drop points on both antlers. On previous hunts I had been fooled more than once by loose hanging velvet giving the impression of drop tines, so I kept that in mind.

A doe was bedded a mere fifteen yards from my only route, but she was upwind and did not notice me or get up as I crawled and slithered by on my hands and knees. I was able to reduce the distance to around 400 yards. With my 10X40 Leitz binoculars, I could clearly see that the drop tines on both antlers were indeed real and not hanging velvet. These drop tines did not seem to be blowing in the strong wind. I could make out other non-typical points as well. This was an exceptionally good non-typical Sitka blacktail buck!

As I began crawling toward the swale where the buck was browsing, I avoided a large pile of very fresh bear poop which was not yet beginning to freeze. It had to be very fresh. The brown bear was nearby. By the gage of its droppings, it had to be a big one.

At about 150 yards, a doe stood up near the feeding buck and stomped a front foot—the universal cervid sign of alarm. The buck's head came up, he looked my way, and charged after the doe as the two deer raced off to the left. With no time to locate a rest and the deer about to go over a small ridge and out of sight, I stood and held just in front of the buck's nose. The 200 grain Hornady reload found his neck and he pitched forward and tumbled out of sight.

My buddy Rob and a cryptorchid buck with "drop" tines that turned out to be hanging velvet blowing in the wind.

My concern was that his fall and tumble downhill would result in broken antler tines. These velvet cryptorchids typically have under-calcified, and therefore fragile headgear. When I got to the fallen deer, the doe stood close by, clearly showing reluctance to leave until I was within less than ten yards of her. I was relieved to see that none of the fallen buck's antler tines were broken, but he'd dropped in a small pocket just below a ridge line, making it a bad spot to be butchering a deer should a bear come homing in on the sound of the shot and approach from the hill above. Kodiak Brown Bears have learned that the sound of a rifle shot means fresh meat is at hand, and the bears have an amazingly accurate homing ability in all weather and wind conditions.

Rob snapped a picture of me when we met that evening.

My work was interrupted by frequent glances in all directions in my effort to intercept the approach of a bear, but I took blood and tissue samples for the cryptorchid study project and had the still twitching meat tied on my packboard in less than twenty-five minutes.

This bilateral cyptorchid is the widest and overall best Sitka buck that I had taken in 43 years of hunting the Kodiak Archipelago. There was no "ground shrink" for this one. Tooth wear indicated an age of about 8.5 years or more.

Unfortunately, my digital camera battery was dead, so I was unable to make any kill site photos, but considering my luck of that day, camera malfunction was a minor factor.

In Alaska, one must remove all usable meat before or at the same time as the trophy is taken from the field. On Kodiak, any material left overnight will be visited by bears, foxes, weasels, bald eagles, ravens, magpies, and sea gulls. A second trip is not a reasonable option, and when necessary, usually results in nothing of use being left at the kill site. Antlers still in the velvet would be chewed and ruined, as well.

This buck was huge in body size, one of the largest I had seen. I estimated it's live body weight at about 250 pounds.

Loaded on the packboard, it's four quarters, back straps, neck, tenderloins and ribs weighed in excess of ninety-five pounds—a good twenty-five to thirty percent more than the meat of the average buck. As my pack weights about twenty-eight pounds when I begin the day, that put a maximum plus load on my two surgically rebuilt knees, but they had been holding up with occasional loads like that for the nearly two years since surgery. Slower, careful travel with care to avoid lateral stresses to the knees and not having to return in the dark was the only way to go.

Jake holding his exceptional Sitka Blacktail taken in 2009.

The lay of the land enabled me to cut across some of the peninsula to reduce my return to about two and a half miles, which, along with the fact that I was no longer actively hunting for a buck to shoot, took me a bit over two hours, arriving at our rendezvous point before dark. It was a great day!

Rob's camera was functioning, so he took a field picture for me.

Unfortunately that inviting high country had offered no buck for Rob to shoot. Yeah, I took what appeared to be the low hand and got dealt an ace!

So, once again, I was reminded that just behind the next bush or around the far bend, may appear an animal of a lifetime. Once again, walking the extra mile, paid off.

Oh, and I may check that area out again in the future.

Joey's Buck

The past two years had been very good to me and my primary deer hunting partner, Rob Coyle. 2010 proved to the third exceptional one in a row. In 2008, Rob took the new #2 SCI Non-typical Sitka Blacktail on a weekend hunt on the north end of the Kodiak Archipelago.

Amazingly, in 2009, Rob and I went to a new area, on a day hunt, and I found what measured out to be the new #7 buck in that category.

In 2010, Rob brought his 14 year old son, Joey, on an eight day hunt with us. We would be using a tent. I've known Joey since he was small enough to be carried in his Dad's back pack as we pursued snowshoe hares and ducks. His enthusiasm for hunting, and everything else he does, has always been of the highest degree. Joey was bent on finding and harvesting a buck larger than his Dad's. Both Rob and I encouraged him. But the likelihood of even seeing such a buck was, well ... not high. Nevertheless, Joey's boundless zeal and energy were inspirational for us all.

Privately I told Rob that if we sighted an exceptional buck, I hoped we could set Joey up to take it.

Rob replied, "I knew you would feel that way, Jake."

We were hunting a new area. After setting up our camp, I walked to the beach to investigate an old Alutique midden site while Rob and Joey explored the country to the east. I returned just at dark and stirred up some supper, highlighted by ground venison burger from the 2009 season. When it was ready, I ate and laid down to read.

About ten o'clock in the evening I woke up and wondered about the absence of my companions. But Rob is one of the most physically fit and level headed hunting partners I have ever had and I suppressed any thoughts

A large bodied 3X3 buck.

Joey with a huge Kodiak Cross fox.

of anxiety. We had seen no sign of bears and both my friends were adequately armed. I went back to sleep.

Shortly thereafter, I heard them coming.

That first day, Joey connected with a very good three point buck. (Western count, meaning the main beam, plus 2 points on each side, with brow tines to boot.) A nice neck shot at over 100 yards anchored his prize! That pleased us all, as Joey's previous best buck was a big two-by-two taken the previous year.

The buck fell at 7:00pm—just before dark, but the hunters got it butchered, loaded on their packs and returned through the unfamiliar country slowly, using their head lights.

In the next few days, we all saw numerous "shooters" and Joey took another nice three pointer. His Dad and I each hung a buck on the meat pole, so we were all well satisfied with this wonderful hunt.

Weather beat us up some, keeping us tent bound due to heavy rain and wind for two days. It's a good idea to carry a book or two and a deck of cards on any Alaskan trip and we were thankful that we had done so. The fresh tenderloins and backstraps were a delicious addition to our menu.

Joey Coyle with his #10 SCI Non typical Sitka Blacktail.

As we calculated the weight limits for the DeHaviland Beaver which was due to pick us up and take us back to Kodiak, we had decided to limit our shooting to two bucks each, unless something really outstanding showed up.

Joey took a dandy cross fox incidental to his deer pursuits.

Time was passing way too fast for us all, when on the next to last day, Rob downed another buck. As he and his son were preparing it for the packboard, Joey glassed a huge non-typical, still carrying velvet. He quickly brought that to his Dad's attention. With more than a mile of rough, steep canyon terrane to negotiate, they wasted no time in covering the first kill to discourage birds and limit smell before they struck off for that extraordinary monster.

I'd collected a second buck to help fill our family's freezer and was back in camp well before dark when I heard Joey whoop as they walked in with his third trophy! The father and son had a quick sandwich, swallowed some mini candy bars, refilled their water bottles and charged back up the mountain to collect Rob's buck. Their day had begun early and it was nearly dark when they started back up for Rob's buck. Most grown men would dread another hike and carryout after a day like that, but in this area, if a deer is left overnight, not much, if anything will be left by morning. Bears, foxes, weasels, eagles, sea gulls and ravens all enjoy eating venison and are quick to find any available edibles.

Joey never flinched at the prospect of two more hours of mountain walking and packing out meat.

More than half of the bucks we saw that November trip were still carrying velvet. In the Kodiak Archipelago that is one clear indication of the animal being cryptorchid, and therefore, sterile. This developmental abnormality has been increasing throughout the region since I harvested my first bilateral cryptorchid in 1994. About 30% of these abnormal bucks also show non typical antlers.

Since I was Joey's age, I have boiled and bleached most of my trophy heads. Joey asked me to help prepare his in the European style also.

It's a little tricky to boil a head and not loose the velvet, especially if the buck was taken in August or September. The velvet of cryptorchids, however, is often retained until the antlers are shed. It is sometimes possible to maintain velvet in place during the skull boiling process, by wrapping the antlers with multiple layers of aluminum foil.

So Joey brought his big buck to my home to boil and bleach. It turned out beautifully and that evening I scored it using the Safari Club International method.

As we totaled the numbers I told him that it was a super buck, but I didn't think it would quite make the top ten of the book.

Joey said "Yes it will, Jake !" He had reviewed the SCI site on the internet and knew his numbers. In fact, that buck was entered in the book as number ten.

Joey Coyle is off to a very good start as a hunter.

Norm Sutliff's Buck

Norm Sutliff was a friend of mine. I met him in Anchorage when he was serving on the Alaska Guide Board. He was plain talking and obviously frustrated with some of the bureaucratic falderal that all boards and committees seem to generate. His way was to avoid the extraneous diversions and get right down to the job that needed to be done. Then go home. I liked that.

"God so loved the world that he did not send a committee," is a quote from a pastor friend that often comes to mind when dealing with boards and working groups.

When I did happen to see Norm at his store, Sutliffs Hardware in Kodiak, he always made time to visit about hunting and fishing. Our discussions led to me visiting him at his home, where he entertained me with interesting stories of Kodiak from before World War II to the present.

Until well into his seventy's he maintained and flew his Piper Super Cub, normally flying it alone or with his wife, Peggy, to his favorite spots for rainbow trout and other species of the abundant wildlife in the Kodiak archipelago. As Norm grew older he began to lose his eyesight and eventually he was unable to read his books—of which he had a large collection. Eventually, he was forced to give up flying.

Norm had lived an enviable life, especially since coming to Kodiak. I encouraged him to write his stories, or find someone who could do so, as many of his experiences were of the sort that would never be repeated. But Norm was a modest man and to my knowledge he never did put his stories on paper.

On Norm's wall was an outstanding mount of a wildly non-typical Sitka Blacktail buck. I had never seen anything like it, but after personally taking

A most remarkable rack for any deer species.

The mounted head as I saw it hanging at Norm Sutliff's home.

dozens of non-typical cryptorchids I recognized the tell-tale signs of cryptorchidism that were clearly displayed by Norm's great buck. When I asked him if that deer had any testicles, he seemed surprised at my question.

Norm verified that the deer had no visible testicles. Furthermore, it was much larger in body and carried far more fat than most deer. The buck gave him the impression that it was quite old, but he did not retain the mandible which would show tooth wear for accurate aging. A single sample tooth would allow the animal to be accurately aged. After his brief, but adequate reply to my question, Norm asked me why I had asked about testicles.

I told Norm that the unusual antlers indicated the hormonal confusion—or disruption—that often manifests itself in wild antler formation of some cryptorchid bucks probably explained his unique trophy. I asked him if he would like me to measure the head for the Safari Club International record book, as I was certain that it would place number one in the non typical Sitka Blacktail category.

But Norm wasn't interested in record book entries. I asked him to tell me the story of how he came upon that remarkable critter.

In his usual matter-of-fact manner he said that one morning back in 1960 or thereabouts, he wanted to get some fresh venison for the table, so he cranked up his super cub and flew out toward Saltery Cove. His wife,

Norm Sutliff's Buck

Norm Sutliff holding his unique deer head.

Peggy went along. They left early and needed to be back in time to open the store. Norm saw several deer that day—and deer were not so numerous on Kodiak Island back then. The first one he came to that was within his time limit to shoot, get to the plane and return to work on time, was the buck on the wall. He knew when he first glanced at it that it was remarkably different from any deer he'd seen before.

So he landed on a nearby lake, made a short stalk, shot the deer, loaded and secured it on a float and was able to open the store on time. The following morning he made a photograph of the head sitting in his canoe near where he tied his float plane.

Due to its highly unusual features, Norm decided to have a shoulder mount made, but in the process the velvet was lost, and it seems that some of the long points, including what appears to be about an eight inch drop point on the right antler, were broken and lost between getting it to the taxidermist and putting it on the wall. Though some scoring points and a lot of character had been lost, it still made an impressive trophy display.

Apparently Norm mentioned my interest in the unusual head to his daughter Barbara, who prevailed upon him to allow me to score it and enter the outstanding trophy in the record book. Barbara called me to say that her Dad was ready for the head to be scored.

This was one of the most complex set of antlers I had ever measured. It was similar to, but far more difficult to score, than the number one non-typical Coes deer head I measured at 182 and 2/8 SCI points in New Mexico in 1987, but after going through the lengths and girths multiple times I arrived at what I believed to be as accurate a total score as possible. That score for Norm's buck was 192 and 2/8.

To fully appreciate the astounding amount of antler grown by this animal, I think it is interesting to note that the number two buck in the category, which was taken by my friend Rob Coyle in 2008, scores 139 points. Norm Sutliff's buck scores almost a third again higher than the number two buck.

This unique shoulder mounted rack hung in Norm Sutliff's hardware store in Kodiak for many years until he retired from active management and took it to his home.

This number one world record head, like the top Coes deer rack in New Mexico had been taken decades before they were ever measured. I often wonder how many more extraordinary trophies remain hidden in garages, attics and such—just under our noses?

At the time I visited with Norm about his remarkable buck, a popular theory in Kodiak was that the cryptorchidism in the archipelago was due to the *Exon Valdez* oil spill in 1989. Oil had reached some of the beaches around Kodiak, but Norm's cryptorchid having been taken in the early 1960s—more than a quarter of a century before the spill—disputed the possibility of that massive accident being the cause.

Gary Cobban's Number One Sitka Blacktail Buck

In June, 1993 I wrote the following story for the Safari Club International monthly magazine. After seeing the beautiful buck hanging at a local sports store, for which I was scoring heads in their annual Big Buck contest, I asked the shop owner if I might measure that mounted head. I told him I was certain it would place at the top of the book. After putting a tape to the rack and Certifying it at 103 5/8 points, I tried to contact Gary Cobban, but he was somewhere between Mobile, Alabama and the Panama Canal, sailing his new, larger boat, named the *F/V LUCRATIVE*, home to Kodiak. Eventually he and I got together for the details of his hunt. This buck was entered in the SCI Record Book of Trophy Animals as the number one typical Sitka Blacktail Deer. It still hangs on the wall at the same sporting goods store in Kodiak.

Gary agreed to the measurement and told me the story of how he can to harvest that buck. The following story varies a bit from the SCI version, but here it is, as told to me by Gary Cobban.

As I sat in the wheelhouse watching my friends climb up the grassy, alder-choked slopes, I felt great. "Just another day in paradise," it seemed—a modified paradise in the rain, wind and snow but paradise, nevertheless.

My friends and I had left Kodiak harbor four days earlier, sailed northwest through Whale Passage then south/southwest via Shelikof Straits to Uganik Island. The weather had been less than cooperative, but my boat—the *FV LUCRATIVE*—provided comfortable and secure transportation. The galley was alive with conversation about the potential for super deer hunting when the wind and rain subsided enough for hunters to hit the beaches and begin stalking. Many deer had been glassed from the deck and anticipation was high, but the storm continued, ignoring the hunters' urgency to begin collecting their winter supply of venison.

Gary Cobban and his former number one Typical Sitka Blacktail buck.

That morning, the wind had finally calmed and the sea lay flat, but fog and drizzle persisted. I assembled a hearty breakfast and rousted my friends from their bunks.

"Coffee's hot and bait's on the table, boys, I think we'd better give it a go this morning," I said. "The radio says another low is tracking this way, so fog and drizzle may be the best we'll get for a few more days."

Those guys inhaled their breakfast and I ferried them ashore in pairs in my rubber raft, then returned to the wheelhouse and my own steaming mug of coffee. The hunters split up and I kicked back. Soon, sounds of rifle shots were rolling off the hills and I knew they wouldn't be coming back skunked. I glassed the hills as deer appeared in small groups and singles across the landscape.

Returning to the wheelhouse after checking the engine room, I began to cruise just offshore to be available to pick up any hunter who came to the beach with a deer.

Standing on a cliff about one hundred feet above the beach I noticed a very large bodied buck with a rack unlike any I had seen before.. A quick check with my binoculars showed this deer to be a really impressive buck. I had decided to forego hunting for myself that day because the trip was half over and my friends had to return to the mainland in three more days—but this buck was just too much. It was the biggest I had ever seen.

I grabbed my boat rifle, a winchester Model 70 in 30:06 caliber, slid open the wheelhouse window and cut the power. The boat's forward motion came to a dead standstill. The swell rocked the boat gently. I had four rounds in the rifle and the first three missed, but on the last shot, the buck dropped. I dropped the anchor, got into the raft and went ashore. In a few minutes I was standing over the huge deer. I drug it to the beach and got it aboard the boat, where I gutted it out and hung it by the antlers, before pouring myself another hot cup of coffee. Less than one hour passed from the time I saw the deer until he was hanging on my boat.

About mid-afternoon, the boys started showing up along the slopes dragging their deer (as it customary in Kodiak) through the grass and moss to the beaches. I picked them up one at a time and motored them back to the *LUCRATIVE*. As each of them climbed over the rail, they let out whoops and hollers at the sight of the rack of my deer. One fellow asked me if I'd called it onto the deck or if it had dropped out of the sky.

They were unaware that I'd left the big boat after dropping them on the beach that morning.

The trip provided a good supply of venison, trophies and memories for all and in spite of another storm, my mainland friends all made their departure dates from the "modified paradise" which is Kodiak and its surrounding islands.

I had a shoulder mount made of my buck and hung it in a local sporting goods store.

Stewardship of Wild Game Resources

It's been said that the boy is the father of the man. In my case, I believe it applies. I'm still a kid when it comes to being intrigued with the many mysteries of our natural world.

So why, readers may wonder, am I devoting so much of this book to the cryptorchid deer of the Kodiak Archipelago? I am doing this in hopes of stimulating the appropriate government agencies to do the job they are paid to do—adequately investigate this alarming situation.

Private organizations like Ducks Unlimited, Trout Unlimited and other "Unlimited" clubs do a lot of good, but so far there is no such group devoted to Sitka Blacktail deer. Perhaps we need one.

My parents emphasized that no animal's life should be taken unnecessarily and those we did kill were to be put to the best possible use. On Christmas day when I was five years old, I got a Daisy BB gun and immediately took it outside before unwrapping my other gifts. In less than an hour I shot two sparrows off a barbed wire fence. When I proudly presented them to our family, gathered for the Christmas celebration, my mother told me to clean them up as I would do on a chicken. I had plenty of experience in plucking domestic fowl. She put them in the roaster with the turkey. I thought they tasted at least as good, maybe even better than the big bird.

When I later presented lizards, snakes, frogs—and the occasional toad, along with an eclectic assortment of large insects and other relatively unpalatable critters from my game bag—or shirt pockets—something had to be done with those things from which I had taken life. Mom did not want to cook many of them—she didn't even want them near her kitchen. In order to justify my collecting such things, I was obliged to purchase rubbing alcohol and preserve my specimens in cleaned, used jars for later scientific study. Most of those jars of specimens were lost in our frequent moves and never put to scientific analysis, but the idea stuck with me. Waste nothing you take from nature, kill nothing without a purpose, and use everything. Admittedly, I stretched the point a bit with some of the insects, and maybe the slimy, warty toads and such.

In Arctic Alaska I worked part time as a biologist and commercial pilot for the Alaska Department of Fish and Game for over twelve years. During those times I was occasionally contracted to work for the State of Alaska, the Bureau of Land Management, the National Park Service, the National Oceanic and Atmospheric Administration, the University of Alaska, and some private agencies. Most of my ADF&G time was spent doing census work on different animals, tracking radio collared individual animals, and evaluating habitat. Some of my contracts focused on hydrology studies, lake and stream fish inventories, investigating magnetism in sea ice crystals, capturing and placing radio collars on tundra swans, basic geological surveys and other pursuits.

I enjoyed some varied and interesting part-time work for many years.

Among the ADF&G activities in which I participated were sedation and live capture of grizzly bears, wolves, and other big game animals from which we drew blood, removed a vestigial mandibular tooth, and took other samples before allowing the sedated animal to recover and move on. I watched and participated as samples were collected and prepared in the field for laboratory analysis.

It has long been clear to me that careful, controlled study of wild game animals is crucial to proper management of wild stocks.

It was equally clear to me that **stewardship** of our wild game is required if we are to have continually sustained populations from which we can harvest animals for human use. This stewardship is a duty of everyone involved—from the government biologists to the individual members of the public, whether they be hunters, guides, photographers or casual observers. Our natural resources are of inestimable worth and must be protected and preserved, as well as put to their best use, which depending on the individual person, may be recreation, food harvest, economic gain, photography or the joy of seeing the animals. Each use has valid justification.

Stewardship of Wild Game Resources

Wild game management in the United States has been remarkably successful overall. The populations of white tailed deer, wild turkeys, wild sheep, elk and other game species are more widespread and healthy now than in the past.

As a life-long dedicated hunter and an Alaskan Master Guide, actively guiding in Alaska since 1967, I have been in a unique position to do more than just give lip service to stewardship. I have endeavored to practice stewardship of the game I pursue to the best of my circumstances and ability. I see it as a responsibility.

When, in 1994 at the age of fifty-two years, I first harvested a cryptorchid buck, I reported it to the local Alaska Department of Fish and Game biologist who dismissed it's significance as just "one of those things." The next year I harvested three sterile bucks and he again seemed to think nothing of it.

During the 1996 season, after I took six cryptorchids and again was met with a dismissive response from the local biologist, I decided to do what I could to spread the word about this increasing and potentially dangerous abnormality.

I began by reading everything I could find at the library on deer and cryptorchidism. Having no experience with a computer, my progress was slow. But I began to form an understanding and appreciation of the situation and the potential deleterious effects of widespread sterility in our local deer herd.

So began what as turned into a twenty-four year endeavor to learn the cause or causes of such an alarming occurrence of cryptorchidism in Sitka Blacktail deer.

In the following discussion I try to not lose readers in the long grass and thickets of too much technological jargon and information.

If you find the information to be too tedious, you could skip on ahead, as I have included some photographs that might be entertaining.

My First Strange Deer from the Kodiak Archipelago

In 1994, my hunting and fishing partner, Tom Dooley, and I were transporting some nonresident hunting guests on his fifty foot seiner, the *F/V REBEL*. We were on the south end of Kodiak. The wind and weather had been frustrating all week with strong wind and high seas during the day, becoming calmer at night, then turning nasty again in the morning. But we were finally able to get ashore. One of the guests commented that landing on that stormy beach was "like Normandy on D day." The wind was blowing a steady forty knots and gusting to sixty against a large sea swell. Luckily the wind was offshore or we would not have been able to land the small skiff to offload the hunters.

The bay we found good enough for landing the skiff was a new one to us, but it would prove to be one of our favorites as the years rolled by.

Bears were thick in that area. I counted sixteen lone bruins—not sows with cubs—in the area I was hunting that day. All bear sightings were from the ground as I walked along, so my twitchy index was set on high and the gusty wind didn't help. Most animals, myself included, are noticeably more nervous in windy conditions.

Due to the bear danger the guests were instructed to hunt in pairs or larger groups. The wind conditions meant Tom had to stay with the boat, so I was alone. I walked into the wind towards some low hills that I figured would probably draw and hold deer on their leeward side. Wild game do not feel comfortable in big winds. Animals, like people, prefer calmer conditions.

After seeing a dozen deer or so, I was plugging along to the windward, looking and hoping for a really outstanding buck in this hitherto unhunted country.

Earlier that week in an area nearby, I found a shed antler lying in the open. I picked it up and noticed that instead of a small protuberance or

Left is the odd base, the Right has a normal "button".

"button" marking where the antler had been attached to the skull, this one showed a noticeable concavity. I wedged it between my pack board and the sack that held my lunch. I'd never before seen such a base on a shed antler.

After pausing to scan the country with my binoculars, I found a single deer browsing on some ferns well below the crest of a ridge on the lee side of the prevailing wind. This animal had the body conformation of a doe, but it was carrying antlers. It was the first week of November, the rut was on, and bucks should be appearing heavier in the front quarters than this one did. Then as I got closer, I noticed some extra points at the base of the antlers, and unless my vision had grown fuzzy, the antlers seemed to be in velvet. Normally these deer shed the velvet in September. So what was the story here, I wondered?

One of the many bears I encountered that day appeared between me and the curious appearing buck. A few late run Silver salmon were still coming up from salt water, so I waited about a half hour until the large

My First Strange Deer from the Kodiak Archipelago

The distinctly feminine appearing neck and front quarters.

brown bear had splashed its way along the creek chasing the struggling salmon. As soon as the bear disappeared around the corner of a hill upwind from me I headed straight for the feeding buck.

The slope the deer was on was much calmer than the exposed areas, but the buck was twitchy and every minute or so he looked up to study the nearby terrane. This is normal behavior for prey species in areas with high populations of predators, and this place was loaded with large predators.

As I drew closer to the object of my attention, I detected lateral points coming from the extraordinarily thick base of each antler. I saw that for sure the antlers were covered in velvet. Now my mind was made up and I really wanted to bag this unusual critter. The unusual or non-typical has always drawn me as strongly as the really large representatives of any species.

Considering the squirrelly wind and the undependable gusts, I was going to need to approach the deer from below, and very slowly, as all game animals tend to keep their eyes on whatever may be in the area just beneath them, but they seldom look up.

Time passed all too rapidly as I edged closer while the buck concentrated on feeding on the dry ferns. Each time he raised his head to look around, I froze in place. I wanted a hundred yard shot or less as I could only see the top of the animal's back, then its head when he lifted it to scrutinize his surroundings. If I didn't drop the deer in its tracks, finding it in the bewildering thicket of ferns, salmon berry bushes and tall grass might be a problem. Then there were the bears to consider. Either I would wait for a sure shot, or not shoot at all.

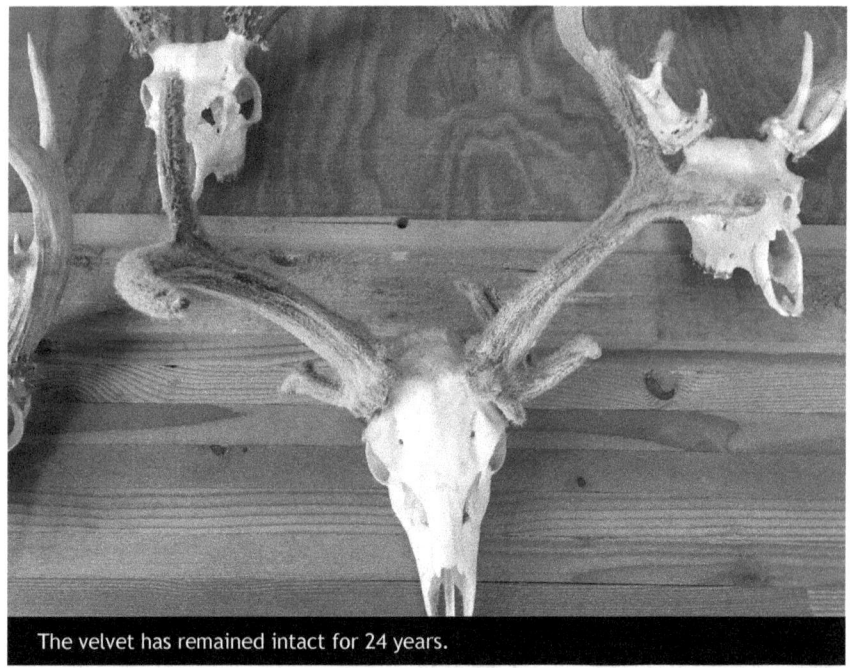
The velvet has remained intact for 24 years.

As per our policy, I needed to be back on the beach with the deer—including al the meat, the head and whatever else I decided to take well before dark so Tom could come in with the skiff in good light. There were plenty of rocks and reefs to avoid between the seiner and the beach. Hitting a rock and disabling the lower unit of the outboard would be a most unhandy thing, so we did our best to minimize that possibility.

With less than two hours before sundown the deer moved to give me the opportunity I needed and I made a neck shot at about one hundred and fifty yards

This skinny necked buck had no scrotum and no testicles. It was rolling in fat and otherwise normal, other than the fact that it did have several spaghetti-like points coming from the extraordinarily thick bases of the antlers, and the antlers were in full velvet in late November.

The pack to the beach was about one and a half miles. Two brown bears had heard my shot. I could see them moving my way. When they got downwind and picked up the scent of the deer, they would come. So I hustled with cutting and loading the meat on my pack board. I got to the beach in time to load into the skiff with the other fellows, each of whom had taken a nice, normal buck.

For years I had been reading the occasional accounts of "cactus bucks" taken in the "lower forty-eight" states, but I'd never seen or even heard of such a deer in Alaska. This was my first grossly non-typical buck after well over forty years of hunting deer.

Back at home, I took special care to wrap the antlers with two layers of aluminum foil to keep the boiling water from touching the velvet. The skull cleaned and bleached up fine for a "European mount" which still hangs over my chair in the living room.

Kodiak had a new biologist, so when we returned to town, I told him about the strange buck. But he was not interested. His attention was focused on the more charismatic brown bears.

So, having no computer or skills to use one, I reviewed my reference books on deer and went to the library, but learned very little about deer with no testes. I did read that those so called "cactus bucks" were cryptorchid animals—meaning their testes have not descended into the scrotum from the abdominal cavity.

Nevertheless my curiosity was piqued and I longed for a return to that same bay. In addition to that non-typical buck, there was the unusual shed antler. The area needed a more thorough investigation. The abundance of brown bears that frequented the area would not deter me from hunting that area again.

Finding the First Undescended Testis

When I harvested my first cryptorchid buck I realized that the testes had not descended but I did not find either one in the gut. I quickly probed and dug around in the abdominal contents, but I really did not know what I was looking for, or where it might be. Also that day I had been hunting alone, but soon had the company of two very interested brown bears that had heard my rifle report and were moving downwind to get my scent. The bears would be at the kill site soon, so I needed to make haste.

My main collaborator at the time, Dr. George Bubenik from the University of Guelph, Ontario mentioned that he had never seen an undescended testis in a deer, and when I asked other biologists what one should look for, their suggestions were vague, as none of them had seen one either.

During the third season of intensive collection of blood, fat, hair follicles, small pieces of meat for DNA and other samples I finally saw an intra—abdominal, ectopic testis. As my partner, Tom Dooley and I were hastily gutting a monorchid deer in hopes of returning to the lighterage skiff well before dark, Tom said, "Well, lookee here, 'pordner', that looks like a liddy biddy testicle." This buck had one normal testis in the scrotum and the other, the intra-abdominal one, was lying there before our eyes—it was lying just next to the heavy nodules of fat which accumulate next to the tenderloins in healthy animals when they are at their heaviest in late fall. That eureka moment took place in November, 2001.

Finally we had located an undescended, intra-abdominal testis! I severed both testicles from their connective tissues and took them to the boat to photograph on a paper plate with a tape measure to serve as a size reference.

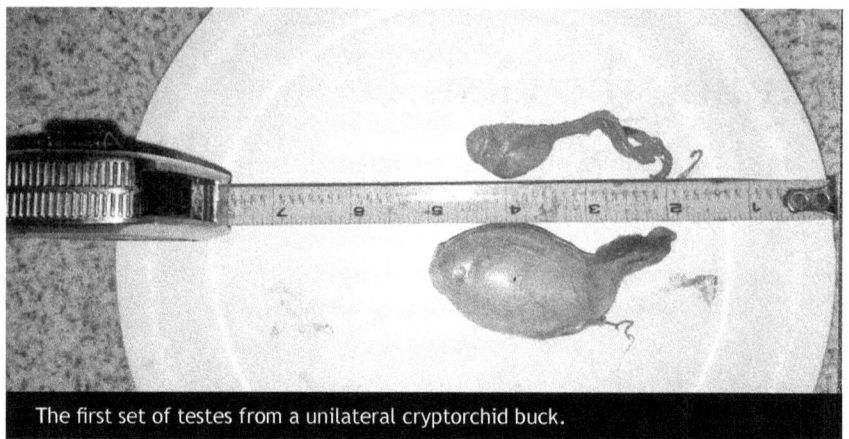

The first set of testes from a unilateral cryptorchid buck.

The undescended testis shown above is a bit smaller than the first one we found. The scrotal testis is of normal size.

Finding the First Undescended Testis

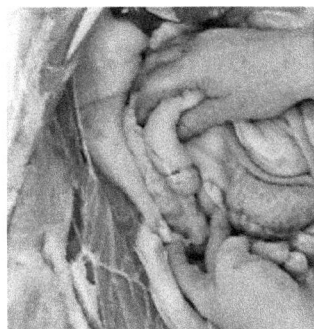

The two undescended, bluish colored testes in a bilaterally cryptorchid buck. The left one was a bit larger than the one on the buck's right side.

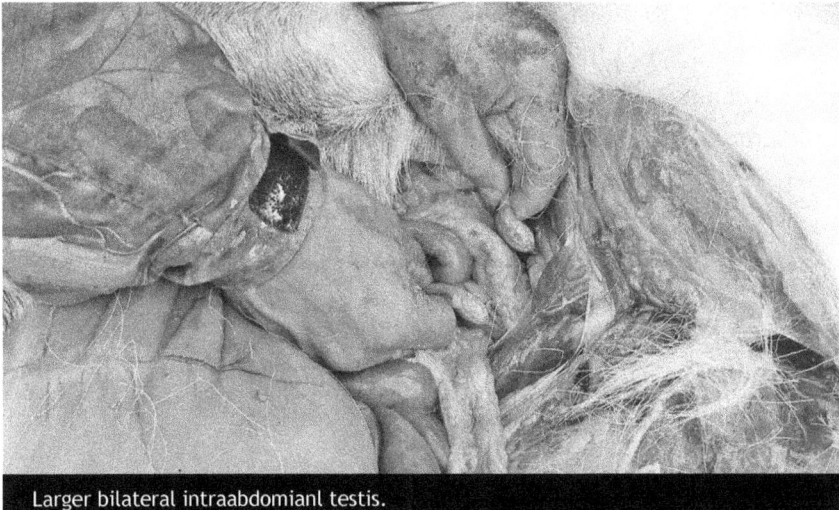

Larger bilateral intraabdomianl testis.

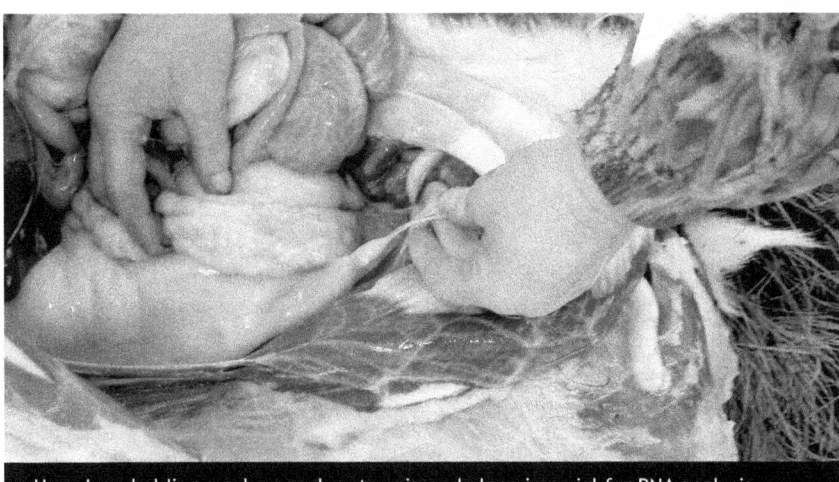

Here, I am holding a gubernaculum to snip and place in a vial for RNA analysis.

Neither Tom nor I would ever miss locating an undescended testis again. I was ecstatic at locating that hidden jewel, but disappointed it had taken over two years to do so. Sometimes I feel like a dummkopf, a real blockhead!

We found undescended testes in the gut always located on a line between the kidneys and the inguinal ring. They vary somewhat in size, with the bilaterally cryptorchid testes being smaller than the undescended organ of a monorchid, or unilateral cryptorchid. Often the ectopic testes have a slightly blue color. Size varies between the large ones at three quarters of an inch in length to the smaller ones at approximately half that dimension.

We found the abnormal testes in the gut with thin, gossamer-like threads connecting them to the area of the inguinal ring. Those threads are called the gubernacula. The testes are found alongside the intestines and often embedded in the gut fat.

Being able to dependably retrieve the abnormal testes gave our project a new impetus. Perhaps the gubernaculum would hold RNA secrets we could begin to unravel.

But this new ability brought with it a new demand. To save RNA for analysis we would have to put the gubernaculum samples in super cold storage from approximately fifteen minutes after the animal's death until it was eventually analyzed at Colorado State University.

We would have to carry dry ice on the boat and in wide mouth insulated thermos bottles in our back packs while we hunted.

Dry Ice and Messenger RNA

As the analysis of samples I sent to Colorado State progressed, I became more aware of the importance of DNA, and later, RNA. Most people are aware that DNA can remain usable for eons, as exemplified by research on Neanderthals, Wooly Mammoths, and other prehistoric creatures, but RNA deteriorates soon after the death of the animal and is less well understood by the general public..

One interesting fact is that DNA is a double-stranded molecule while RNA is a single stranded molecule.

DNA and RNA perform different functions in humans, and probably similar functions in other higher animals. DNA is responsible for storing and transferring genetic information while RNA directly codes for amino acids and as acts as a messenger between DNA and ribosomes to make proteins.

DNA functions as long-term storage of genetic information for transmission of genetic information to make other cells and new organisms.

To boil that down to basics, it is believed that messenger RNA (or mRNA) functions to send signals to developing organs as they mature.

Dr. Rupert Amann of CSU explained to me that unlike DNA, RNA deteriorates rapidly after an animal's death and must be collected as soon as possible from our sampled deer—within fifteen minutes or sooner. As soon as possible was the rule I followed. Furthermore, the sample tissues must be placed in minus 80 degree storage immediately, and kept that cold, for it to be accurately analyzed.

The gubernaculum is a gossamer like filament that serves to draw the intra- abdominal testis through the inguinal canal and into the scrotum, whereupon the testis begins a rapid increase in size. It was thought that the retention of the developing testes in the abdomen was a result of a malfunction of messenger RNA and corresponding malfunction of the gubernaculum.

Messenger RNA would show up in the gubernaculum.

Dry ice is frozen carbon dioxide with a temperature of minus 109.3 degrees Fahrenheit, or minus 78.5 degrees celsius.

We could collect usable RNA in the field if we carried dry ice in wide mouth thermos bottles, placed the samples in their individual containers in the dry ice, then transferred the samples to larger containers with dry ice when we returned to the boat. We kept enough dry ice aboard to last for weeks—until we returned to Kodiak.

So, my partner, Tom Dooley, and I added a thermos of dry ice to our packs every time we went deer hunting.

When we returned to Kodiak I took the super frozen samples to the Fish Tech for storage in their minus eighty degree freezer.

To get these valuable samples, which we gathered at so much expense and inconvenience to CSU before the dry ice in their container had disappeared, I carried some in my checked luggage to Fort Collins.

The only public source of dry ice in Kodiak was at the Safeway grocery store and after a couple years of collecting samples for RNA analysis, Safeway discontinued selling dry ice.

Colorado State University sent me dry ice blocks by UPS, but by the time they arrived, they had sublimated to a very small size, which was much too small for our use. Plus we had to get the RNA samples back to CSU in a super cooled state.

Then, by wondrously good timing, a liquid solution called "RNA later" was developed which allowed us to place the samples in the small vials of solution and store it in a household refrigerator.

The Sample Collection Procedure

The processes of collecting a complete sampling of an individual deer took a minimum of twenty minutes in the field and had to be done as soon as possible after the animal was killed—not only to get usable RNA within as short a time as possible, but also to avoid conflicts with bears which often come rapidly to the sound of even a single gunshot. The most effective and efficient order of events was to collect two vials of blood from the femoral artery, then open the gut cavity and locate the small undescended testis. After placing in labeled containers the gubernaculua were placed in either dry ice or, after 2005, the "RNA later" solution. Last, a quick search for other abnormalities in the abdominal cavity was done. The fat, hair follicles and meat for DNA could be gathered once the salvaged parts of the animal were on the boat.

In 2009 Dr. Rupert Amann, PhD, of Colorado State University came to spend a week with us on the boat to observe the deer and my technique in collecting and preserving the samples, first hand.

Of course the meat of the deer had to be salvaged according to State regulations—as well as for ethical and practical reasons. No animal should be harvested unless it is completely utilized. The flesh is excellent table fare and local venison has made up a major part of my family's diet for the past five decades. My method was to cut free and strip the back strap meat from the back of the ears to the rump. The four quarters were removed, the ribs were removed and finally, the tenderloins, heart and liver were collected. All that remained for the birds, foxes, bears and weasels was the guts, the hide, and the nearly meatless spinal column. The meat and head were secured to my pack board, the blood and other samples was placed in my pack sack. The load was transported on foot to the beach, then to the boat.

Dr. Amman resting in a bear den.

Dr. Rupert Amann of CSU came to see the cryptorchids first hand. He holds a bilaterally cryptorchid buck.

The Sample Collection Procedure

Kodiak Brown bears often come quickly to the sound of a rifle shot.

Packing out the meat, samples and head of a buck.

Each jaw was labeled, incisor tooth to be removed later.

Separation of serum and other lab work after supper.

Back on the boat, after the evening meal I prepared sections of the testis and the various other samples as required. Of course the individual samples were clearly labeled and I avoided cross contamination of each sample with those of others. I used rubber gloves for all lab work to avoid cross contamination of samples, rather than for my own protection.

Finally the serum was pipetted off from the blood tubes and placed in 1.2ml vials which were then frozen. The time required for the serum to separate from the whole blood varies. In some cases the serum—which appears as a clear or pinkish colored liquid—appeared as a separate layer in the blood tubes by the time I unloaded my pack board at the boat the same day the deer was killed. But other times it took a day or two for the separation to take place. I have no idea why serum separation varies so greatly. No centrifuge was used or necessary. I placed the blood tubes upright in a clean coffee cup and left them in the galley of the boat, well away from the stove. After extracting the serum, the remains of the whole blood were discarded.

The mandibles were labeled and saved, primarily for use of an incisor tooth to determine age of the animal.

On average, I spent a minimum of thirty minutes during the evening on preparation of samples for each deer harvested. We sometimes had four or five hunters in addition to Tom Dooley and myself, so some days six or seven bucks were taken, which made for a long evening of sample preparation.

My preparation of samples had changed immensely from the early days of pinning insects to a board and dropping lizards into an alcohol filled fruit jar.

Our guest hunters were eager to cooperate and nearly all collected their animal's samples willingly and efficiently, with the exception of the gubernaculum, which is a bit demanding to identify for inexperienced collectors.

Collecting fetuses

In 2008 no information was available regarding the maturation sequencing and in utero development of Sitka BlackTail Deer (SBTD). The most pressing question for us was the timing of descent of the testes from the abdominal cavity through the inguinal ring and into the scrotum. The question was: if a male fawn was born with one or both testes still in the gut, would it remain so throughout its life, or might the testes descend sometime after birth? Post-parturition descent of the testis is not documented in other species, so we assumed, it would be unlikely in these deer, but we needed to know the answer to this and many other questions.

I was becoming alarmed at the marked increase in the number of fawns I observed nursing their mothers in late November and even December. In 2008 I recorded more late-nursing fawns than ever before. This would seem to indicate a shortage of fertile bucks during the previous rutting season.

During our scheduled autumn hunts in October, November, and December of 2008, I collected does which gave us some baseline data, but we needed to investigate the progress of the male fetus maturation, especially regarding the migration of the developing testes from their original site near the kidneys in their tail-ward passage through the abdominal cavity, and finally through the inguinal ring and into the scrotum.

Fortunately for the needs of our study, the Subsistence season for deer in the Kodiak Archipelago is extended through January and as a local resident, I qualified for collecting deer until January 31. To get fetuses as advanced in maturation as possible, I went to the south end of Kodiak and hunted for a week near Lazy Bay in late January, 2009.

I took the mail plane to the Lazy Bay cannery where I had arranged with the winter man, John Garber, to be quartered while collecting the

The cannery in Lazy Bay. Photo taken in early November.

does for the study. I had known John for years and had met some of his relatives the year I arrived in Alaska—in 1967. He was a wonderful host and we had great reminiscences during and after dinner each evening.

The physical accommodations were the best imaginable for a project like this. I had access to walk-in coolers and walk-in freezers, as well as a warm, dry place to sleep. In January in the southern areas of the Kodiak Archipelago, refrigerated facilities are seldom needed, as the outside air temperature normally remains in the high teens and mid-twenties, however the coolers provided good insurance that the samples would be handled under ideal conditions and the fresh meat was safe from prowling bears.

Days are short in January in the north country, but I was comfortably ensconced in the middle of prime deer country. A thirty minute walk from the cannery put me on public ground open to hunting, amidst large numbers of deer that collect in that area during winter.

Five of the seven days of my trip were suitable for hunting and each day I walked out from the cannery to public land. Every day I saw scores of deer and late in the afternoon of each day I harvested one female after spending most of the daylight hours observing the animals. The local Alaska

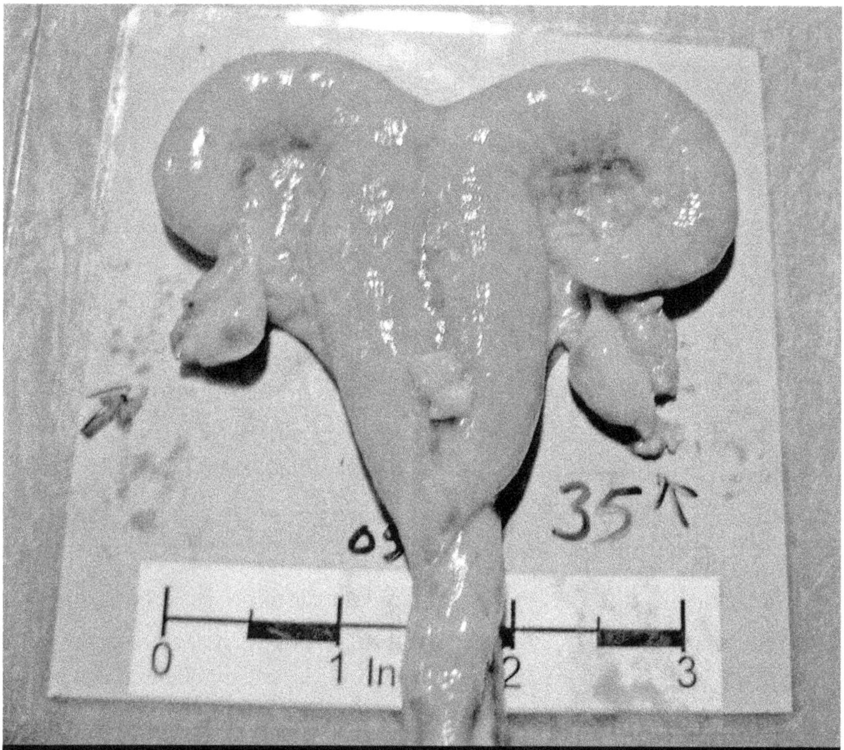

Collecting fetuses

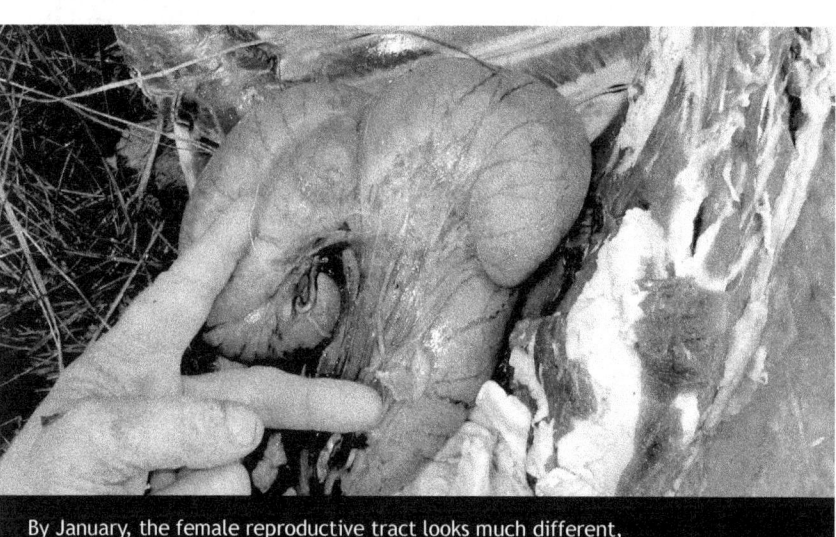

Uterus, fallopian tubes and ovaries from a doe taken in November. The ovaries, indicated by the arrows, are about the size of a small bean.

By January, the female reproductive tract looks much different, with two growing fetuses.

Fish and Game biologist had stated publicly that cryptorchid bucks do not shed their antlers, to which I responded that such was not the case. I kept alert for any bucks still carrying antlers in late January, but of the several hundred deer I counted, not one was carrying even a single antler. I was alarmed at seeing about twenty percent of the does with small fawns remaining close by. Normally this time of year the fawns are more independent of their mother.

Similar to the procedure used on males, I took femoral blood, from which I separated the serum, collected some patches of hide with hair follicles, some samples of meat for DNA, and some fat. I also removed the uterus, fallopian tubes and ovaries from each animal.

The fertilized egg remains in the fallopian tube for some hours before it moves slowly through the tube to the uterus where it attaches—a process called, implantation—and remains until birth.

Upon fertilization the egg begins rapid division into differentiating cells and tissues and is called an embryo. After the eighth week the developing baby is referred to as a fetus.

It would have been ideal to return to Lazy Bay in late March and early April to collect more fetuses, but I was unable to get a collection permit for does during the closed season which ran from February 1 through July 31. Our study especially needed male fetuses harvested around March 30.

So I spoke with the Alaska State Troopers, the U.S. Coast Guard Police and the Kodiak City Police, explaining our need for fetuses. I offered to come on call at any time of the day or night to collect samples from road killed does. Furthermore, after collecting the sample tissues I would deliver the carcasses to which ever charitable agency or other location the police preferred.

All the local law enforcement agencies were cooperative and primarily through the efforts of one ADF&G Wildlife Trooper, Alan Jones, I was able to collect half a dozen fetuses from does struck by automobiles on the road between Kodiak town and the airport. These collections were randomly spaced, but provided us the information we needed regarding the timing of normal descent of the testes into the scrotum.

Recounting the collection of samples during January would be incomplete with mention of unexpected, complicating situations.

Collecting fetuses

Red foxes on Kodiak often come to "help" with butchering any time of the year.

When I arrived at Lazy Bay snow and ice covered the ground, making ideal conditions for hunting. However on day three, a warm front moved in and brought wind and rain which made everything icy slick and brought out some bears, as well.

Warm conditions sometimes cause the sleeping bruins to become wet and chilled, so they emerge from their dens and amble around nearby. Normally in a few days the conditions cool off, the dens freeze up and the bears go back to resume their hibernation. But bears will take advantage of any feeding opportunities in situations like this and can surprise unsuspecting hunters. In fact, some bears stay out of dens for the entire winter in the Kodiak Archipelago.

On day four I saw tracks of two single bears of medium size—each was about a seven or eight footer. I did not see either animal, but the tracks were fresh and the alders were thick enough to easily hide a bear, so I was extra cautious. I spent the morning and half of the afternoon observing about three hundred undisturbed deer as they browsed and went about their daily routine. I held off taking a doe, unaccompanied by a fawn, until late that afternoon and waited until I found one in an open area which would be less subject to a concealed approach by a bruin. Kodiak bears have become aware that the sound of a gunshot can mean fresh deer meat and their ability to home in on the location of the sound is uncanny in its accuracy.

On day four I shot a mature doe in the head and was hurrying along with the sampling, as the sun was low and I wanted to avoid returning to the cannery, slipping and stumbling in the dark. As I began to remove the back straps I heard a loud rasping bark a few feet behind me, which caused me to startle and grab my rifle, immediately jacking a bullet into the chamber, in case of need. I knew the bark was that of a red fox (Vulpes vulpes), but bears were on my mind, and that put me into an automatic defensive mode.

A large female Cross fox was standing less than ten feet from me. I laughed and tossed the vixen a piece of fat from the gut and went about my hurried butchering, then loaded the meat on my pack board.

The next day I glassed the kill site and saw that nothing remained of the carcass and hide. At least one bear had enjoyed a mid-winter treat. I crossed paths with those two bears multiple times during the next two days, but I never did catch a glimpse of either one.

As it turned out, the collection of road killed fetuses was the most important part of the effort to sequence the descent of the testes ... and it was the least expensive in terms of effort and financial outlay, thanks primarily to the efforts of Trooper Alan Jones.

We found both normal and cryptorchid embryo bucks in does struck and killed on the road between Kodiak town and the airport. And I began to see bucks with abnormal antlers nearby—even in my own yard, a short distance outside the city limits. I was surprised to see that three of the five male fetuses taken from road killed does showed testes descent was incomplete, indicating they would have become cryptorchid bucks.

Deer "Horns"

How many times have you heard a hunter refer to deer "horns", or inappropriately used that term yourself?

I've seen some rare examples of cases in which the term "horns" is perhaps applicable, but only among cryptorchid Sitka bucks.

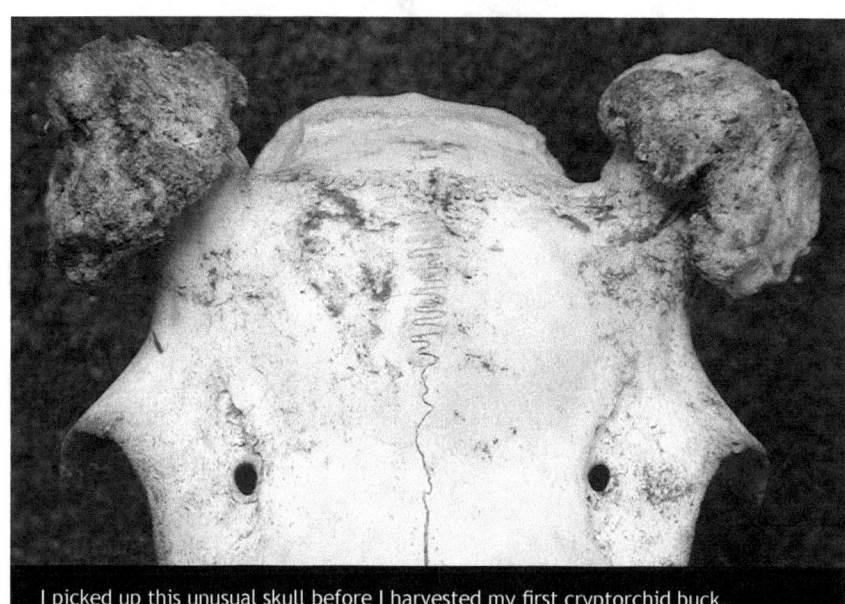

I picked up this unusual skull before I harvested my first cryptorchid buck. I wondered what was going on with this thing.

When this young appearing cryptorchid hit the ground, both antlers popped off, leaving the boss-like stumps. I had never before seen such a situation.

Deer "Horns"

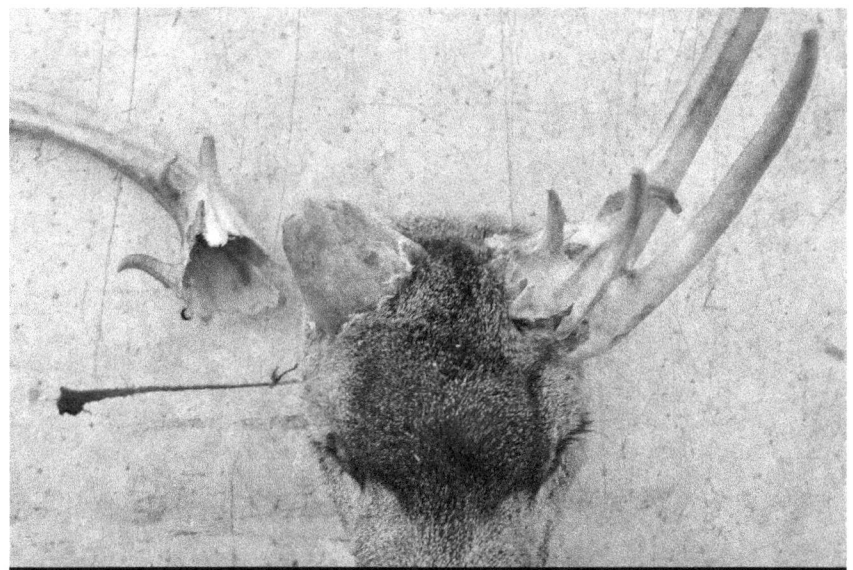

When I got to the boat with my pack loaded with meat and the head, the right antler of this older buck slid off, and before I boiled the skull the other had sipped off, as well. Strange appearing, to say the least.

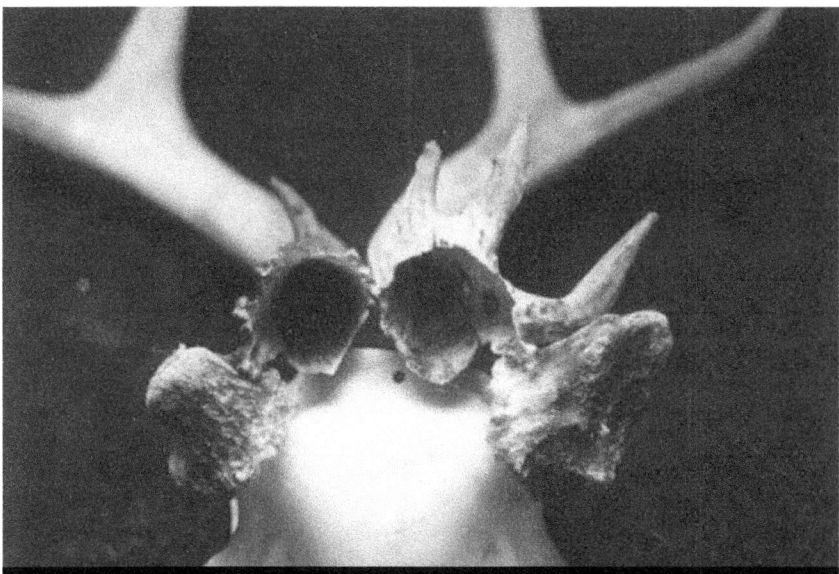

In 52 years of hunting Sitka Blacktail deer I have only harvested the two "horned" bucks shown here and below. Both were cryptorchids taken on the Aliulik Peninsula, on the south end of Kodiak.

The two strange racks shown together.

I have never seen photographs of such oddly formed antlers in other species of deer or from anyplace but the Kodiak Archipelago. Deer biologists in other states tell me that they have never seen such strange antlers on whitetail or mule deer.

Cryptorchid Bucks: Common Myths and Misconceptions

One can use Google to find a few peer review pieces on Cryptorchidis. Most of those were written by our collaborators in investigating the Sterile Sitka deer phenomenon in the Kodiak Archipelago - Dr. George Bubenik, Dr. Rao Verramacaneni, Dr. Rupert Amann and Dr. Emily K. Latch.

I believe the average deer hunter will shy away from such purely scientific papers due to the unfamiliar language and lack of eye-catching photographs. Nevertheless, in attempting to be thorough in addressing the issue, I pursued scholarly papers on cryptorchidism, epizootic hemorrhagic disease, chronic wasting disease and other abnormalities, as well as the more crowd-pleasing publications with photographs of unusual antlers.

Using the popular vernacular, if one looks for articles on "cactus bucks", the seeker is immediately gratified with many pictures of outstanding non-typical deer. This begins to be fun. Most deer hunters would call it eye candy—perhaps akin to pornography for deer hunters.

For the past several years I have googled up "cactus bucks" and have found some interesting photographs of what obviously are cryptorchid bucks from other states, including Mule Deer from Utah, Colorado, Nevada, New Mexico, Arizona, Washington and Oregon. White Tail cactus bucks have been reported in Oklahoma and Alabama. If I searched intensely enough I suspect I would find reports of such abnormal deer from every state, except perhaps Hawaii.

Reports of wildly non-typical deer are becoming more frequent in the literature of the United States.

It's often difficult to impossible to get specifics regarding location, habitat, and other pertinent details of each photographed deer, but many of those intriguing photographs have gone viral on the internet. Few of the stories mention whether or not the animal had one or two testicles in the scrotum. I believe most hunters are so mesmerized by the amazing set of antlers they neglect to thoroughly check other aspects of their trophy.

Sometimes I find information in scholarly papers that I believe to be partially or completely untrue—based on the 355 Sitka Blacktail bucks I have studied and sampled in the Kodiak Archipelago from 1994 to the present. Here are some quotes from internet stories I have found about cactus bucks.

I have underlined the salient points, with which I disagree.

My comments are noted in bold print.

From the Oregon Division of Fish and Wildlife:

What are characteristics of "cactus bucks"

"Cactus bucks are male deer with antlers with abnormal growth patterns that retain the velvet due to alterations in testosterone level usually as a result of testicular trauma, undescended testicles or from the effects of disease affecting the blood supply to the testicles. These animals often have multiple short misshapen points and excess "globs" of velvet hanging from their antlers giving rise to the name "cactus buck". These animals also have small or unapparent testicles.

However, we have never found evidence of testicular trauma or small testicles (Hypogonadism) in the 355 Sitka Blacktail deer I have sampled in our project on cryptorchidism in the Kodiak Archipelago. The undescended testes are much smaller than the scrotal testes, but this is not typical hypogonadism.

"Why has there been an increase in sightings and harvested deer with this condition in Oregon and where are the majority of these animals being found?"

There have been increased reports throughout central and eastern Oregon in addition to eastern Washington in the last few years (2013-2016). The primary reason for this condition is thought to be a response to previous infections with hemorrhagic disease such as epizootic hemorrhagic disease (EHD) or bluetongue (BT) viruses. ODFW has documented both viruses in mule deer and white-tailed deer populations during 2014-15 in several locations in Oregon.

"What causes abnormal antler growth in Cactus Bucks"

"A number of "cactus bucks" were evaluated in Colorado. Necropsies and virus evaluation indicated an association with EHD or BT viral exposure and development of abnormal antlers. Mule deer are more resistant to infection and mortality caused by the viruses but also suffer long-term impacts of inflamed blood vessels of the testicles which can result in chronic inflammation and a regression of testicular tissue. Antler abnormalities usually result in the next season of antler growth which is why we likely see a delay in animals with this condition a year or two after a hemorrhagic disease outbreak.

There are no reports of epizootic hemorrhagic disease or blue tongue in any Alaskan deer. And no records of EHD or bluetongue have been described in Sitka Blacktail deer studies.

From 2003 to 2008 the State of Alaska conducted a survey of deer on Kodiak, funded by the Alaska Chapter of Safari Club International, searching for evidence of Chronic Wasting Disease or other communicable pathologies, but no evidence of such abnormalities was found in Kodiak.

The caption on one photograph of a wildly non-typical deer stated: ""This deer was an "antlered doe," which is one of the most common causes of cactus buck syndrome."

Male pseudohermophrodites are does with antlers. These animals have female external genitalia, but have male organs (testicles) internally.

Cryptorchid bucks do have one or two internal or intra abdominal testicles, but I have found none with female external genitalia (vagina).

In the hundreds of non-typical Sitka Blacktail deer I examined, not one was a doe.

A Kingscamo* story:

Long Story—On Ghost Buck -Interesting Points

"What is a "cactus" buck?
Every year, we see pictures of deer that have bizarre, velvet-covered antlers that have a mass of knobby points and abnormally heavy bases. These are the type of deer usually known as cactus bucks. There has been a great deal of research done on what causes a deer to grow such an uncontrollable glob of velvet and I believe you'll find the results interesting."

"So what do testosterone levels have to do with cactus bucks? Well, everything. <u>In most cactus buck documentations, a buck had the misfortune to turn "himself" into an "it." The buck's testes, the major testosterone producer, may have been left on a barbwire fence line or seriously injured in any number of ways. These castrations continuously result in "cactus" formation antlers with permanent velvet.</u>"

None of the bucks we studied showed any sign of scrotal or testicular injury, let alone castration. Nor have I ever found any testicles dangling from a barbed wire fence or hanging on a stalk of devil's club.

In a publication of the Isaac Walton League of America I read:

"A second unique male antler anomaly is a "cactus" buck. These bucks suffer from very low testosterone production due to hypogonadism or cryptorchidism (i.e., their testicles are the size of a green pea or never descend from the body cavity). **(I doubt this reader has ever seen an undescended testis.)** Because they never experience a fall surge of testosterone, <u>the antlers are never shed. Each year new velvet and antler material is grown over and around the existing antler.</u> Over time this gives the antlers the look of a

---

* http://www.kingscamo.com/Got-Testosterone-An-Overview-of-Cactus-Bucks_b_13.html

gnarly "cactus." These bucks are not common, but a couple are reported killed in Virginia each year.

Continual growth and lack of shedding of antlers of affected bucks is, I believe, one of the most common (and perhaps the most erroneous) fallacies associated with cactus bucks. For more than fifty years I have observed Sitka Blacktail deer in the Kodiak Archipelago and I have never seen a deer still carrying antlers past the middle of February. Most shed their head gear in December. So though permanent retention of antlers may occur in Virginia deer, I have not seen or heard of it in Sitka blacktails

For the past several years I have seen photographs in different magazines that appear to be cryptorchid bucks, but none were identified as such. I called several guides and outfitters connected with the pictures to try to get an idea of what percentages of abnormal deer they were finding, but none responded.**

"The condition of the buck's antlers depends on when the injury occurs. If a deer is castrated as a fawn, it will never grow antlers in the first place. If the injury happens while the buck already has hardened antlers, the buck will usually shed their antlers almost immediately."

"On the other hand, if a buck is injured after it has shed its antlers, next season it will grow its last and permanent set, which will never be shed." "Finally, when a buck is injured while still growing its antlers, it will keep them—and the velvet cover—for the rest of its life."

"Bucks with "permanent velvet" are the ones that end up with remarkable cactus-like growths. Does that grow antlers may also sometimes assume the same appearance, as do deer suffering from other conditions, so it is sometimes hard to identify a cactus buck."

Again, I have never seen a Sitka blacktail with antlers after normal shedding time. Considering the high incidence of cryptorchidism in Kodiak deer—up to 70 percent in some areas for the past two decades—if it were true that cryptorchid bucks never shed their antlers, surely there would have been multiple observations of antlered bucks throughout the year, but this is not the case.

** https://www.outdoorhub.com/stories/2015/05/19/
7-freaky-examples-cactus-buck-syndrome/

Paunsaugunt cactus buck study AST EDITED ON Sep-03-16 AT 02:09 PM in Utah, the incidence of cryptorchid bucks has increased to the point that the Division of Wildlife Research "asked for, and got from the Wildlife Board, some one-time (supposedly) permits (10) on the Pauns (Paunsaugunt) for a study regarding the unusual number of cactus bucks on that unit. 10 people in the depredation pool will each pay $80 and be accompanied by a UDWR employee or Alton CWMU personnel to shoot a cactus buck and provide samples (blood, tissue, lymph, stomach contents, sperm, etc.) for a study as to the cause of the phenomena per genetics, habitat, disease, nutrition, or what-have-you. No waiting periods or points are involved and the hunter gets to keep the deer sans the samples. The results, if they can be identified, should be interesting ... maybe we'll find some unintended consequences of trophy management. Or maybe not!

In any case, I, for one am looking forward to the study.

EDITED: I found it interesting to learn that those cactus bucks are NOT counted as part of the buck to doe ratios, or in the case of the Pauns and Henrys, as part of the percentage of bucks over 4 years old."

So, it appears that cryptorchidism has reached the level in Utah that game managers are concerned and are acting to reduce the numbers of these "wierd," non-reproducing ,deer in their management areas.

Attempting to Generate Interest

In 1994 I reported the first abnormal buck I harvested. The deer had no visible scrotum or testes. It was a cryptorchid. The local Alaska Department of Fish and Game biologist said the "cactus buck" was just one of those phenomena that is sometimes encountered. Initially, I was content with that.

In 1995 I harvested three more such deer. It was obvious that something was amiss. When I discussed this with the biologist he told me we should not be alarmed. He said the problem would likely just go away.

In 1996 I began to notice features that alerted me that an animal was sterile. Often the antler tips were sharper than normal. About a third of the different bucks still carried velvet as late as November. Velvet is normally shed in September. Most of the cryptorchids were noticeably larger in body size than other deer, and most were light in the shoulders and neck, similar to a doe. That would draw my attention from a distance. That year I harvested six sterile bucks. None showed any sign of a scrotum or damage to the scrotal area. The average age of deer taken in the area is 3.5 years, but these cryptorchids averaged 8.5 years.

Again, the ADF&G biologist attached no significance to the increasing presence of sterile bucks. He was interested in bears.

Not satisfied with the disinterest displayed by the officials, I began to write to other hunters and biologists. I distributed copies of my photographs to anyone who seemed genuinely interested.

By 1999 I was corresponding with more than a dozen wildlife managers and biologists. Most of our emails were addressed to the entire group. A biologist from Saskatoon, Saskatchewan, sent an email asking to use some of my photographs in an article he was writing for wildlife veterinary magazine. I told him that he was welcome to use my photos and I need not be credited. I wanted to get this information distributed as widely as possible.

The email group included a veterinarian from Fairbanks who was a government employee. That year I shipped an entire carcass of a cryptorchid buck, as well as organ samples from the kidneys, adrenal glands and other tissues to him. He told me that he saw great research potential in the issue. That same vet immediately advised the fellow in Saskatoon to not write an article about cryptorchid Sitka Blacktail bucks, as the literature was full of such pieces and the article would make the writer look foolish.

The vet had hit his "reply all" key. We all got a copy of his advice to the Saskatoon man.

That same day I wrote to the vet, asking for references in the literature. I had found only one which dealt with hypogonadism or undersized scrotal testes in a mule deer buck found on the Hanford Nuclear Reservation near the Columbia River in Washington. No mention was made of cryptorchidism in that area which has serious nuclear contamination.

Two others on the email list also requested references, but the veterinarian never answered any of our requests and never again participated in our email exchanges.

This seemed strange. I resolved to do what I could to explore and alert others to this issue.

In late November, 1999 a new area biologist took over in Kodiak. He asked me to bring him blood serum from any cryptorchid bucks we took that season. We made one trip in December. We took five bilateral cryptorchids from which I drew blood. I separated two 1.8 milliliter vials of serum from each deer. The serum was kept frozen until I delivered the samples to the biologist.

I told the biologist that I would collect serum or other samples for him, my only request was that he keep me informed regarding the analysis of the samples.

In April, 2000 I asked the biologist about results.

The man laughed as he told me he had destroyed the samples because they were frozen.

My face flushed. I asked him how he took care of serum. Frozen serum will keep for years, but left at room temperature it quickly deteriorates. I realized the cryptorchid phenomenon would not be addressed by the State of Alaska.

In 1999 Dr. George Bubenik of the University of Guelph, Ontario, a participant in the email group, offered to analyze blood serum if I would collect and forward it to him. Dr. Bubenik was offended by the response of the man from Fairbanks and incensed at hearing of the destruction of the serum samples.

The following year we co-authored a paper and over the next two years we published other peer review reports. See the references at end of this chapter.

In 2002 Dr. Bubenik informed me that he was going to retire and there was no one at the University of Guelph, Ontario to take his place on our research project.

By good fortune and timing an article appeared in the *Alaska Magazine* describing some of my observations and showing a photograph of a non-typical cryptorchid buck I had collected, which follows verbatim:

August 2003 *ALASKA Magazine* p.57
STERILE BUCKS CONCERN KODIAK ISLAND HUNTER

Jake Jacobson wonders why so many Sitka black-tailed bucks on Kodiak Island have a defect known as "cryptorchidism"—the failure of the testes to descend into the scrotum. The condition causes sterility, and it's on the increase, he said.

"Nontypical critters have always been fascinating to me," Jacobson said.

Fairly nontypical himself, Jacobson has degrees in dentistry and biology. He has hunted Kodiak Island's deer since 1967.

Since 1994, the first time Jacobson shot a buck that had no testes in its scrotum, he has seen many others, he said. On a three-day Kodiak

Island hunt last November (2002), he and three other hunters bagged twelve bucks, eight of which were cryptorchids.

Cryptorchid bucks display antler formations that vary from wildly nontypical to normal, but usually with very sharp tine tips, Jacobson said. Some retain all of the velvet until shedding their antlers, while others have normal, polished antlers, he said.

To date, Jacobson has been unable to get government game managers to investigate cryptorchidism on Kodiak. He said most biologists blame inbreeding for the defect. He disagrees. Kodiak's deer population originated with the relocation of twenty-five deer from Southeast in the 1920s and 1930s. Other deer populations originating from much smaller relocations don't have the defect, he said.

Jacobson speculates that heavy metals may be causing the defect. He is interested enough that—without state or federal aid—he has been collecting blood, fat, teeth and hair samples from bucks and having them analyzed. "More than just a curiosity, this rapidly accelerating cryptorchidism constitutes a threat of as yet unquantified dimensions," Jacobson said. If you have information or theories about cryptorchism in Sitka blacktails, you can call Jacobson at (907)486-5253 or e-mail him at huntfish@ak.net.

After I presented our data and concerns, on July 17, 2003 the Kodiak Island Borough Assembly passed Resolution No.2003-23, which ended with:

NOW, THEREFORE, BE IT RESOLVED BY THE ASSEMBLY OF THE KODIAK ISLAND BOROUGH that the Assembly supports grant funding to Dr. Jacobson and Dr. Bubenik to continue and expand their research into the cause or causes of abnormal cryptorchism in Sitka Blacktail Deer in the Kodiak Archipelago.

ADOPTED BY THE ASSEMBLY OF THE KODIAK ISLAND BOROUGH THIS SEVENTEENTH DAY OF JULY, 2003.

Gabrielle LeDoux, Mayor
Judith A. Nielsen, CMC Borough Clerk

During the two months following the *Alaska Magazine* article, I received calls and emails from biologists in Germany, Czechoslovakia, South Africa, Canada, and several other countries as well as a half dozen American institutions. All offered to participate in the investigation of the sterility of Kodiak deer.

Dr. Rupert Amann, a retired Professor Emeritus in Andrology—the study of male reproductive systems—from Colorado State University asked me if I thought Dr. Bubenik would share samples of serum and other materials. I was certain that Dr. Bubenik would share. I introduced the scientists. Cooperative efforts began and Dr. Amann became the driving force in researching cryptorchidism from that date forward.

That summer I was interrupted by a telephone call. The caller claimed he was with a federal agency. He requested that I give him my deer samples. I told him that I had duplicates of most samples and with proper notification and a written request I would share with him.

The fellow angrily told me that those samples were property of the U.S. government and could be seized at any time, if necessary.

The samples were collected from legally taken deer and like the antlers and meat, they belonged to me. I hung up. I should have gotten him to talk more and taken his name. I heard no more on this issue, but I became concerned that my samples might be seized.

Colorado State University researchers requested that I send serum and other samples to them.

Relieved to have the samples in secure storage, I sent my entire collection via frozen air freight to Dr. Rupert Amann at C.S.U. in Fort Collins, Colorado.

CSU provided me with sample kits for collecting blood and other things. From 2003 forward all the samples I collected were sent to that institution.

We published several more peer review papers. These research treatises can be found by going to Google and typing "Sterile Sitka Blacktail Deer."

Laboratory analysis by Dr. Amann and Dr. Rao Veeramachaneni at CSU and Dr. E.K. Latch, of Purdue University, indicated inbreeding was not the cause. An endocrine disruptor or mimic were likely responsible. The pregnant does were being exposed to something that was disrupting normal development of the male fetuses.

Meanwhile, microscopic examination of slices of testicles by CSU scientists revealed four types of carcinoma present in ninety percent of the abnormal testes, and in fifty percent of the normal, scrotal testes of deer taken on Aliulik Peninsula—the location of the original "hot zone" of sterile deer. The cancers found were: Seminoma, Sertoli cell tumors, Leydig cell tumors, and Stromal cell tumors.

These cancers and other lesions are rare in the general deer population. The cancers put a new urgency on the research.

In the spring of 2003 I received a telephone call from a State of Alaska official who suggested that I cease and desist my Sitka deer investigations or possibly face criminal charges for "unauthorized research."

What was going on with that?

Visiting the Kodiak Court House I searched the law books for "unauthorized research" and found nothing in the statutes. I contacted the Kodiak District Attorney and explained my suspicion that for some reason, someone was trying to scare me away from further deer research. The DA confirmed that no such crime existed. He urged me to continue investigating and wished me well.

An Attempt to Lobby for Funding

In August, 2006 Sarah Palin defeated the sitting Governor Frank Murkowski in the Republican primary. She went on to defeat former Democratic Governor Tony Knowles in the general election that November.

I was one of Sarah Palin's active supporters. When she visited Kodiak in September, 2006 I hosted her and drove her around Kodiak. I sat beside her at a fund raiser in Kodiak. I explained the situation regarding the alarming increase in cryptorchid bucks in the entire Archipelago and I asked for her help when she was elected. She assured me that the situation would receive state attention.

After Sarah Palin's inauguration in 2007 she was busy with efforts to write new oil tax rules to give Alaskans a much better deal than had been negotiated by her predecessors. Alaska's Clear and Equitable Share (ACES) was put in place and did as its name implies regarding oil revenues. Alaska's fiscal picture was looking rosy, as its coffers filled with oil revenue.

That seemed the best time for our group to pursue state funding for a modest, but thorough research project dealing with cryptorchidism in Kodiak.

After explaining my expectation for success in obtaining state funding, Dr. Amann from Colorado State University and Dr. Loren Buck from the University of Alaska, Anchorage, put together a proposal for a state grant.

As an active conservative, I took a resolution to the District 36 Republican Committee in 2007 and convinced them to pass:

RESOLUTION 2: The State of Alaska should approve adequate funding to determine cause(s) of the alarming increase of sterility in Sitka Blacktail Deer in the Kodiak Archipelago.

In Kodiak, I took another resolution to the local borough assembly after conversations with the mayor and others, emphasizing the high incidence of cancers in the affected bucks. We overcame resistance by the local Alaska Department of Fish and Game office and its area biologist. The resolution was passed.

A RESOLUTION OF THE KODIAK ISLAND BOROUGH ASSEMBLY REQUESTING STATE FUNDING OF RESEARCH INTO THE CAUSE OF BIRTH DEFECTS IN SITKA BLACKTAIL DEER IN THE KODIAK ARCHIPELAGO, AND HOW TO ADDRESS THE PROBLEM

WHEREAS, since 1994, the population of Sitka black-tail deer on the Kodiak Archipelago, especially on Aliulik Peninsula with 70% affected males, increasingly has displayed a birth defect termed bilateral cryptorchidism, rendering males sterile because their testes never descend into the scrotum (another 6% on Aliulik Peninsula have only 1 scrotal testis); and

WHEREAS, an unusually high incidence of cancer cells has been found in scrotal testes of otherwise normal appearing male Sitka black-tail deer on the Aliulik Peninsula; and

WHEREAS, because wildlife often serve as a sentinel for human afflictions, the incidence of testicular cancer and cryptorchidism in Sitka black-tailed deer on the Kodiak Archipelago has implications for the health of residents of this Borough; and

WHEREAS, this birth defect is a threat to the deer population of the Archipelago, because of reduced numbers of fertile breeding males and possible yet undetected defects occurring in female deer; and

WHEREAS, sport hunting and wildlife viewing are important to the economy of Kodiak Borough, and these activities and local subsistence hunting may be negatively affected by these birth defects; and

WHEREAS, study of the nature and magnitude of this problem afflicting Sitka black-tailed deer on the Kodiak Archipelago has been spearheaded by Dr. James P "Jake" Jacobson, of Kodiak, and publications by he and colleagues in peer-reviewed journals (eg, Environ Health Persp 114(Suppl 1): 41-59, 2006) have been accomplished without funding by the State of Alaska; and

WHEREAS, ignoring this multi-faceted problem in Kodiak's deer population would be imprudent; and

WHEREAS, the National Institutes of Health or similar Federal agencies are unlikely to fund a study of deer movement patterns, favored browse, or content of potential causative agents in browse;

NOW, THEREFORE, BE IT RESOLVED BY THE ASSEMBLY OF THE KODIAK ISLAND BOROUGH THAT the Assembly urges the State of Alaska to fund a project, potentially led by Dr .C. Loren Buck of the University of Alaska Anchorage with assistance of Dr Jacobson and others, to study movement patterns, favored browse, and fetuses of female Sitka Black-tailed deer and also to analyze and link concentrations of potential causative agents in body tissues and browse, with the goal of identifying the underlying cause of these birth defects in deer and publishing the results, so that wildlife personnel can recommend a course of action.

This was the second resolution passed by the assembly on the same issue, urging the same action. I felt this endorsement should lead to the granting of our funding request from the State of Alaska.

On to Juneau

With Dr.Loren Buck, a field research professor from the University of Alaska, Anchorage, and one Vice Chancellor from UAA, I traveled to Juneau in February 2008 with a proposal for a grant to be administered by the University. This proposal was designed by Dr. Amann (CSU) and Dr. Buck. I would be a field participant, but would have nothing to do with administration of the grant money, or analysis of the biological samples. I would remain a field collector and observer—a willing "grunt".

As I ascended the capitol steps with Dr. Loren Buck, and the Vice Chancellor, we were met by the Commissioner of Fish and Game. The Commissioner was confrontational in demeanor. He asked me what I was doing in Juneau.

I responded that he knew what I was doing and that was why he was there to intercept and discourage us.

He mentioned that even if we were to discover the cause of the sterility, there would be little we could do about it.

"Unless and until we have an idea of the cause, there is surely nothing we could do about it," I told him.

Furthermore I told him that I had nothing new to add to the mountain of evidence and scientific data already presented to his department and many other individuals and organizations, and that if he did not assist us in securing grant money, I suggested that he would have his own neck stuck out.

The commissioner huffed, turned away, and stomped back up the steps into the capitol building.

Members of the Alaska Legislature were courteous and receptive.

Two of the Senators mentioned that they knew of me, had seen my hunting videos and read newspaper accounts and other articles about the deer. They were in favor of my efforts to get a grant for the University to administer in this critical effort to discover the cause or causes of sterility in deer.

While addressing one large gathering of lawmakers, after my presentation of facts, including mention of the larger average body size and age of the sterile bucks, their higher winter survival rate and so forth, one of the Senators asked me about the meat.

"Oh, the meat of Sitka Blacktail deer is fine. It is absolutely the most delicious of all venison that I had been privileged to taste, including that from many other places in the world. And the larger bodied, sterile animals make harvesting the animal more attractive", I assured them.

By being a Federal "Designated Hunter" I could legally harvest a full limit of three deer for myself and each family member, as well as for anyone else who asked me to fill their tags. Some seasons I harvested more than a dozen deer. With so much meat on my hands, I distributed it widely in the community of Kodiak. Many families benefited from that aspect of our research efforts.

The samples of all the deer I harvested were processed quickly and completely.

"But, aren't you a bit reluctant to eat the meat of those abnormal deer?" the Senator asked.

"Oh no, in fact I prefer the flesh of these natural "steer deer" as it is a bit more tender than that of the normal animals. Venison has been a main part of my family diet for generations," I replied.

I could sense that wheels were turning rapidly in some of the legislators minds. After a pause to let their concerns ferment, I broke the silence.

"But, I believe I understand what your are concerned about, Senator, and as a matter of fact, I need to tell you that my last two children were born without testicles."

A murmur ran through the room. I heard two women shriek. I got some strange looks from several in the front row of the group. I saw grimaces and disgust. Some people shifted in their seats. Discomfort was taking hold of the large group of attendees.

Now I really had their attention!

"But my last two kids were girls, so it's a good thing they developed no testicles."

Some of the Legislators got a good laugh at my little joke. I believe interjecting a bit of humor in serious discussions often has benefits.

Laughter and relief replaced the shock and worry. I thought I had the Legislative body going in my favor on the issue. Surely adequate grant funding would be forthcoming.

Several of the gathered legislators came up to shake my hand and congratulate me on my efforts to solve this mystery and for my sincere and long standing efforts in stewardship of the public game resources.

Our proposal which I carried to the State Legislature on February 25, 2008 is detailed below:

Plans to Unravel the Problem

Until the cause of this uniquely high incidence of sterile cryptorchid male Sitka Blacktail Deer is known, and the mechanism by which such changes are inflicted on male fetuses is understood, the extent of threats to other wildlife in the Kodiak Archipelago, and humans of the area, will remain unknown. The feral reindeer on Kodiak Island is one additional species possibly affected by cryptrochidism.

> Ignoring this problem is not good stewardship of Alaska's wildlife.
> Ignoring this problem is not good public health policy.
> Ignoring the problem is not good game management policy.

Given appropriate funding from the State of Alaska, we plan to identify the cause of the problem and recommend a course of action, based on what is found, including:

> Learning the extent of movement of female deer on Aliulik Peninsula and favored browsing areas; are deer likely to move in/out of the Aliulik Peninsula? Study to be done using GPS collars, led by University of Alaska Anchorage scientists.

> To get at the cause of the problem, analysis of samples of browse, water, fat, and blood serum for estrogenic agents, both of plant origin and man-made origin should be done. Many analyses can be done at University of Alaska Anchorage; some may need to be performed elsewhere.

> Gene expression in male fetuses at the time of testis descent would be examined, using specially harvested tissues, many of which are already collected and await analysis.

Funding should be provided for fetuses sampled at or near one-third of the way through gestation, and analyses run at Colorado State University.

> To allow firmer conclusions on possibilities of a classic gene mutation or altered epigenetic regulation of gene expression, sequences of selected genes and promoters would be analyzed at Colorado State University.

> Characterization of both normal and pre-cancerous cells in abdominal and scrotal testes from SBTD on the Aliulik Peninsula and elsewhere in the Archipelago. State-of-the-art analyses to be performed at Colorado State University.

> Results and conclusions from this 3-year effort will be made public, as all our other studies have been.

❯We anticipate better evidence for a most probable cause of the problem, and possibly identification of the causative agent(s).

❯Although females are not a focus of planned studies, we might draw conclusions on the threat to female fetuses from the currently unknown agent affecting male fetuses.

❯We anticipate making conclusions if the agent or vector should be a concern for human health.

❯We anticipate a conclusion if the problem in Sitka Blacktail Deer on Kodiak Island could be reduced or eliminated and, if so, recommendations on how to proceed.

The Alaska Department of Fish and Game officials strongly argued against state funding, though not in my presence. They refused to engage in an open debate. I believe ADF&G feared that somehow they would lose some potential funding for their department if our grant for the University was approved. Also, since their own biologists had not deemed the anomaly important, they opposed it.

Or were the ADF&G people motivated by something else?

For years some people suggested that we were witnessing a government cover-up. Could it be that some means of inducing sterility had been experimented with at Kodiak that had gone awry and now was affecting deer? Or was it an effort to eliminate deer?

Personally, I did not believe this theory held much chance of validity. Why would Kodiak be chosen for any such experiment? And more important, how could such a plan be implemented and kept secret? I felt that someone involved with such a program would blow the whistle.

On the other hand, since deer were introduced to the Kodiak Archipelago and were therefore "not native", perhaps that might lead government folks to experiment with that species. The Archipelago is relatively remote and the chances of the condition spreading to other locations was slight.

But our proposal was successfully blocked by the Alaska Department of Fish and Game, and we received no funding from the State of Alaska.

Seeking Grant Funding

As I have never attempted to write a grant proposal and have no experience or interest in administering a project involving many other people from disciplines with which I was not familiar, I left other efforts to secure government funding to the professionals at Colorado State University.

Word came to me that the National Institutes of Health refused to fund our study primarily because Sitka blacktail deer are not a recognized study animal species, like some strains of rats, mice, pigs and monkeys. So they felt it inappropriate to deal with a big game wild animal species. I wonder at their inflexibility.

The National Science Foundation turned down the grant proposal because the directors perceived cryptorchidism to be a disease. That is disappointing, as cryptorchidism is a developmental condition, not a disease, and it is not contagious.

To fully fund analysis of all the samples I had sent to Colorado would be prohibitively expensive for me. I had already spent about thirty thousand dollars on the issue. The analytical work had been funded by CSU, while the State of Alaska and federal departments offered no financial support.

Analysis of kelp, ferns, and other food materials of deer in the search for phytoestrogens and contaminants is costly. I gathered a large volume of samples which sits in secure storage at Colorado State University awaiting funds for proper analysis.

Some basic data: on the Aliulik Peninsula alone, among 187 male Sitka Blacktail Deer (SBTD) examined by myself in 1999-2007 hunting seasons, 70% were bilateral cryptorchids and another 6% had only one scrotal testis. Among the bilateral cryptorchids, 35% had abnormal, or non-typical antlers. Elsewhere on the Kodiak Archipelago approximately 12% of the male Sitka Blacktail deer that I harvested or observed the carcasses of, were cryptorchid.

We had accumulated a vast collection of samples—far larger than most studies of this nature collected. From 1999 through 2010 I collected samples from 355 individual Sitka deer. Only about 20 were females.

Finally, in early January of 2010 we learned that the President of the University of Alaska elected to not include the deer project in the appropriation request. This news came through the University of Alaska, Anchorage

Provost. The primary reason given for his decision appears to be the lack of buy-in by ADF&G and USFWS. However, there seems to be much more to this that the Provost did not feel comfortable sending via e-mail.

People trying to help us secure funding informed me that considerable effort was spent to get the support of Alaska Department of Fish and Game and the U.S. Fish and Wildlife Service. This effort resulted in verbal support from ADF&G as well as from the USF&W refuge manager for Kodiak Island who said he would prioritize our research because of the diet work we were proposing. But none of these individuals were willing to write letters of support for fear of overstepping their bounds with their upper administration personnel. Though supported fairly far up the bureaucratic chain, apparently there was stiff resistance at the higher levels.

It was the non-support at the highest levels of ADF&G and the USF&W Service that killed things at the University of Alaska on the Statewide level.

This confirmed for me that for undisclosed reasons, state and federal government officials in high positions did not want the cryptorchidism issue in the Kodiak Archipelago to be investigated further and they preferred that it be ignored or suppressed.

2010 Harvest Report Questions

Nevertheless, I kept after the issue. After months of discussions with the local biologist in Kodiak, in 2009 I prevailed upon him to have the ADF&G include in the hunter harvest report a simple section which follows:

2010 Kodiak Archipelago Deer Questionnaire

Sitka black-tailed deer live throughout the Kodiak Archipelago. They bring hunters to the area and provide food for local residents. Most deer appear to be healthy, but anecdotal reports of altered development persist. Some deer might have non-descended testes or abnormal antlers. Meat from such deer is fit for human consumption. Please help us learn if there is a problem and where normal or abnormal deer were shot.

For each deer, please fill in the month and number of area where shot (see map), and circle the other appropriate answers. Then mail card.

Area of Harvest	For males: number of testes in scrotum 2, 1, or none	Antlers: *Typical, Velvet, or Non-typical*
Month of Kill		
Sex: *male or female*		**Comments:**

If you have any questions or comments, you can contact us at: 907-486-1880 or larry.vandaele@alaska.gov

When the reports were tabulated, the ADF&G figures were comparable with my percentages of bilateral and unilateral cryptorchid bucks from the areas we hunted. I hoped that would bring ADF&G fully into the effort to find out why so many bucks were sterile. However, the survey has been deleted since 2010.

Still I wonder how any government agency charged with management of any species should avoid collection of data as important, and as easily and inexpensively obtained, as this?

In 2010 the Alaska Department of Fish and Game printed a notice for hunters:

Kodiak Deer Condition Survey – 2010
Kodiak deer condition survey—2010

Most Kodiak deer are productive, but some have been found with abnormal testicular development. This may cause reduced sperm production and abnormal antlers that may stay on throughout the year. **(This has not been shown to be the case in the Kodiak Archipelago.- Jake's note.)** There is absolutely no indication that these abnormalities impact the quality of the meat for human consumption, but they can reduce the productivity of the herd. We would like your help in learning where these anomalies occur and how common they are.

It is important for us to hear about all the deer you harvested; both male and female, normal and abnormal.

Please fill in the information below and circle the appropriate answers.

When you are finished please give the completed questionnaire to your transporter or drop it in the mail.

After the 2010 ADF&G survey, the notice was stopped. I believe ending this inexpensive data gathering, after only one year, was unconscionable. Once again, it seemed to me that the Alaska Department of Fish and Game wanted to suppress or ignore the cryptorchidism that was affecting a high percentage of Sitka Blacktail deer in the Kodiak Archipelago.

In late November 2007, on the Aliulik Peninsula, Drs Buck and Jacobson observed large, branched-antlered bucks seemingly uninterested while small spike bucks were actively breeding nearby does. Large numbers of unusually small, nursing fawns also were observed. Late nursing means late birth due to late breeding. Was there a shortage of sexually competent, fertile bucks? Were all the inactive large branched-antlered bucks Bilateral Cryptorchids? Those that we collected were.

Repetition of this scenario might adversely affect the SBTD population on the Aliulik Peninsula and elsewhere.

Regional Advisory Committee

All rural Alaskan subsistence users have the opportunity to comment and offer input on subsistence issues at Council meetings. They meet to develop proposals to change Federal subsistence regulations, review proposals submitted by others, and provide an open forum for public expressions, opinions, and concerns regarding any matter related to subsistence.

On February 11, 2015 I was asked to give my views on the sterile deer situation to the Regional Advisory Committee (RAC). My presentation is summarized below:

Several conclusions have been reached:
1. The non-descent of the testes is a developmental problem -not a disease.
2. Inbreeding is not the cause of cryptorchidism.
3. For Sitka Blacktail bucks on the Aliulik Peninsula, there was no genetic difference between non-cryptorchid versus cryptorchid males detected via microsatellite DNA.
4. The incidence of DDT & Lindane (antiquated, toxic pesticides that

were once used extensively worldwide) is higher in Kodiak deer than in deer from SE Alaska.
5. On the Aliulik Peninsula, a whopping 70% or more of all bucks were bilateral cryptorchids and therefore sterile. Other similar areas exist in the island group.
6. TUMORS: Carcinoma in situ was found in 90% of the undescended testes and in 50% of the "normal" testes of bucks taken on Aliulik Peninsula. These same types of cancers are increasing in the human population.
7. Colorado State University scientists consider ongoing exposure to an estrogenic endocrine disruptor as the most likely cause of the multiple problems seen in SBTD on the Aliulik Peninsula. Is the causative agent man-made or natural? We need to find out!

The does are apparently exposed to the agent while they carry their fawns. In 2008 we found 3 out of 5 road killed does between Kodiak and the airport had cryptorchid bucks en utero.

In October, 2014, I spent 4 days walking and 2 days boating in Alitak Bay, accompanied by a retired ADF&G biologist. We saw an average of 8 deer per day in areas that held 80 to 100 deer from 1998 through 2008. We saw no branch antlered bucks. We each shot two spike bucks, all four of which showed cryptorchidism (three were bilateral, one was unilaterally cryptrochid). I believe the deer population in the Alitak Bay area is not recovering from the harsh winter of 2011/2012 due to a lack of fertile bucks.

A huge sample collection is in appropriate storage at Colorado State University. More complete analysis can be done if funding is secured.

Further research into this alarming situation is warranted.

That ended my presentation to the RAC.

The Alaska Department of Fish and Game had biologists in attendance at the RAC meeting. I suggested that the least ADF&G could do would include the questionnaire of 2010 on all future deer harvest reports.

At the RAC meeting the new resident biologist agreed that was a good idea. I expected him to put the questionnaire in the harvest report. I hoped that the new man would see the common sense in at least collecting the data.

When I visited him in his office a week later, he said that his superiors told him it could not be included in the harvest report due to the cost of compilation of data.

So, it appeared that again the decision to suppress research came from higher ups.

To me it seems absolutely nonsensical for ADF&G to refuse to include the questions regarding number of testes in the scrotum and condition of antlers (in velvet or not) in their required harvest reports. Cost of collection and interpretation of such data would be minimal, but the value would be inestimable.

Is the ADF&G simply blind to the significance of this unheard of degree of cryptorchidism, or is there another, darker reason for their reluctance to address the issue?

Influential, in-the-know people have told me how bureaucracies, like the military work: Typically, if the person closest to the issue is unconvinced that there's a problem, that view will percolate all the way up. In terms of state government, if the underlings don't see it as an issue, it's extremely rare for a commissioner or Governor to intervene. The chain of command is seldom violated.

I wonder.

Widespread sterility in the deer of Kodiak is not going away. It is increasing and spreading.

References

https://www.ncbi.nlm.nih.gov/pmc/articles/PMC1874179/
Dilemma and hypothesis
How do antler malformation, cryptorchidism, induction of abnormalities in all four primordial testicular cell types, and lack of hypospadias tie together?

- Bubenik GA, Jacobson JP. *Testicular histology of cryptorchid black-tailed deer (Odocoileus hemionus sitkensis) of Kodiak Island, Alaska.* Z Jagdwiss. 2002;48:234–243.

- Bubenik GA, Jacobson JP, Schams KD, Barto? L. *Cryptorchidism, hypogonadism and antler malformation in black-tailed deer (Odocoileus hemionus sitkensis) of Kodiak Island.* Z Jagdwiss. 2001;47:241–252.

Horns, Pronghorns and Antlers by George Bubenik and Anthony Bubenik

JJacobson JP. 2003. *Sterile Bucks Concern Kodiak Island Hunters.* Alaska, 69 August:

Testis and Antler Dysgenesis in Sitka Black-Tailed Deer on Kodiak Island, Alaska: Sequela of Environmental Endocrine Disruption?

D.N. Rao Veeramachaneni,1 Rupert P. Amann,1 and James P. Jacobson2

Competing hypotheses for the etiology of cryptorchidism in Sitka black-tailed deer: an evaluation of evolutionary alternatives

E. K. Latch, *Department of Forestry and Natural Resources*, Purdue University, West Lafayette, IN, USA

R. P. Amann, *Animal Reproduction and Biotechnology Laboratory*, Colorado State University, Fort Collins, CO, USA

Search for more papers by this author

J. P. Jacobson, *Arctic Rivers Guide & Booking Service*, Kodiak, AK, USA

Cryptorchidism and its impact on male fertility: a state of art review of current literature, Eric Chung, MBBS, FRACS and Gerald B. Brock, MD, FRCSC

https://academic.oup.com/humupd/article/14/1/49/823056
Epidemiology and pathogenesis of cryptorchidism
H.E. Virtanen J. Toppari, *Human Reproduction Update,* Volume 14, Issue 1, 1 Jan 2008

http://onlinelibrary.wiley.com/doi/10.1002/j.1939-4640.2003.tb02654.x/full
Cryptorchidism: Incidence, Risk Factors, and Potential Role of Environment; An Update Authors Patrick F. Thonneau, Peggy Candia,Roger Mieusse

https://www.ncbi.nlm.nih.gov/pubmed/8621244
Risks of testicular cancer and cryptorchidism in relation to socio-economic status and related factors: case-control studies in Denmark.
Møller H1, Skakkebaek NE.

https://www.ncbi.nlm.nih.gov/pubmed/15094270
Lancet. 2004 Apr 17;363(9417):1264-9. *Difference in prevalence of congenital cryptorchidism in infants between two Nordic countries.*

Boisen KA1, Kaleva M, Main KM, Virtanen HE, Haavisto AM, Schmidt IM, Chellakooty M, Damgaard IN, Mau C, Reunanen M, Skakkebaek NE, Toppari J.

Various Considerations

Consanguineous Unions or Inbreeding

Commonly, when discussing the alarming degree of cryptorchidism in the Kodiak Archipelago, the first thing that comes to people's minds is inbreeding.

The Kodiak deer herd, widespread and vast as it is with an occasionally estimated population of over 100,000 animals, is isolated. No new genes have been added to the pool for the last eighty years or so, except by natural mutation, which is minimal.

Given that sterility is the central issue, one would think the condition will simply breed itself out of existence.

I worked with mendelian charts. Could it be that a recessive gene is responsible? It would take pairing of two recessive genes to result in sterility. That rarely happens.

We have found sterility to be only in male deer. I examined dozens of ovaries of female deer. All showed scarring, which indicates previous ovulation and apparent fertility, I found no female deer that had unscarred ovaries which would indicate sterility.

We must keep in mind that the deer captured in Southeast Alaska for the three introductions to Kodiak came from widely separated areas, thus likely providing a broad degree of genetic diversity to the deer that founded the population in the Kodiak Archipelago. It is generally accepted that the higher the genetic variation—the more diverse the gene pool—within a breeding population, the less likely it is to suffer from inbreeding depression.

If a genetic mutation is responsible, could it be a mutation of multiple genes?

This is a complex issue, however research indicates that the sterility we are investigating is not caused by genetic mutation.

I found welcome peace of mind after sending samples of Kodiak deer to Dr. Emily Latch of Purdue University. After analyzing the samples I provided she dispelled concerns about inbreeding being a factor in the high numbers of deer we were finding.

A Research Peer Review Paper follows:

Competing hypotheses for the etiology of cryptorchidism in Sitka black-tailed deer: an evaluation of evolutionary alternatives

E. K. Latch, Department of Forestry and Natural Resources, Purdue University, West Lafayette, IN, USA

R. P. Amann, Animal Reproduction and Biotechnology Laboratory,

Colorado State University, Fort Collins, CO, USA
Search for more papers by this author

J. P. Jacobson, Arctic Rivers Guide & Booking Service, Kodiak, AK, USA

O. E. Rhodes Jr.

Abstract

On the Aliulik Peninsula (AP) of Kodiak Island, Alaska, 70% of male Sitka black-tailed deer (SBTD; Odocoileus hemionus sitkensis) are bilaterally cryptorchid (both testes fail to descend; male is sterile). Both genetic and environmental factors have been proposed as possible causes of this problem. We investigated the possibility that population genetic processes (isolation, inbreeding and genetic drift) have contributed to an increased frequency of cryptorchidism in this population. Overall, SBTD on major islands throughout Alaska have unusually low levels of genetic diversity, though we identified a likely glacial refugium on Prince of Wales Island in the Alexander Archipelago. Within the Kodiak Archipelago, deer on the AP did not exhibit the patterns of genetic isolation, inbreeding and drift that would be expected if cryptorchidism in this population was the result of a founder mutation(s). **Instead, our data favor exposure to environmental contaminants as a likely alternative mechanism causing high prevalence of cryptorchidism on the AP (Aliulik Peninsula).**

Another possibility is androgen insensitivity. As I mentioned before, androgen is produced by the testis, but also by the adrenal glands. Thus both male and females normally have an androgen (testosterone) titer.

None of the characteristics of androgen insensitivity were seen in any of the cryptorchid bucks we harvested. All the bucks had a normal appearing penis, no sign of a uterus, and no sign of an external scrotum or damage to the scrotal area.

However receptivity at the androgen receiver sites could play a role, as androgen regulated genes are critical for the development and maintenance of the male sexual characteristics.

Water

Many times in the last fifty years in remote, rural Alaska I have noticed an oily sheen on small pools of stagnant water. I have seen such water commonly in stagnant pools from well north of the Arctic Circle to Kodiak Island. To eliminate contaminated water as a possible cause of the cryptorchidism in Kodiak deer, we sampled water from various sites and sent them to Colorado State University for analysis. Analysis did not reveal any unusual or dangerous contamination in the water samples I collected.

Plants

Phytoestrogens are estrogens (any of a group of steroid hormones that promote the development and maintenance of female characteristics of the body.) found in some natural wild plants. The fact that they are not generated by the endocrine system of the animal that digested them led to the interesting alternate term: **xenoestrogen**—i.e. "strange or foreign" estrogen.

Estrogens are animal-generated hormones that give female characteristics and fertility to females. It has been speculated that plants generate phytoestrogens as a defense against overpopulation of animals that consume the plant by reducing female fertility. This is believed to occur because the molecular similarities of phytoestrogens consumed as food and animal generated estrogens can lead to mimicking or substitution for the animal's estrogens, which could lead to reduced fertility. The plant estrogens take the place of the animal generated estrogens and interfere with the animal's normal maturation process. (This, to me, seems incredible and leads to the questions—do plants think? Can plants act in their own defense—or revenge? Also animal generated estrogens are deposited directly into the blood. They do not go through the digestive tract where stomach acids would likely change them significantly.) But this phytoestrogen phenomenon is well documented and generally felt to be valid.

This phytoestrogen mimicry is akin to the situation whereby a super-immunity to the smallpox virus can give relief to people suffering from herpes simplex virus, because the molecular structures are similar enough to mimmic one another. In the 1970s I vaccinated one of my children seven times over as many weeks to cause a high titer of smallpox antibodies in hope of providing immunity to Herpes simplex, often manifested as "cold sores". The procedure worked and she no longer was plagued by recurring cold sores. She has been clear for the past thirty-five years since her last vaccination.

With intuitive reasoning, one might suspect that if the pregnant female is subjected to a high level of phytoestrogens, that might lead to interruption or modification of maturation processes in the developing fetus that depend on endocrines for its development.

Compared with other big game species in North America, little basic research has been done on Sitka blacktail deer. Some minor studies have been done on deer fecal material which indicate the diet of these deer is made up of approximately 15 percent grasses, while 85 percent of their food comes from browse, such as leaves and stems of herbs, lichens, sedges and other plants common to the area. These are easier to digest than most grasses.

Accurate analysis of plants and stomach contents to determine and quantify presence of phytoestrogens has not been done, due to the high cost. This is something that should be undertaken. I collected many samples which await funding to be analyzed.

At the request of the andrologists (Andrology is the branch of physiology and medicine that deals with diseases and conditions specific to males) at Colorado State University I collected samples of ferns, forbs, sedges, and other plants that are commonly browsed by deer. These samples were placed in special paper containers avoiding any contact of the collected plants with plastics. Merely being transported in plastic bags could skew the analysis.

My rifle on a large deposit of fermenting kelp on a beach of Aliulik Peninsula.

Beach Kelp

Kelp washes ashore in many areas of the Kodiak Archipelago and both deer and brown bears feed on it. High tides deposit the kelp on the beach. Twice daily, high tides deposit more kelp and it builds up until an extra high tide or a storm removes the kelp deposits and washes them out to sea. Kelp may accumulate in some locations for years. In places the kelp may be piled several feet high, especially on beaches of the south east aspect, or Gulf of Alaska side of the island.

On several occasions I noticed a smell similar to that of farm silage. The distinctive odor was that of fermentation.

What, if any, effects might moldy or fermented beach kelp have on Sitka deer that feed on it? We don't know, but to find out, it will take some serious and expensive laboratory analysis.

Ocean And Wind Currents

Beaches throughout Alaska are typically littered with debris from local fishing boats which includes garbage of all sorts, plastic, nets, buoys, and other gear. Large ocean going vessels are known to have pumped and rinsed their bilges (they called it "Butterworthing" due to the appearance of the bilge oils) in Gulf of Alaska waters for decades. Debris from distant parts of the world, especially the Pacific Ocean show up regularly in Alaska.

Following the Fukushima Daiichi nuclear plant accident on March 11, 2011 debris from Japan began showing up on Alaskan beaches from the panhandle to the Aleutians, including the Kodiak Archipelago. Many types of flotsam from plastic containers to entire fishing boats began to appear in Alaskan waters, confirming that major ocean currents bring all types of material from far away to the remote beaches of Kodiak.

Cryptorchidism had been appearing in the Kodiak island group since long before the Fukushima nuclear accident. Obviously no link exists between these two events and the cryptorchidism phenomenon. The point is, pollutants from all over the Pacific have made their way to the Emerald Isle for centuries—since the beginning of time, actually.

Some people speculated that the Valdez oil spill in 1989 led to the cryptorchidism in Kodiak deer, but the largest cryptorchid so far measured was taken in 1960. (See story: Norm Sutliff's buck in this publication.) Though oil from that spill did reach some Kodiak beaches in 1989, I do not believe that the oil spill played a role in the problem of deer sterility in the Kodiak Archipelago.

The Alaska Stream and the Alaska Coastal Currents both flow from northeast to southwest and embrace the Kodiak Archipelago. The land mass and its continental shelf slow the currents. The large tides and deep island fjords tend to leave much debris isolated and deposited at or above the high tide line. Many "artificial" debris products take a very long time to deteriorate and some undergo chemical changes.

Just as PCBs, DDT, and other industrial products and pollutants travel by air, these and many more potentially harmful products undoubtedly reach, and have been reaching the island group for a long time.

Given the air masses and the constant ocean tides and currents, the presence of pollutants normally associated with urban populations, factories, etc. should be of no surprise when found in the Kodiak biosphere.

Lindane and DDT Contamination~

Among the tissues we collected from each deer we harvested was fat. Analysis of the fat samples by Colorado State University researchers showed that in the 32 samples analyzed, DDT metabolites, Lindane and PCBs were similar for deer from throughout the Kodiak Archipelago, but DDT was up to ten times higher in Kodiak deer, than deer from southeast Alaska.

I was assured that the concentration of DDT and other trace pollutants in Kodiak deer does not constitute a threat to humans who consume the flesh of these deer. I trust this, as my family and I have consumed large amounts of venison for more than five decades. Annually Kodiak venison constitutes between 20 and 60% of the red meat diet of my family—and we eat a lot of meat.

Ongoing research has proven that DDT is very persistent in the environment. DDT accumulates in fatty tissues, and it has been dispersed over wide areas in the upper atmosphere. DDT is one of many persistent organic pollutants still used in parts of the world. Each sovereign nation makes the decision to allow use of DDT or not. DDT has long been banned in the US and the United Kingdom.

One can reasonably assume that DDT, Lindane and other likely pernicious contaminants have reached and continue to reach the Kodiak Archipelago on the winds and with the tides. Most of our storms come from the southwest. They may carry DDT and other pollutants from Asia.

Government Reluctance to Investigate

The USF&W has a Congressional mandate—a directive from Washington, D.C.—to remove non-indigenous species from lands they administer, as was done with the Hagemeister Island reindeer herd in 1992.

In this chapter I quote freely and verbatim from publications listed with the internet address.

I quote from the *Alaska Journal*, December 26,1992. (http://www.nytimes.com/1992/12/26/us/alaska-journal-reality-destroys-a-fairy-tale-image.html)

Hagemeister Island

"They killed 790 reindeer. But only 172 carcasses were removed, dressed and distributed to native villages; the rest were left to decay. On Nov. 29 the government suspended what it had labeled a "mercy killing". Villagers are angry at the way the government handled the first round of shooting. "It's the worst wanton waste case since the buffalo," said Moses Kritz, a member of the tribal elders. Mr. Steiglitz … (USF&W) emphasized that his concern was for the lichen. **If I have to choose reindeer or lichen, I have to chose lichen. It's tougher to grow back.**"

https://en.wikipedia.org/wiki/Aleutian_wild_cattle

Aleutian wild cattle are feral wild cattle found on some of the Alaskan Aleutian islands. Several attempts have been made to round up these cattle for ranching. In 1985–6 the cattle on the Shumagin Islands were eliminated by the U.S. Fish and Wildlife Service, but they still remained on Umnak Island and Chirikof Island.

https://www.alaskapublic.org/2015/07/06/
caribou-emigrate-from-adak-feds-struggle-to-stop-the-spread/

Caribou Emigrate From Adak; Feds Struggle to Stop the Spread
By Lauren Rosenthal, APRN Contributor -July 6, 2015

It's no mystery how caribou wound up on Adak Island. They were imported in the late 1950s so Navy personnel would have something to hunt.

Now the Navy is gone and the island is a prime spot for big game hunters. But there are not enough of them, says Steve Ebbert, a wildlife biologist for the Alaska Maritime National Wildlife Refuge.

After an environmental assessment, the Fish and Wildlife Service decided the best way (to avoid spread of caribou) was to organize a hunt on Kagalaska Island, near Adak.

The team bagged nine male caribou. U.S. Sen. Lisa Murkowski isn't impressed.

The hunt cost $58,000, plus another $13,000 to butcher and salvage the meat. That was requested by Murkowski and other officials. Going forward, the senator wants to see a different approach.

My comment is: $71,000 is a lot to spend to unnecessarily eliminate nine caribou.
Other groups of feral animals have been destroyed. At this time USF&W does not seem to be actively pursuing removal of deer from Kodiak. Apparently that agency is unable, or unwilling, to engage in normal management of deer because the deer are not native to the area.
Benign neglect may suffice to eliminate the deer.
This seems to be an instance of an ill conceived government edict resulting in a "head up and locked" policy. Clearly each individual case of

so-called "invasive or non-indigenous species" should be evaluated and carefully considered before drastic action—or inaction is taken.

Feral reindeer on Kodiak Island
https://www.fws.gov/refuge/Kodiak/what_we_do/science/ungulate/reindeer.html

BACKGROUND

Thirty-two reindeer were introduced to the Lazy Bay region of Kodiak Island in 1921, and granted to the native peoples by the Department of the Interior. A cooperative was formed ("The Alitak Native Reindeer Corporation") in 1931 to manage the reindeer. Residents of Akhiok managed the herd, and the population grew throughout the 1940s and 1950s. The population reached a peak of approximately 3,000 head by 1950. A wildfire in the early 1950s destroyed a large portion of reindeer range, and an estimated 1,200 reindeer escaped into the wild. Active management of the herds ended in 1961. Federal grazing leases were allowed to expire in 1964. Reindeer were not removed from the formerly leased lands, despite a letter from the U.S. Bureau of Sport Fisheries and Wildlife which declared that any property not removed from the leased area would become US government property (June 10, 1963). The following year, the State of Alaska declared the reindeer to be feral and established an open season, no bag limit hunt on feral reindeer, with no same-day-airborne harvest.

Shareholders of the Alitak Native Reindeer Corporation disputed the government's claim. After negotiations with lawmakers, they agreed to sell the herd to the State for $10 a head. However, the deal was never sealed for unclear reasons. Despite this, harvest regulations continued to remain unchanged for the following 40 years.

Historical estimates of reindeer populations are vague due to a lack of formal surveys. Reindeer were not surveyed until the late 1970s, when 250 reindeer were counted near the Ayakulik and Sturgeon Rivers.

Since then, the population appears to have remained relatively stable at approximately 250 to 300 animals in the same region.

In 2002, the Alaska Department of Fish and Game authorized same-day-airborne hunting of reindeer. However, concerns over a perceived decline in herd abundance prompted the Alaska Board of Game to reinstate a ban on same-day-airborne hunts in 2010. The change further restricted harvest potential by instituting a six month hunting season, and limiting annual take to one reindeer per hunter. The impacts of these regulatory changes on the reindeer are unknown. However, there is concern that these changes may increase reindeer abundance and lead to associated degradation in fragile tundra habitat. Understanding the relationship between regulatory changes and reindeer abundances requires robust annual estimates of population levels. In attempt to quantify the effect of harvest management on reindeer abundances, Kodiak National Wildlife Refuge initiated annual surveys of reindeer abundance.

It seemed that the Alaska Department of Fish and Game and the U.S. Fish and Wildlife Service preferred to see the feral reindeer eliminated completely as they feared the ungulates would cause severe damage to ferns and other plant species.

Roland Ruoss and I, both Kodiak residents who opposed the total demise of reindeer, wrote proposals to the Alaska Board of Game in 2009 to end same day airborne hunting of feral reindeer on Kodiak Island and to place a limit of one animal per hunter per year. The board approved the proposals and placed those restrictions on the hunt.

The Alaska Department of Fish and Game is charged with game management for sustained yield as its main mission. Yet, after more than twenty-four years and multiple anecdotal and scientific reports, the State of Alaska's response to the increasingly widespread cryptorchidism in the Kodiak Archipelago has been to ignore or discourage efforts and requests for research funding into possible causes and relationships.

The cryptorchid, sterility problem is not going away. It is causing a severe drop in the deer numbers in Alitak Bay and other areas. After the 2010 Harvest Reports were counted and the degree of cryptorchidism was shown to be consistent with what we had reported, the Alaska Department of Fish and Game refused to include further questions regarding antlers and testicles on Hunt Reports. How can this official stance can be justified?

It is my belief that eventually proper research will be engaged and the cause or causes of the alarming sterility will be found. But how long must we wait for this?

References

Papers which I wrote or co-authored.
Abnormal Sitka Black-Tailed Deer on Kodiak Island prepared by Jake Jacobson, Arctic Rivers Guide & Booking Service, Kodiak, AK.

Dec. 2001 Cryptorchism, hypogonadism and antler malformations in black-tailed deer (Odocoileus hemionus sitkensis) of Kodiak Island

GA Bubenik, J. P. Jacobson · D. Schams · L. Bartoš -

Jan. 2001 Histologie des testicules de chevreuils à queue noire (Odocoileus hemionus sitkensis) cryptorchides de l'Ile de Kodiak en Alaska G. A. Bubenik J. P. Jacobson

Dec. 2001. Testicular histology of cryptorchid black-tailed deer (Odocoileus hemionus sitkensis) of Kodiak island, Alaska by G.A.Bubenik, Guelph, and J. P. Jacobson, Kodiak.

By G.A. BUBENIK, Guelph, J.P. JACOBSON, Kodiak, D. S

CHAMS, Freising, and L. BARTOS, Prague

Summary

Distinct antler malformations, (such as lack of points, distortion of antler forms, incomplete velvet shedding, casting above the coronet and a diagonal separation of cast antlers), were detected in Sitka deer (Odocoileus hemionus sitkensis) of the Kodiak Island (Alaska, USA). Many of these deer were also unilateral or bilateral cryptorchids and a few exhibited a moderate or severe separation of frontal skull bones. Radioimmunoassay analyses of serum revealed signs of hypogonadism: we found higher concentrations of LH ($P=0.05$) and lower concentrations of T ($P=0.037$) in bilateral cryptorchids as compared to intact bucks. There was no apparent impairment of spermatogenesis in the remaining testis of the unilateral cryptorchid deer. Unfortunately, no ectopic testes were so far recovered in cryptorchid deer. **Surprisingly, only about half of deer with bilateral cryptorchism exhibited hypogonadic symptoms. In the other half of cryptorchid deer, the antlers appeared completely normal and the concentrations of LH or testosterone in the serum of several bucks were in the range of intact deer.** It has been postulated that in some cryptorchid deer, ectopic testes can produce sufficient amount of testosterone, which prevents obvious antler and skull malformations, as well as reduces the compensatory elevation of LH. The possible causes of the hypogonadism resulting in cryptorchism and antler mal-formations are discussed.

2006. Cryptorchism, hypogonadism and antler malformations in black-tailed deer (Odocoileus hemionus sitkensis) of Kodiak island

3. Environ Health Perspect. 2006 April; 114(S-1): 51–59.
Published online 2005 October 21. doi: 10.1289/ehp.8052
PMCID: PMC1874179
Copyright This is an Open Access article: verbatim copying and redistribution of this article are permitted in all media for any purpose, provided this notice is preserved along with the article's original DOI

Monograph

Testis and Antler Dysgenesis in Sitka Black-Tailed Deer on Kodiak Island, Alaska: Sequela of Environmental Endocrine Disruption?

D.N. Rao Veeramachaneni,[1] Rupert P. Amann,[1] and James P. Jacobson[2]

[1] Animal Reproduction and Biotechnology Laboratory, Colorado State University, Fort Collins, Colorado, USA

[2] Arctic Rivers Guide Service, Kodiak, Alaska, USA

Address correspondence to D.N. Rao Veeramachaneni, Animal Reproduction and Biotechnology Laboratory, Campus Delivery 1683, Colorado State University, Fort Collins, CO 80523.

The authors declare they have no competing financial interests.

Received January 31, 2005; Accepted July 13, 2005.

Abstract

It had been observed that many male Sitka black-tailed deer (Odocoileus hemionus sitkensis) on Kodiak Island, Alaska, had abnormal antlers, were cryptorchid, and presented no evidence of hypospadias. We sought to better understand the problem and investigated 171 male deer for phenotypic aberrations and 12 for detailed testicular histopathology. For the low-lying Aliulik Peninsula (AP), 61 of 94 deer were bilateral cryptorchids (BCOs); 70% of these had abnormal antlers. Elsewhere on the Kodiak Archipelago, only 5 of 65 deer were BCOs. All 11 abdominal testes examined had no spermatogenesis but contained abnormalities including carcinoma in situ–like cells, possible precursors of seminoma; Sertoli cell, Leydig cell, and stromal cell tumors; carcinoma and adenoma of rete testis; and microlithiasis or calcifications. Cysts also were evident within the excurrent ducts. Two of 10 scrotal testes contained similar abnormalities, although spermatogenesis was ongoing. We cannot rule out that these abnormalities are linked sequelae of a mutation(s) in a founder animal, followed by transmission over many years and causing high prevalence only on the AP. However, based on lesions observed, we hypothesize that it is more likely that this testis–antler dysgenesis resulted from continuing exposure of pregnant females to an estrogenic environmental agent(s), thereby transforming testicular cells, affecting development of primordial antler pedicles, and blocking transabdominal descent of fetal testes. A browse (e.g., kelp) favored by deer in this locale might carry the putative estrogenic agent(s).

Keywords: antler dysgenesis, CIS, cryptorchidism, Leydig cell tumor, microlithiasis, rete carcinoma, seminoma, Sertoli cell tumor

Cryptorchidism & associated problems in animals R. P. Amann & D. N. R. Veeramachaneni Animal Reproduction & Biotechnology Laboratory Colorado State University, Fort Collins, CO 80523-1683 USA.

In 2008 Dr. E.K.Latch of Purdue University published the following paper:

Competing hypotheses for the etiology of cryptorchidism in Sitka black-tailed deer: an evaluation of evolutionary alternatives E. K. Latch1, R. P. Amann2, J. P. Jacobson3 & O. E. Rhodes, Jr.1

1 Department of Forestry and Natural Resources, Purdue University, West Lafayette, IN, USA

2 Animal Reproduction and Biotechnology Laboratory, Colorado

Percentage of sterile Kodiak deer on the rise Guest Opinion
Article published on Friday, Jan. 7, 2005 By Jake Jacobson *Kodiak Daily Mirror*

Books and papers which I reviewed but did not write or co-author.

Horns, Pronghorns And Antlers by George A. Bubenik and Anthony B. Bubenik (Evolution, Morphology, Physiology, and Social Significance)

Deer of the Southwest by Jim Heffelfinger

Deer of the World by Valerius Geist

Mule Deer by Valerius Geist

Abnorme Bock by Ulrich Herbst

The Deer Of North America by Leonard Lee Rue III

Deer; The Wildlife Series edited by Duane Gerlach, Sally Atwater and Judith Schnell

Alaskan Wildlife Diseases, University of Alaska, Fairbanks

Mule and Black-Tailed Deer of North America by Olof C. Wallmo

Google
    evolution of StikaBTD

GEIST
    https://retrieverman.net/2012/01/23/a-species-younger-than-the-domestic-dog/

PLEISTOCENE
    https://en.wikipedia.org/wiki/Pleistocene

WTD
    https://www.google.com/#q=White+tailed+deer

*** https://en.wikipedia.org/wiki/Deer

https://en.wikipedia.org/wiki/Preorbital_gland

http://www.fieldandstream.com/articles/hunting/2009/11/how-whitetail-glands-work

https://en.wikipedia.org/wiki/Capreolinae

References

Metatarsals: http://digitalcommons.unl.edu/cgi/viewcontent.cgi?article=1015&context=nebgamepubs

http://tpwd.texas.gov/huntwild/wild/game_management/deer/age/

average age of harvested deer
http://www.vtfishandwildlife.com/UserFiles/Servers/Server_73079/File/Hunt/deer/2015%20Deer%20Age%20Report.pdf

http://northernwoodlands.org/outside_story/article/buck-meets-doe

Origins of Sitka Blacktail Deer on Kodiak Island
https://www.google.com/#q=ORIGINS+OF+SITKA+BLACKTAIL+DEER+ON+KODIAK+ISLAND

ADF&G
http://www.adfg.alaska.gov/index.cfm?adfg=wildlifenews.view_article&articles_id=109

McCrea Cobb, USF&W -history of non-native mammal mgmt on Kodiak:

UAF
http://www.uaf.edu/files/ces/cnipm/annualinvasivespeciesconference/13thAnnualMeetingProceedings/Cobb.pdf

https://ghr.nlm.nih.gov/condition/androgen-insensitivity-syndrome

https://flutrackers.com/forum/forum/earth-weather-astronomy-environment/pollution-incl-gulf-of-mexico-oil-disaster/121734-dramatic-increase-in-sterility-of-male-sitka-blacktail-deer-in-alaska-believed-to-be-due-to-environmental-contamination

Phytoestrogens
https://en.wikipedia.org/wiki/Phytoestrogens

Fermentation & Phytoestrogens
http://www.koreascience.or.kr/article/ArticleFullRecord.jsp?cn=SPGHB5_2000_v32n4_936

Lindane
https://www.theguardian.com/environment/2015/jun/24/insecticide-lindane-found-to-cause-cancer

DDT
https://www.epa.gov/ingredients-used-pesticide-products/ddt-brief-history-and-status

Photos

Some interesting cryptorchid Sitka Blacktail Bucks taken by us or our friends in the Kodiak Archipelago.

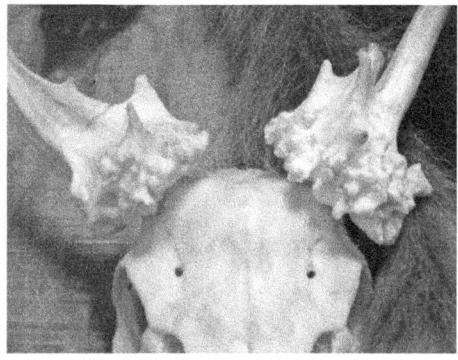

KODIAK ALASKA DEER

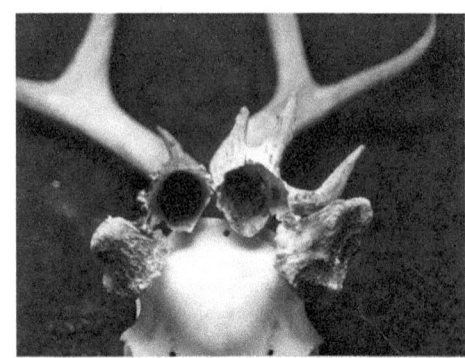

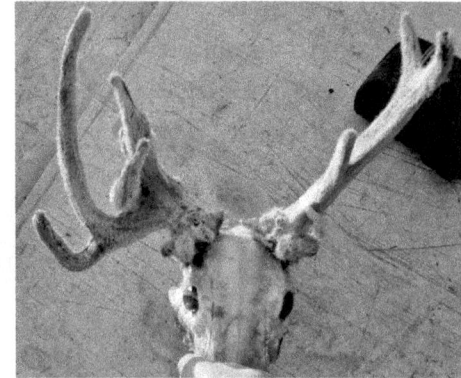

KODIAK ALASKA DEER

Photos

www.ingramcontent.com/pod-product-compliance
Lightning Source LLC
Chambersburg PA
CBHW071703160426
43195CB00012B/1561